CLERGY WOMEN
AND THEIR
WORLDVIEWS

CLERGY WOMEN
AND THEIR
WORLDVIEWS

Calling
For A New Age

Martha Long Ice

PRAEGER

New York
Westport, Connecticut
London

Library of Congress Cataloging-in-Publication Data

Ice, Martha Long.
  Clergy women and their worldviews.

  Bibliography: p.
  1. Women clergy—Attitudes. I. Title.
BV676.I32   1987   253′.088042   87-7001
ISBN 0-275-92643-5 (alk. paper)

Library of Congress Catalog Card Number: 87-7001
ISBN: 0-275-92643-5

First published in 1987

Praeger Publishers, One Madison Avenue, New York, NY 10010
A division of Greenwood Press, Inc.

Printed in the United States of America

∞™

The paper used in this book complies with the
Permanent Paper Standard issued by the National
Information Standards Organization (Z39.48-1984).

10 9 8 7 6 5 4 3 2 1

For My Family

Contents

Preface

My decision to investigate the worldviews of clergywomen, and to evaluate those views against the literature of worldview paradigm shift, was a decision born of longstanding interests. As a minister's daughter, a minister's wife, and a frequent participant in various lay ministries, I had a continuing fascination with the dynamics of religious communities and the consequences of various styles of leadership.

I was one of those many women who, upon marriage (in 1948), decided to be essentially at home, caring for a growing family (which came to be three sons and three daughters by 1960). I continued to read, maintained a schedule of volunteer commitments and speaking engagements, and imagined that, were I ever to engage in serious scholarly writing, it would likely be an attempt to articulate the convergences I saw in certain religious and secular paradigms of reality.

In recent years it became possible for me to do a doctoral program at the University of Michigan. From the beginning I assumed that my dissertation would be the aforementioned theoretical study. Meanwhile, I took a university course in the methodology of "naturalistic research" (a phenomenological approach to data-gathering) and was required, as a class assignment, to interview four persons occupying some role in common. I chose clergywomen, largely because I judged them relatively accessible to me; I preferred to devote available time to interviews and writing rather than to setting up the project.

Ease of access, level of interviewer/informant rapport, and richness of data gathered made the project one of the least burdensome, most rewarding academic pursuits I had undertaken. As I finished classwork and moved toward candidacy, I included it in a small list of possible dissertation themes that I presented to some of the faculty in consultations devised to help me finalize my choice; but I didn't see it as tapping a wide enough spectrum of my interests. Several people challenged my apparent reluctance to give serious consideration to the topic of clergywomen. They pointed out that (1) research on clergywomen could provide a concrete focus for relevant development of my theoretical interests; (2) I was showing unmistakable enthusiasm about the approach and findings of the already completed interviews; and (3) my life experiences fostered alertness to religious/personal nuances in documenting and analyzing interview content.

I found myself increasingly stimulated to think about how I would do such a study. In the end I simply recognized that my intention to research women ministers had put down roots. My plan was to compare their worldviews with some of those emerging in contemporary religious and scientific thought.

My model was the kind of scholarship from which I had profited most. I owe much to thinkers who gathered a wide range of observations and insights into fresh articulations, which fed my eagerness to see whatever I could—not just of the nature of reality, but of the ways to be in that reality on behalf of self and species.

Although my completed work had to pass muster before an official academic group, my envisioned audience was more a group of persons who simply wonder about clergywomen: what kind of women go into ministry, how life is for them as ministers, what they hope to accomplish, and so on. I wanted to deliver a study that would not lack empirical and logical rigor but that, nonetheless, would be digestible beyond the boundaries of a professional specialty.

Clearly a gap exists between the discourse modes in professional scholarship and everyday conversation. Complex distinctions require precise verbal labels for discussing them. Yet it seems to me that scholars must do what they can to lay their efforts before interested audiences outside a profession, especially before the groups who are the subjects of the observations.

Thus I planned that the informants would be in a position to evaluate me informally as a person, through face-to-face interviews; that they would be able, if they cared, to read what I am writing about them; and that they might, if so inclined, develop their own discourse with the content of the study.

Lillian Rubin's introduction to *Worlds of Pain* contains the following lines:

We have attitude studies and behavior studies; . . . We have probability statistics; . . . but they tell us nothing of the experience of flesh-and-blood women and men who make up the numbers. This is not a failure of those studies; they are not designed to do so. Still they leave us with only a fragment of knowledge. Therefore, we need . . . qualitative studies that can capture the fullness of experience, the richness of living. (1976: 13–14)

Doing this study at sixty years of age, I have accumulated a vast indebtedness to mentors who form a procession of helpful guides in my life; they have made valuable contributions to my intellectual and personal development.

I thank all the members of my dissertation committee: Walter Allen; Ann Hartman; Gayl Ness; Rafe Ezekiel, in whose class this project was born; and chairman Max Heirich, whose critical challenges were a unique blend of supportiveness for my work and stimulus to improve it. I much appreciated having a dissertation director whose questions and comments not only pointed to working problems but also illuminated their solutions.

I am profoundly grateful to the seventeen clergywomen who provided the interview data. Their grace made my task a pleasant one.

Additionally, I want to acknowledge the steady support and encouragement of family and friends, as well as the magical word-processing skills of Lisa Baum and Jo Engelhardt.

Finally, my appreciation goes to Alison Bricken, whose author-friendly editorial approach smoothed the final stages of manuscript preparation.

Chapter 1

The Project

This is a study of 17 clergywomen.[1] It is an attempt to document carefully their own reports of their life experiences. The investigation seeks to understand what appear to be changes not only in the role-status characteristics of U.S. religious institutions, but also in the ways these institutions may be coming to orient their constituencies toward cosmic reality, the social order, and personal experience.

Surveys already are yielding comparisons of male and female ministers, looking at gender-based differences in such things as background experiences, education, work circumstances, status mobility patterns, and attitudes (Carroll, Hargrove, and Lummis 1983). Complementary research focuses on congregational responses (e.g., attitude changes, satisfaction with leadership, etc.; Lehman 1985). Such large statistical "portraits" offer useful indications of shifting parameters; but they have difficulty capturing the kinds of processes that underlie the role enactments—processes that affect the social meanings exchanged in personal encounters with individual humans and with societal systems.

In-depth interviews with the clergywomen in the study have provided an empirical foundation of autobiographical data for analysis. The resulting descriptive tapestry has yielded resources for interpreting the existential significance of current survey findings.

I have been especially attentive to the women's subjective constructions of (1) self-image, (2) notions of ministry, (3) views of institutional settings, and (4) ultimate preoccupations. My goal has been to know and report these intersubjective realities in a way that illuminates crucial dynamics in religious institutional development. Carroll, Hargrove, and Lummis refer to Paul Tillich's thinking that religious institutions may function as social change agents through (1) exercising direct political power, (2) offering credible prophetic criticism, or (3) interpenetrating with society, offering exemplary behavior in critical areas of action. This study suggests that, in the latter sense, clergywomen's presence in U.S. religion may be a potent factor in a major worldview shift already under way.

THE MINISTERIAL TASKS

Influenced by equalitarian ideals and pressures, U.S. institutions have recently begun to permit women to occupy leadership roles formerly held exclusively by males. This means that traditional gender role norms that have been assumed broadly applicable in public and private life no longer can be counted on as offering dependable social guidelines.

In the religious sector, a number of mainstream U.S. denominations now ordain women into official clergy status. Certain things about church structure have made it possible for relatively larger numbers to gain access to influential positions than is true, say, in economic or political institutions. Denominations vary considerably as to number of women employed and amount of influence the women have in shaping the institutional course. It is notable that during the short periods of time most churches have admitted women as clergy aspirants, female students have come to make up as much as half of the seminarian aggregate in some schools. This, in itself, signals a truly dramatic change in the structure of religious organizations. Much attention and speculation center on its possible consequences. People wonder about the effect on the women, the role, the institutions, and the society. There are, of course, profound implications for the evolving content and style of the various ministerial functions.

As women have sought ordination, much controversy has focused on the traditional understanding of the clergy as "sacredly masculine" (Carroll, Hargrove, and Lummis 1983). Insofar as women are allowed into the role, the organizational structure of denominations is confronted with revision of a potentially radical sort.

Western religions have tended toward an image of God as the ultimate patriarch, the seat of cosmic control. One consequence has been an intensely *yang* (or, roughly, "male") emphasis. *Yin* (or more "female") aspects of the religious traditions have been ignored or submerged routinely, although they are often officially recognized.

Customarily the clergy role has been endowed with broad social permission to assume the patriarchal prerogatives of defining and interpreting reality, organizing public action, and intervening in personal affairs. Classical Western assumptions of patriarchy, scientism, and world mastery thus are challenged by the simple presence of females in the crucial religious role of clergy authority, let alone by how women, as persons, come to exercise their options.

By way of models for cosmic truth, and by way of personal-ethical counseling around the establishment of communal ideals, the various denominations substantiate their commitments and build traditions encompassing the range of symbols, concepts, practices, and sentiments that make up belief systems. It is logical to anticipate change in all these factors due to a systematic shift in social types used as leadership personnel.

The religious enterprise, and therefore the ministerial role within it, is counted on to clarify for people what is true, what's best to do, and what are the social arrangements under which human life prospers most. Religious leaders fulfill functions, then, that are theological, ethical, and pastoral.

In their theological work they conceptualize and articulate traditional beliefs in terms credible for the present moment. Professional ministers regularly are called on to ''do theology''—to think through and speak about the connections they find among their ideas of God, their religious practices, and existential issues.

Closely related is the task of ethical instruction. People seem to have more pressing conscious needs for legitimation of their action choices than for legitimation of their thought categories. The ministerial role typically carries authority to formulate and teach decisional principles and personal attitudes that promote a social order in keeping with the stated beliefs. Ministers are looked to for normative assessments that offer guidance in everyday choices.

A third expectation in society for religion, and within religion for itself, is that ministers will lead their believer communities in establishing some unifying and mutually supportive ways to live together. Such communal ventures ideally tap the central tenets of the faith, providing integrative images and models for both personal development and group interactive processes. Religions thus bear a burden of responsibility for exhibiting utopian human association, at once supremely rational and transcendently nurturant.

Though individual ministers may lean toward excellence in some one of the major leadership tasks at the expense of the others, the functions are so imbedded in each other that it is hardly possible during a professional career to escape substantial involvement in all three.

GENDER DIFFERENCES

In addition to a small list of sex differences clearly determined by genetic heritage, many gender distinctions stemming from developmental socialization in U.S. society have been found to exist. Wide-ranging empirical evidence supports the conclusion that male and female cognitive, decisional, and relational styles emphasize contrasting themes and criteria.

I certainly do not want to imply that male and female characteristics separate neatly into mutually exclusive sets. Their distribution is represented by overlapping normal curves; *human* characteristics are shared across the sex categories, but the frequencies differ systematically by sex. Thus certain human traits may be met in women more often than in men, either because more women than men are found to exhibit them or because women tend to show them more strongly (i.e., in more instances and/or contexts) than do men.

Faced from birth with gender differences in social expectations, obligations, and entitlements, males and females develop quite different perceptual/conceptual grids as they try to make sense of what's happening to them. For the purposes of this research some of the most pertinent suggested polarities are listed below. (They are also some of the most generally accepted distinctions mentioned throughout the gender differentiation literature.)

Females are disposed to develop skills of personal nurturance, integrative thinking, peer negotiation, and intuitive judgment, excelling in creative adaptation to environmental particulars. They tend to focus on complex systems, as such, and see the parts in terms of the whole. Males are more apt to develop skills of abstract analysis, linear logic, and visual/spatial judgment, aggressively imposing rational control on dynamic processes toward some desired goal or accomplishment. They are likely to concentrate with high intensity on limited aspects of phenomena and to understand wholes as assemblages of discreet component items.

Males tend to conceptualize ethical issues in terms of abstract principles and hierarchical entitlements. Females are more inclined to weigh both the competing ethical responsibilities for maintaining supportive relationships and the possibilities for maximizing collective well-being.

Men typically enter relationships for what may be accomplished through the association. Friendships for men take the form of companionship in a desired project or activity, with the activity forming the primary focus of the contact. Women form friendships more for their intrinsic value, developing trust and closeness through extended processes of mutual self-disclosure, mutual nurturing, and informal trust-building negotiations. In work associations women still maintain a primary focus on the relationship aspect; and in personal relationships men continue to accent the joint activity aspect.

Women commonly report the clearest and most satisfying sense of who they are occurs within the context of intimacy. Men, rather, seem to experience strong threats to their self-boundary maintenance from close associations. Separation, for men, provides the most unmistakable affirmation of individual identity.

Whereas leadership may be imaged by men as a high position in a hierarchy of command and dominance, women often image leadership more naturally as a central facilitating position in a network of peer-negotiated operations.

Penetrating all the other gender differences is the most persistent and pervasive difference of all—the difference in social power. Males receive the primary entitlement in U.S. society to "say what's *really* so" publicly, normatively, and officially, putting females traditionally under social judgment as defective or derivative, by male standards. (It is supposed by some that the primal origins of sexist domination by adult males in human societies lies in females' intimi-

datability due to smaller size, inferior short-term strength, and periodic inca-
pacitation from childbearing and lactation.)

Current scholarship continues to deliver a rich outpouring of theoretical and
empirical work focused on the gender role distinctions outlined above and their
sources. An extensive literature documents the differences within U.S. society
and seeks to explain their existence in terms of human biogenetic heritage and
the circumstances of childhood socialization. Chafetz, Chodorow, Gilligan, Maccoby and Jacklin, Rossi, Rubin, Stockard and Johnson, Block, and others have
built on the insights of earlier thinkers, such as Freud, Jung, Mead, Piaget, and
Erikson, to create a sophisticated and credible understanding of sex role divisions.

Insofar as the basic infant attachment is typically with an adult female, the
psychological ego-separation project presents different problems for boys and
girls. Identity formation, for boys, calls forth recognition, at some level, that
maleness requires the budding ego to deny in itself those qualities in the mother
that socially define her as female. Most specifically these are the qualities of
nurturance: personal service, empathic communication, cooperative adaptation,
emotional display. Masculinity, as such, is not only presented to young males
in more abstract terms (such as courage, strength, objectivity, rationality, being
in control, winning in combat) but, in addition, adult male models, doing their
culturally defined male tasks, are not as pervasively present to small boys in
twentieth century U.S. society as are women. Boys must negatively value womanly qualities in themselves in order to achieve the culturally mandated repression; and, thereafter, women (in their most characteristic manifestations) become
a ready reference point for what a male is not. This means that socialization,
through imitation of adults and identification with them, is more problematic for
boys than for girls. It is a more conscious accomplishment and more conflictive.

The need to achieve a separate self against the pull of personal intimacy may
explain why men continue throughout life to feel that somehow maleness must
continue to be "proved" or won anew in endless contests of power—lest they
cease to be. Relationships with women are fraught with potential, on the one
hand, for restoring the old, spiritually satisfying pre-Oedipal merger, but on the
other hand, for threatening loss of the identity that was successfully wrested
from a woman at high personal cost.

Females, by comparison, appear to have an easy go of it in the identity
construction process. Yet, perhaps more because of this ease than in spite of it,
and because of strong and pervasive operational norms, women show a tendency
not to complete adequately or to maintain confidently an adult identity separation.
They may drift toward merger with others, may let themselves be co-opted into
others' needs and agendas, they sometimes develop subversive identities within
a merged dyad, or are apt to fear and condemn ego-separation as selfish (even
while feeling stifled), and embrace self-sacrifice as a feminine virtue (even while
knowing it is personally and socially destructive). Conclusions are deductively
obvious. Such theoretical explanations imply that until and unless human babies

are presented, from birth, with available intimacy involving both male and female adults (adults who engage in respectful, mutually satisfying cooperative arrangements), the identity separation project will not culminate successfully in self-confident, generative adults with adequate peer discourse skills.

This study cannot test the correctness of the widely noted gender distinctions often described as typical of males and females in U.S. culture. It seeks to avoid either simplistic acceptance or dismissal of such comparisons by searching in the deep structure of biographical data from women clergy for indications of how religious institutions may be affected by female leadership. Empirical evidence for the broader significance of my findings must come from other procedures in other studies.

INTEGRATION OF TASK AND GENDER THEMES IN WORLDVIEW

As women enter professional religious ministries, surely we might expect their differences from men (in thoughts, feelings, and intentions) to find expression in the institutions to which they newly bring leadership. There are several possibilities for such expression (discounting, as unlikely, that they would or could simply adopt the male-constructed role and conform wholly to its traditional expectations). Women might devise a specialized female clergy role consistent with the version of womanliness they represent; or the sponsoring institutions might evolve a new view of the ministerial role—a synergetic product of male and female perspectives; or the ministers and the churches might come to participate consciously (either prophetically or opportunistically) in what some social thinkers regard as a worldwide shift in paradigms of reality.

The latter two options are closely related. Clergywomen may now be in a pivotal role at a time of significant change in world events and human consciousness. The setting (religion) and the role (female clergy) may combine special stimuli and expressive channels for generating innovative images of an evolving coherence that merges worldview, institutional structure, and personal identity in fresh ways. One black informant with lengthy ministerial experience seems to imply this when she says:

• Women are taking the church into the twenty-first century. The time has come to move the whole message beyond the pulpit—to come together in community from all sides—to fulfill the work of Jesus by being more of service in communities.[2]

Beyond the gender differentiation literature itself there is an expanding literature of world-order analysis and futurism, calling attention to the rather newly noticed deformity of social orders in which narrow male modalities dominate social structures. Many social thinkers (Capra, Berger, Bellah, Satin, Naisbitt, and others) have stated their conviction that we are now living in a critical period of major conceptual upheaval and that our current decades will be seen by future centuries as marking a radical revision in worldview.

Writers addressing themselves to this perceived transition often speak of the powerful challenges brought now from equalitarian, holistic, and world partnership ideals against such "obsolete" assumptions as patriarchy, scientism, and world mastery, for example. Traditionally the former ideals have been associated more with female life modes and the latter with male. Increasingly, some maintain, the former ideals constitute a core of ideological tenets that simplify and integrate social meanings in a humane and practical set of commitments. These commitments are proposed as more comprehensive and appropriate than traditional ones for addressing contemporary social issues and stabilizing social order, amidst what is assumed to be an unstoppable escalation of social variety and change.

Implicitly and explicitly the "new view" calls for new recognition that there is creative dialectical completion of *yin* and *yang* aspects of reality in each other. When they are pitted against each other as separate alternatives, and especially when one side (in the U.S. case, the *yang* side) is given systematic preference over the other, then a social pathology of personal and institutional formation is the result. As with all social phenomena, people can learn to take such pathology for granted as "the way things are and always should be." Nevertheless, numerous voices are now questioning the collective wisdom of addressing social exigencies with this skewed set of resources.

Until recently, institutionally legitimated religious rights of women have not tended to include the right to make official statements of the faith in preaching, administration, scholarship, or sacred acts. Now journalistic reports are alerting us to nontrivial modifications in religious perceptions and expressions connected with women's presence in strategic leadership roles. This means that as women become more numerous in the ranks of theology doers and sayers, theology may sound a very different tone than it has in the past.

Since women have been the integrative specialists and theology is an essentially integrative discipline, it is not surprising to hear some male seminary personnel report intellectual ferment in theological discussion connected with the presence of female students. In the past, they say, male students have often shown little patience with scholarly theology, but now are being drawn along with women students into consideration of its foundation in common experience.

It is interesting to speculate on how some of the following gender-associated polarities might be incorporated over time into religious views and structures (including architectural and other artistic expressions):

God as the "radically other"—a totally underived and transcendent identity; or God as absolutely merged with humanity—the totally empathic nurturer

God atop the hierarchy—the ultimate boss; or God as perfect peer connection—a loving, respectful partner

God as imposer—the shaper and giver from "out there"; or God as infuser—the center of life "in here"

God as abstract being; or God as "earthed," embodied, particularized

Such polarities also inform moral judgments in gender-specific ways. Women are known (Gilligan 1982) to have approaches different from those of men when puzzling through ethical issues and when offering guidance regarding humane decisions. Mention was made earlier of the leanings toward principle, policy, and entitlement as bases for male morality; toward personal need and collective well-being as bases for female morality.

Often studies of power entitlement have noted that groups wielding public power (in most cases male) tend to construct, legitimate, and maintain social institutions congruent with male conceptual categories. Power holders seldom are pressed to consider dissonant possibilities and easily reject them, if considered, by applying familiar standards of judgment. Groups denied public power usually go through "double socialization"—social adjustment that recognizes both their own point of view (out of their own social location) and the official or dominant point of view about what is *really* real, according to the powerful social leaders. Ordinarily, so that they can maximize their advantages in connection with the powerful, people with a low power status must develop a dual awareness of personal and official realities.

If then, as the world-order prophets are saying, we are moving steadily and inevitably toward social crises needing holistic solutions, androgynous conceptualizations, and simultaneous advances in "high tech and high touch" (to use a Naisbitt phrase), people *not* accustomed to power entitlement may well have the crucial experience and imagination for speedy, creative adaptation to the requisite conceptual frames and transitional roles. This study offers concrete examples of how such adaptation may happen.

Women, thus, are in the possibly advantageous transitional position of having been socialized into both their own and traditional male views. In many cases they will have worked hard to reconcile the two into a fruitful synergy. It seems certain that societal ethics will shift considerably over time if both men and women are allowed to give public counsel in matters of social goodness.

Likewise, in the third task area we have considered, it makes sense to expect that shared male/female leadership will modify the styles of community building prevalent among religious groups. The person-centeredness of female orientation in general supports the suspicion that the move toward gender balance in clergy rosters will be accompanied by gradual redress of the current tilt toward rigidly rationalized associations.

All religious traditions require ongoing community bases for sustained credibility. An important aspect of all such communities is the continuing project of establishing and maintaining ideal ways to be together as humans. In doing this the groups must develop reasonably satisfying and commonly acceptable explanations for such experiences as death, catastrophe, injustice, suffering, irony, and tragedy. This is not solely a theological exercise in an intellectual sense; it is an exercise in communal/personal solidarity. Such explanations must penetrate the sentiments of a people and mark their exchanges of meanings. The belief vernacular of males and females is gender-distinctive. One difference is the apparent sturdier connectives between scholarly and mundane levels of theological articulation among women as compared to men.

In Western history, as males have devised intentional communities, they have tended to impose an abstract organizational design on existential phenomena, either as a logical extension of philosophic ideals or as a rational progression toward some goal. Churches could hardly escape at least some structural revision due to the leadership of women clergy with a contrasting disposition to order communal life according to consideration for ecological factors and anticipated individual/personal consequences.

As black people in the United States found out in the 1960s, churches can be strategic places for certain social interest groups to promote change, both by investing in political-prophetic stands and by offering revised worldviews. The social location of women ministers forces them to encounter attitudes (within and around themselves) that specially alert them both to the community changes they themselves represent and to the cost/benefit balance of becoming vocal advocates and interpreters of the change momentum. They are in a key spot to image and facilitate experimental models of religious community. We should expect such models to point in the direction of more equalitarian relationships, more androgynous identities and roles, and "more flat" institutional organization (i.e., networks rather than hierarchies).

There are some probable areas of conflict between existing congregations and female ministers. Insofar as membership needs are interpreted and felt as needs for external authority regarding correctness about cognitive and normative principles, women clergy may be disorienting and offensive, both symbolically and stylistically. For persons expecting disagreements to be settled through assertion of rationally superior arguments or through strategic application of social sanctions, interpersonal process (which is the more characteristic female mode) may seem exceedingly insecure, muddled, hazardous, and interminable.

There are also predictable conflicts between traditional male leaders and women ministers. Contemporary ferment and anxiety among males and females in the areas of self-image, self-presentation, interpersonal technique, conceptual style, personal choice, and vocational choice are well documented in an expanding literature. For women, the ferment heightens awareness of old griefs and new possibilities. The desire to press for equal consideration as humans can easily erupt in impatience and anger, if movement is slow or turns against them. For men, it is often unsettling and irritating to be associated with peers who are challenging familiar and honored vocational assumptions. Understandably, the demand for a high consciousness regarding such matters does not tend to be welcomed by all men as a stimulus for healthy self-assessment and growth, but may be seen as a gratuitous aggravation and a deflection from central vocational pursuits. Effective conflict resolution most creatively involves the modal techniques of both genders in a developmental counterpoint. That is, on one level, rational analysis and contractual agreements may facilitate specific strategies of short-term cooperation; on another level, good faith exchanges of information may foster mutual sensitivity, empathy, and support for long-term trust. As religious institutions distribute the clergy role among male and female ministers, the usual ways of building nurturant solidarity must undergo change of some sort. It remains to be seen what kind of change is indeed occurring. I am interested in what type of religious community is coming into being and how it accommodates and expresses the presence of women clergy.

METHODOLOGY

It seemed clear that if I wanted to discover the essential personal thrust of my informants it was imperative to use a low-structure methodology that interfered as little as possible with spontaneous delivery of self-report about self-situation and self-understanding, on the informant's own terms. To this end I shaped a qualitative investigation, primarily using data from in-depth interviews with seventeen clergywomen. A phenomenological mode of inquiry, searching out social processes and imbedded meanings that inform the ways human actors image human happenings, seemed best to fit what I wanted to know and say about women in ministry and how I wanted to be in relationship with them as an investigator.

The research perspective and techniques adopted for this project are controversial in sociology. Given the frequency of voiced doubts about whether such qualitative sociological analysis is sufficiently hard, empirical, or real science, I choose to be as clear as possible in explaining why I have pursued such an approach for the research at hand—why I see my chosen approach as best, and indeed required, for answering the specific questions that interest me.

Sophisticated quantitative analysis procedures in contemporary academic sociology have become so effective and attractive in describing and explaining social phenomena that their use has tended to eclipse other perspectives. Stunningly crisp parametric pictures of complex social data emerge at all levels of social inquiry and in all substantive areas. Distributive dimensions of variable social occurrences are captured aptly with such methods; parameters can be compared across categories and across time; coincidence of variability in different social factors can be determined; support for specific theoretical hypotheses can be built by testing repeatedly for evidence of refutation. But translating empirical data into numerical equivalencies, and seeking insight through mathematical-statistical modeling of data relationships simply does not work well for answering some important social questions or for clarifying certain social issues. (No matter how awesome the transportation powers of a supersonic jet plane, it cannot help me get across the street to see my sick neighbor!)

Quantitative methods do not serve my purposes if I want to explore the multifaceted and often exceedingly subtle strategies and transformations through which new social influences (e.g., innovative adaptations and motivating ideologies) first appear, develop, and build credibility. Crucial aspects of social reality often tumble, unremarked, through the grids of formalized research instruments that are not designed specifically to spot them. The characteristic emphasis of quantitative studies is on the location and measurement of central social dominances; the perspective is unprepared to illuminate phenomena that are not yet noted and at least familiar enough to the researcher that appropriate measuring tools can be invented.

Alternative techniques are needed for discovering social facts that lie outside the awareness of the investigator or that rest heavily upon empathically hearing and recording narrative accounts of experience. Documentary sources and formalized questionnaire responses typically elide even such interpretive nuances as: whether respondents were apathetic or cynical about the research stimuli; whether they internally dismissed the choices as absurd or irrelevant to their situations; whether they suspected they were part of a typical/untypical response pattern (and what difference this might make to them); what they held as a rationale for their responses; how committed they were to their answers, as stated; under what circumstances they judged they would have made different responses; or what ideals and intentions might foreshadow social changes of nontrivial proportions.

Professional investigators often recognize this risk of missing valuable or critical information due to precision of formal probes. They may attempt compensation through less formal ''pre-study'' phases of research, intended to elicit subject-expressed cues as to what might be the most fruitful questions.

But personalistic studies must not be considered merely a preparatory function for gathering actual empirical facts. Expertly documented reports of subjective social experience can move very close to the pulsing heart of social life as it is known *empirically* in the living of it. Facts about how real people regard and describe the social processes of their days can stand as scientific data in their own right (except in a thoroughly positivistic, reductionist view of science), and can provide solid core information that transcends mere ''human interest'' drama. The strength of phenomenological data-gathering is not just that it generates more lively, colorful accounts; it accesses realities different from those revealed by quantitative methodology. If I want to know how clergywomen trace the routes by which they came to be ordained—if I want to know how they see their own professional intentions relative to their canopy institutions—if I want to know what options they see for themselves and how they arrive at decisions— if I want to know the thoughts and the conscious commitments of these women who are affecting a major institutional sector—in short, if I want to examine processes and subjective impressions, then there are clear scientific advantages in positioning myself to hear the women's stories firsthand, at considerable length, and with few formal restrictions. Scientific findings, documented in verbal imagery, can be as sociologically valid as those recorded in charts and tables.

Each has special potency for social illumination; each is ill-suited to capture the substance of the other; each requires rigorous professional discipline and unqualified devotion to the undistorted disclosure of findings. (Each method, it should be noted, is also subject to popular projection beyond its area of legitimate application.)

I see myself transporting a bit of social reality, experienced by real people, through to the gaze of other (or, for that matter, the same) real people. My contribution to scientific objectivity lies in careful, accurate, personally accountable articulation of the subjective meanings, interactions, and processes revealed in the stories they tell. The clergywomen are the experts about what they see and feel. As a researcher, I am expert only in the sense that I bring a certain connoisseurship to the listening and again to the telling—placing it all within a larger arena of classical and contemporary social discourse.

While it is not helpful in reporting findings to display everything said by an informant in a lengthy interview, a responsible qualitative researcher honors objectivity by showing all statements that illuminate the study focus and suppressing nothing that provides discrepant information for consideration. It is important that, overall, quoted interview selections be a reasonably balanced use of information from all interviewees and not just the expression of a few.[3]

The post-interview ordering of spontaneously delivered ideas requires a researcher discipline that is both artistic and scientific. There must be devotion to the criterion of accuracy in reporting informant sense; this demands editing judgments that select passages, make cuts, and occasionally alter the exact words in the interest of preserving the truest possible portrayal of the informant's thinking. The following are examples of editing strategies I used.

If essentially the same idea was stated in several congruent ways by one woman, I sometimes collapsed them into a single complete statement containing the most revealing phrases from all. In such cases I was alert to the need for scrupulous care that the resulting "collage" in no way blur or distort the meaning intended, but enhance its clarity. (Instances: quotations on pp. 48, 52)

Similarly, related offerings on the same subject that were not continuous in the actual interview were often grouped together in the quotations, so that the breadth of thinking on a certain issue would be apparent. (Instances: quotations on p. 69)

I consistently opted for meaning clarity over literal use of word sequences used by informants. Thus, "I feel safe with my doubts in God's presence" is rendered by me as "In God's presence I feel safe with my doubts." The context shows the latter to be the woman's intended meaning; reporting her words verbatim would leave room for another interpretation that does not really represent her thinking.

In planning my work I leaned heavily on Raphaël Ezekiel's "naturalistic research" methods and on Shulamit Reinharz's suggestions for "experiential analysis," while also profiting from the rationale and work plans of other qualitative researchers, such as John Lofland, Barney Glaser, Anselm Strauss, Kai Erikson, Mirra Komorovsky, and Lillian Rubin. They all emphasize the concrete situatedness of social events and meanings. The resulting modified phenomenological frame that I chose employed an open-agenda format for the interviews, allowing subjects to tell their own stories and to set their own priorities, minimally stimulated by researcher questions and comments. There were two 2-hour interviews with each woman and one 3-hour meeting of the group to respond firsthand to each other and to my reported findings.

Since I have been curious about possible commonalities in clergy role enactment, I attempted in the informant selection process to secure as wide a range of demographic and personal types as possible. The variety is dramatically evident in the content of Chapter 2. The group is heterogeneous as regards age, race, professional tenure, denominational affiliation, and sexual orientation. My hope has been to guard thereby against cheap generation of trivial hypotheses regarding what is going on among these women. Where it was possible to obtain such information, I selected women regarded highly by colleagues as having potential for influence and leadership, in order to minimize bias from interviewing persons with little to lose through adopting nonconformist positions vis-à-vis establishment views. This strategy also was thought to provide more trustworthy indicators for locating the trajectory of institutional change.

The selected persons are not a scientific sampling from the population of all clergywomen. They do not "represent" all clergywomen, except in the special sense that they are true cases of women who function as ordained professional clergy. They are not presented as "average" types. They are persons who, for various reasons, are seen in their institutions as having an impact. Therefore, they are well suited as a resource for understanding and describing the focal concerns of this study—namely, the processes that shape and constitute the influence of female clergy on other persons and on institutional formation.

In a letter prior to the first interview, and again during the informal conversation initiating that occasion, I encouraged each woman to include autobiographical material covering such things as memory of early experiences; early social locations (e.g., family, household, race, class, religion, ethnicity, region); educational background; personal faith history; personal traumas; belief changes; work history; goals, plans, and hopes; worries, fears, frustrations, and ambivalent feelings; satisfactions, joys, and achievements; general health; employment conditions and professional moves; typical days; personal life (e.g., mating, parenting, friendships, leisure, hobbies, special interests, and ideal models for being and doing). Usually sharing memories of early childhood became the most comfortable point of entry into telling about themselves.

Sociological dimensions emerge from the documented particulars of the informants' life stories. They become theoretical grist for the construction of hypotheses about the connections of clergywomen with certain institutional trends and reality paradigms. This study, though, does not encompass the testing of such emergent hypotheses; nor does it encompass comparisons of the gathered data with data from other relevant categories, such as clergymen, women in other institutions, or clergywomen in other times.

Research is just beginning to address such questions. Important insights await (1) comparisons of female and male clergy (e.g., as to self-perception, institutional functions, or macrostructural influences); (2) comparisons of levels of orthodoxy among denominations with ease of access (for women) to ordained status; (3) assessment of effect, over time, of women clergy on both official and popular versions of theology.

My case focus provides information for interpreting the "life sense" of statistical parameters from other studies; the data also constitute a fertile ground for generating hypotheses and stating them in terms indigenous to the experience world of the informants; most importantly, the data have intrinsic sociological value and interest.

The study nests comfortably in a set of questions C. Wright Mills calls a third "intellectual pivot" of classical thought (along with structural analysis and historical analysis):

What varieties of men and women now prevail in this society and in this period? And what varieties are coming to prevail? In what ways are they selected and formed, liberated and represented, made sensitive and blunted? What kinds of "human nature" are revealed in the conduct and character we observe in this society in this period? (1959; 5–7)

When Mills eloquently proposed "sociological imagination" as a "most needed quality of mind," he envisioned a populist type of scholarship pursued with openly reformist intentions. He advocated a broadly utilitarian sociology— a practical use of knowledge and rationality to help people make better sense of their surroundings and their inner states.

He saw a vast audience of persons needing credible bases for confident decisions in their daily lives. Above all, he admonished sociology professionals to demonstrate the peculiar double vision that clarifies human events by regarding them as, at once, structurally and existentially real—understandable only in thoughtful consideration of how social settings and personal meanings intersect.

This chapter has revealed the perspectives, intentions, and questions I brought to the project. Chapters 2 through 10 will show what I found and what I think it all may signify.

Chapter 2 introduces the women, so that the reader is able to envision the persons whose ideas will be encountered.

Chapter 3 discusses gender orientation and establishes that the informants exhibit an epi-normative, androgynous version of female social responses.

Chapter 4 digresses into a consideration of some pertinent sociological concepts.

Chapter 5 deals with key informant views of authority and with the function of "struggle" in the informants' lives.

Chapter 6 takes up the clergywomen's approach to the task of administration in religious communities.

Chapter 7 looks at how the women conceptualize moral leadership.

Chapter 8 examines the way they arrive at truth—how they do theology—and includes consideration of their feminist and linguistic issues.

Chapter 9 reviews a large body of "futurist" literature and demonstrates its connection with the informants' perspectives.

Chapter 10 draws on sociological analyses to illuminate the import of the research findings and to suggest subsequent steps in scientific investigation of the questions raised.

NOTES

1. In the title, "clergy women" is two words, for emphasis. Hereafter, this will be a single word—the parallel to "clergymen".

2. Throughout the study, the large dot will signal an informant speaking. In a series of quotations each dot will mark the shift to a different informant.

3. In this study, about 75 percent of the gathered information is shared with the reader. The unused material comes mostly from the biographical details in the interviews.

Chapter 2

The Women

This chapter presents the women whose voices you will be hearing throughout the study. The information comes from their own shared observations about their lives and from firsthand observations I made during the interviews.

I met them and talked with them in their offices, in their living rooms, or, occasionally, in a classroom or a retreat center. The striking variety in personal appearance heralds the variety in personal styles and backgrounds. They are short and tall; heavy and slight; young and old. Some have brown eyes, some blue eyes; they may have dark skin or light skin; short, curly black hair or long, straight blond hair. They wear business suits with ruffly blouses and clerical collars with ski sweaters and slacks.

Though I selected only Michigan and Ohio informants, the seventeen women come from all over the eastern half of the United States: New England, Mississippi, Florida, Iowa, Georgia, New York, Illinois, Delaware, Tennessee, South Carolina, Ohio, and Michigan. One grew up in India (the part that is now Pakistan), and one had a lengthy and significant (young adult) experience working as a teacher in Indonesia. Another accompanied her military husband overseas and spent three years in Turkey while her children were young. Several were in Europe during their college years for special study programs.

Since I had started the project with the intention of including women from major U.S. denominations, I consulted the various regional headquarters to augment my own knowledge of who the women are and where they are located. I specified only that the persons referred be non-marginal in the institutions; that is, that they be ministers who influence their church groups through notably capable leadership, unique status, or both. "Unique status" involves here such high-visibility factors as "only woman serving this area in our denomination" or "a wonderful woman who was ordained in her seventies after retirement from a state social service job." Unusual status gives a woman a certain influence simply from being a focus of attention, regardless of her personal potential. It might be argued credibly that *all* clergywomen share a "unique status," since it is true that they tend to be their community's and their congregation's "firsts"; but, denominationally, some are no longer rare simply because they are female.

During the selection process I remained alert to news media items, word-of-mouth descriptions, and comments in denominational publications. As I began contacting people and firming agreements for interviews, I took great care to arrange for diversity in age, race, marital status, and ministerial milieu, in addition to denominational diversity. I leaned toward choices of women in congregational ministries rather than, for example, agency administration, hospital and prison chaplaincies, or campus outreach. Only two of the seventeen are in specialized, non-congregational roles—one as a pastoral counselor with cancer patients and their families, one as a campus ministry team member.

Among them, the women are affiliated with 12 religious denominations. They are Presbyterian, Reformed Church in America (2), United Church of Christ (3), Episcopal (2), African Methodist Episcopal, United Methodist, American Baptist, Progressive National Baptist, Unity, Lutheran, Reform Jewish, and Roman Catholic.

The Roman Catholic woman is the only informant not officially ordained into her denomination's priestly ministry. For various reasons, Catholic parishes in the United States face a current shortage of priest personnel. During this crisis many "women religious" from the church's orders are functioning quite fully in pastoral roles. In many cases they are theologically sophisticated and come into the work with extensive prior experience in ministries of counseling, teaching, spiritual formation, and so on. To date, the Vatican authorities have ruled against ordination legitimizing the priestly role for women; nonetheless, I have included one such Catholic sister among the ministers studied because, functionally, she qualifies as clergy.

The greater number of women from the United Church of Christ reflects, in part, the fact that there has been greater ease of access to ordination for women in that denomination over a longer period of time; hence, a larger candidate pool was available to me for achieving range in other respects.

Of the 15 informants serving in congregations, nine are in relatively large urban parishes (i.e., 200 or more in membership). Three of these are the sole ministers in their parishes; the other six, in multiple-staff ministries (one in the "senior" staff position at a prestige location in that denomination; five in "associate" or "assistant" positions). Two women are at smaller urban churches[1] as the only professional. Four are located in rural towns. Three of these latter are alone as clergy with fairly small congregations; one is an assistant in a sizable parish that draws widely from the surrounding countryside.

Three of the women have organized new congregations for their dominations. Two, at interview time, were in building programs. In one case, the structure was a "first" for a congregation that had been meeting for three years in rented quarters; in the other case, the construction was a major expansion and improvement after 20 years of this woman's pastorate.

The women range in age from the mid-twenties to the mid-seventies, with a mean age of about 40 years. I did not ask specifically for age information, but often it was volunteered and it is deduced easily from other biographical data. The reader should keep in mind that, regardless of age, these women are quite new as clergy. The example above of a 20-year tenure is exceptional in the group. Only one other woman has been ordained nearly as long. Even when these two are included, the average time since ordination is only a little more than six years. The mean drops to four and a half years if the *three* who have been ordained longest are omitted from the list.

Ordination carries different implications across the groups. For example, some candidates face a two-stage ordination, as deacon and as elder; some are ordained immediately upon completing formal preparatory requirements; some cannot be ordained until they have secured a denominationally approved position in a congregation or church agency; most, but not all, need a four-year undergraduate degree from an accredited college in addition to religious instruction from boards or seminaries of the religious body.

At this point in history the correlation between age and years of professional ministry generally is not strong among women. When U.S. denominations began approving women for ordination, many middle-aged single and married women entered the seminaries. It is not clear how this picture may change in the future. Obviously, as more young females have the clergy option made evident to them, more are choosing it. And the reservoir of late age aspirants, built up by former restrictions, should drain down rather quickly. But women and men are tending toward less conventional career strategies in recent years. Later stabilization of vocational commitments, mid-life career changes, and shifts in labor market requirements make students of "nontraditional" ages more and more common in many specialties. Perhaps even more unpredictable is the response, over time, of youthful cohorts of women to the envisioned rigors of practicing parental and pastoral ideals simultaneously as mothers and ministers.

There is considerable variety in personal style of presentation among the women. Some are vivacious, almost hyper-fluent communicators; others are reserved and quiet, with calm, measured speech. They present distinctive combinations of joviality, seriousness, piety, contemporaneity, sociability, gentleness, contemplativeness, innovation, flamboyance, and conventionality. Yet, with all the differences, some qualities are strong throughout the group. They are outwardly a remarkably pleasant, self-confident lot—able articulators of concepts, experiences, and problems. They like being women and they like being clergy. Their assertiveness tends to be couched spontaneously in empathic terms, lending a flavor of commitment and concern rather than self-absorption or inclination to manipulate others.

Such presentation is a clear asset to public ministerial performance and doubtless interacts with the role selection process as well as with the development of the role. It is also a critical factor in gaining acceptance over time with parishioners and colleagues who may doubt or deny the suitability of females for the clergy position. Many of them report being told, prior to their selection of their vocation, "You would make a good minister." This was often said by people who may not have considered such a role an actual or legitimate possibility.

Four of the women are black, 13 white. The previously mentioned women with longest professional experience as ministers are black women. Marital status takes many different forms even in this small group. Eight of my informants are single and nine are married. Of the eight singles, five have never been married and three are divorced. One of the singles identifies herself as lesbian. Seven of the nine who are married are in a first marriage; two are in a second marriage after a divorce. Five of the women are presently married to ordained clergymen. Three of the latter marriages are first marriages for both mates; two are second marriages for both mates. Four of the ordained male spouses are active as professional ministers. Only one of these is in a joint ministry with his wife. One husband, who was formerly a clergyman, has moved into an industrial/commercial position that, he is said to feel, suits him better. The other husbands are working as music teacher, labor consultant, medical doctor, business technician, and federal agency executive.

No one at this point reports being in a troubled marriage. In fact, all the presently married clergywomen indicate strong support from their husbands for their vocational choice and for their personal development. Of the nine married informants, five had decided on the clergy vocation before marrying the present spouse; four were married before considering and choosing the vocation. Except for the clergy spouses leading other church communities, the husbands are all described as active in the congregations their wives serve. Most participate in more than token ways, as choir directors, religious school teachers, committee members, and special program coordinators.

Among the 12 women who are or who have been married, the average number of children is slightly above two. The largest number for any one mother is four, and several are childless. One is committed to childlessness because she is a known genetic carrier of a debilitating pathology.

All have high school diplomas and all but three have completed bachelor's degrees. Denominational requirements for ordination vary a great deal, but most of the informants have had at least three years of professional/theological study, four at prestigious Ivy League seminaries. Most also have had extensive, supervised practical experience of some sort, usually formal internships.

Five of the women grew up in families with fathers in professional roles: two doctors, a clergyman, a corporate business executive, and a school superintendent who also held a post in local government. Four fathers managed small business enterprises. Eight informants have clear working-class origins, with fathers mostly in factory labor, skilled and unskilled. Of these, one father was in agricultural work; another was a bus driver.

Ten mothers of clergywomen in this study were in the traditional housewife role during the childrearing years, though several of them were notably active in volunteer services outside the household. An informant whose (traditional housewife) mother died when the future clergy daughter was only two tells of a very concerned father who worked hard to hold his family together by enlisting the assistance of relatives and friends until his remarriage five years later. Two women had mothers who worked for pay outside the home only infrequently and for short periods of time. The remaining five mothers were regularly employed for extensive periods of time as their children grew: two as public school teachers, two in health care (as a doctor, a nurse), and one as a saleswoman. An informant whose mother worked at home remembers the mother's great pride in the maternal grandmother's status as a pharmacist in Europe.

Three parental marriages were terminated in divorce, one after the clergy daughter was an adult. Three were disrupted by the death of one spouse. A father and two mothers died before the clergy daughter's adulthood—at infancy for one informant, at high school and college stages for the others.

For 14 of the informants the religious dimension of life was well integrated into the childhood home experience and was central in family organization. For the other three it was an important early experience, but the parents themselves were not active in religious communities. The parents either allowed or arranged religious instruction for the children.

The Jewish woman recalls growing up in a thoroughly Jewish world. Until high school she had no real exposure to or knowledge of a non-Jewish way of life. She describes her parents as knowledgeable but not traditionally observant Jews. Holidays were celebrated in her home, but the family was not active in the synagogue. When she asked her father, "Why don't we go to synagogue?" he responded, "Why do we need it? It's what you do in the street that's important." She says that it is still hard for her to make meaningful distinctions between religious and cultural elements of Jewishness, since it was as late as her seminary years that she was put in touch with many specifically religious ideas of Judaism. She speaks of a bustling, people-filled environment:

• Bunches of kids running in and out of houses . . . *always* lots of company . . . *always* lots of relatives around . . . mothers calling across to each other from back windows of apartments . . . many working mothers, but some [like hers] always home to look out for their own children and others'.

None of the other informants talk about such complete fusion of cultural and religious background. Yet the integration of religious perspectives with the whole of life is certainly a common theme in the remembered childhood happenings for these women, who are now professionally articulating such integration. Roughly two-thirds of the 17 women indicate much regular church activity and/or religious observance shared by family members.

Among these 17 women, birth order appears to be an important factor. Eight are the oldest or only children in their families. Three more are the oldest or only *daughters*, with one or more older brothers. These findings are consistent with the literature indicating positive correlation of oldest child status with achievement orientation and with social recognition for achievement. However, the women of this study exhibit, in addition, high levels of interpersonal competence and affiliative behavior—traits associated more strongly, as a rule, with youngest children in families, but also correlated more strongly with femaleness than with maleness.

Without exception, the women recall childhood reputations as "bright kids" and remember "eating up" learning in school and out. There are some skipped grades in their elementary school experiences. Even the one with the most disadvantageous educational beginning reports being a good student and "loving" school. She was a child in the segregated rural South, where black children worked in the fields from the age of three or four years, picking crops and carrying water, and being allowed to attend a little two-room school between Thanksgiving and March planting. Her teacher was the same one her father had had—a woman who, according to my informant, possibly had not received a high school diploma and surely had not gone to college. On the little girl's first day at school, a trick was played on her that was so confusing and upsetting that she did not return to school until the following year. It is interesting to note that, in spite of the inauspicious start, this woman now holds city, state, and national awards for outstanding community leadership.

In addition to the recognition received by the informants for learning achievement at school, over half of them remember recognition at an early age for other talents and skills: musical, dramatic, forensic, memorizing, dance, group leadership, or teaching. Significantly for this study, such positive feedback in their lives is connected strongly with church-related activities.

The story of one informant is illustrative. She recounts an early taste of leadership while attending church meetings with her grandmother. The girl had learned many of the songs used in these meetings. One of them ("A Charge to Keep I Have and a God to Glorify") required individuals to sing out parts in turn, and the whole group would then join in a choral response. They were singing one day when she took a turn, something she had not previously tried. The women came right back with the customary answer. She was all at once startled, abashed, excited, and pleased as she savored this moment of being somebody who could elicit the appropriate musical response, just like the grown women. She thinks she was eight or nine at the time and the only child in the group.

With few exceptions (three, or possibly four, from the information I have) the women also were considered "good kids," that is, generally cooperative, helpful, independent, and responsible in the eyes of significant adults. Many of them had had rather remarkable, deeply formative friendships with adults outside their nuclear families even while the girls were still in grade school. Sometimes the friendships stemmed from school contact; sometimes they came via parental friendship networks.

One informant grew up in a racially integrated working-class neighborhood where there was extensive interracial mingling of children and adults, with little consciousness of color, according to her memory. Her parents, who still live there, were not political activists but (by example) "taught healthy self-respect and respect for others, regardless of category or situation."

As a white child she had had a black teacher (the same person in both third and sixth grades) who was especially influential in her development. She adored this woman and hoped to be like her someday. The young girl was devastated, then, when this excellent instructor and warm, affirming friend was fired from her teaching job and arrested for forging credentials. The positive influence was preserved, however, when the teacher wrote a personal letter to her former pupil, expressing regret for "letting her down," and offering further information that allowed the child to cross the bridge from disappointment to renewed understanding and respect. The girl never again saw her beloved teacher, but continues to remember her as one of the *big* people of her life.

In another case, the adult friend was a school principal who, together with the principal's husband, provided a haven of surrogate parenting in their home for this child from an unhappy family situation. The girl and her siblings were showered with comfortable attention from the childless couple, who seemed to enjoy having young visitors as household add-ons.

A musically talented informant who dismayed her parents by turning away from a stage career toward a religious vocation recalls with profound appreciation a woman choir director and her husband, who "were neat people" and whose friendship is remembered as a very important developmental influence. This friendship overlapped in time with another strong growth stimulus from the girl's senior pastor, a man instrumental in opening up her "cabined religious views" and alerting her to international issues of social justice.

For the minister-informant whose childhood was spent largely in India/Pakistan, her parents' participation as medical doctors in the missionary community drew her into a loving, caring extended-family type of association with many adults, as well as with other children. Social events often brought the adults and children together as peers on "fun nights"—social occasions in which all ages joined for musical entertainment, games, drama, or informal clowning. Among the many adult friends she remembers from her childhood years, one stands out: a man whose extensive library she was allowed to use. He entered into thought-provoking conversations with her over a long period of time and always treated her "like an adult." He died while she was still very young and willed her his fine library, a gesture with no small impact on her life.

She speaks of him with affection and gratitude. When, from ages ten to fourteen, she spent many months each year at a boarding school some distance from home and family, she added to the number of adults who were both friends and models in her development.

The following woman had a circle of friends that almost entirely coincided with that of her mother, though she did not single out special adult friendships beyond the ones with her parents. She was born in the South to a mother and father whose lives centered in their religious community, as had their families'. From the grandparents streamed sturdy traditions of family solidarity and church service. Her paternal grandfather was a choir director; her maternal grandfather, who ran a country store, was also a church "regular." As an only daughter, she was, from birth to adulthood, her mother's constant and willing companion, a "sister," and a friend. She remembers this close association with fondness.

• You have to understand what a complete social center the church has been in Negro life. We went everywhere together. Negro girls had two safe places—home and church; and we went back and forth between them, visiting shut-ins, attending meetings and conferences, taking trips. Church events were touching-down places for important Negro personages passing through the area: we met famous political figures, educators, actors, musicians. It was a beautiful world! God was seen and known in nature, and in Scripture [which her family studied and memorized extensively].

In her early years she became familiar with classical music, varied literature, studies of other cultures, and museum collections. She speaks of racial and cultural diversity, using metaphors of esthetic delight, such as "human bouquet"—a perspective brought along into her late years from her early learning.

I asked her to tell me about her consistent choice of the term "Negro" where I have learned to say "black." She prefers "Negro" because, for her, it "emphasizes cultural heritage more than color and sounds more dignified."

Incidentally, this woman's father desperately wanted his daughter to be musical and bought the child a violin. Teacher and pupil never transcended the left-handedness of the novice, so a violinist she was not to be. She did succeed at piano and organ.

The theme of strong father-daughter and/or mother-daughter friendships appears in approximately half of the stories, about equally divided between male and female parents. While most of the girlhood social networks are not so overwhelmingly adult-integrated as the last two mentioned, wherever child-parent (or child-grandparent) companionships were strong, the child tended to become acquainted early with many arenas of adult activity as part of such closeness.

Early images for one woman center around the family grocery. A childhood aspiration was to remain, as an adult, in this enterprise, where she often helped out in small ways. She and her father worked well together, she remembers, but when he heard of her idea to be in the store as an adult he was firmly against it: "A father shouldn't be an employer!"

She remembers him as "warm and playful, though also gruff and blustery sometimes—a man who swore a lot and was a stern disciplinarian, but who could also apologize and displayed really good values." When she confided in him one day about her wanting to be a minister, this man who, in her experience, had shown little interest in religion, shared the recollection of his family's desire that he become a priest. He was pleased by her decision. It strengthened the bond between them.

A father taught his future clergy daughter to read, starting her at age three with his own old primer featuring "Tommy and His Airplanes." Later on, he took her to the racetrack regularly, and to baseball games, teaching her how to handicap horses and figure batting averages. Her family "took great pride in learning, always emphasizing excellence" and encouraging her to think that she "could do anything." It therefore "made no sense" to her when her father also remarked, "Boys don't like girls who are too smart."

The smell of turpentine and paint inevitably brings to one informant memories of her painter-father.

• He was always quiet but very warm and affectionate. When I was little I used to run down the sidewalk to meet him at the end of his workday. He would put me on his bicycle and ride me home with him.

Mother friendships in the data center around a variety of church, school, community, and explicitly social activities, long walks in one case, and personal services for needy relatives, neighbors, or friends.

One clergywoman tells of an especially close and companionable relationship with her mother, who is pictured as a veritable social work agency: "With her, religion was never an excuse for not acting on behalf of others in their need." She took in people who required nursing care, painted a house for someone who couldn't get it done otherwise, got an alcoholic relative "straightened around and sober for the last twenty years of his life," and, in general, helped unpretentiously wherever she could with both her extended family and nonrelatives. At one point, her husband and children moved with her to a place where she could care for them along with another family whose mother had died.

This informant's home is remembered as an especially happy environment. She "felt *much* loved" by her deeply religious immigrant parents, whose love for each other was also evident to the children. She remembers much praise and few stated rules, but a constant expectation that she would act *responsibly*. There was comfortable cooperation between the parents, according to this daughter. The mother was recognized widely as the dynamic center of the extended family, a woman "who never ceased to grow and change with the times and who cared about *everyone*." In spite of the mother's vast outpouring of energy in the larger kinship and community networks, the informant recalls many pleasant times within the nuclear family unit as well. She suspects that her parents' primary diversion was having fun with their children. She reports, for example, "simple celebrations, little surprises, nice but inexpensive gifts, picnics, drives to the airport to see the planes,'' and so on. Interestingly, while the mother is such a powerful model of thoughtfulness and loving compassion, and the informant identifies strongly with her, it is the father who is remembered more for his ever-ready warmth and affection.

Grandparents are often mentioned in early life accounts, too, as powerful positive contributors to developmental well-being. The mother-daughter-church closeness described in one of the cases above is echoed in another, but now with a paternal grandmother who exercised a lasting influence. The grandmother is recalled as ''a strong, serious, strict, but kindly woman—respected throughout the community for her high ideals.'' The informant (oldest of ten siblings) speaks of the deep pride she felt as a child in being with Grandma as they walked along the country road, watching knots of gambling men quietly disperse when they approached. My informant remembers her grandmother as firm, yet comfortable to be with, and more approachable and understanding than the child's parents in many instances. The same clergy informant was close to other forebears. At least one great-grandmother, with memories of life as a slave, was nearby, working on her farm and serving as a midwife in the neighborhood while the informant was a small child. The occasion of the great-grandmother's death at 84 is held to be a miraculous occurrence. The old woman often voiced her hope that she would die without great suffering. One day she walked toward the barn at milking time, reeled, and fell down dead. The family experienced it as ''a beautiful thing,'' a blessing on this woman who ''never wanted to suffer more.''

A paternal grandfather is strong in the memory of one informant, whose household included him while she was small. She thinks back to the times when he would read stories as, for her, the most memorable feature of his presence in her childhood home.

One grandmother is called a ''second mother.'' The informant lived with her during family furloughs in the United States and later became the ''family representative'' at the grandmother's funeral.

From age eleven until she left for college, an informant lived in a household composed of herself, a sister, their mother, and their grandmother. Her words capture the tone struck by other women who had grandparents knit into the family: ''Intergenerational living can be *very* rich.'' This same informant says of her other grandmother, ''She provided all the dress-up stuff—the occasional opera, restaurant meal, or theater performance.'' From other sources we know that intergenerational living can also be highly stressful and rancorous, but in the lives of these particular women the skew is dramatically positive. There is only a glimmer of this negative potential in one or two of the stories, where invalid grandparents were in the homes for long periods of time. What the grandparents' presence meant in the parents' lives is, of course, a different question. For these informants, though, the grandparents' nearness tends to rest warmly in their memories.

The images of parents and grandparents carried along by informants in their own versions of their lives cannot be put forth as a dependably objective description of those relatives *as they actually are or were*. The images certainly can be offered as an objective account of the *informants' experiences* of those persons, and the latter view is an important focus in this study.

When the data are considered as a whole, there is a clear dominance of certain types of mothers, fathers, and mother/father combinations among the informants. At least through the eyes of these daughters, all but four mothers emerge as admirably competent because of various accomplishments. (Grandmothers are also notable in this respect.) Even the four exceptions are exceptions only by default; that is, the spontaneously delivered descriptions simply do not contain information that allows me to make pertinent judgments in their cases.

Eight clergywomen either remember their fathers as very warm, cooperative men or the relationship with them as a warm and comfortable one. The other nine father memories are distributed across other types: unstable/compulsive, omnicompetent/distant, domineering/exploitative, harsh/angry, and so on. The data also contain unmistakable signs of adequate-to-superior competence throughout the father group (as with the mothers) in chosen occupations and activities. Yet the daughters tend to emphasize the manner of the relationship to the family as they talk about their fathers. This may be either because father work competence is taken for granted (not considered especially noteworthy) or because it is not as directly observable by one's children. A third possibility is that the clergywomen, as women are said to do (in the gender role literature), tend to value quality of relationship more than objective achievement, a point that cannot explain the more direct references to competence among the mothers.

The combination of a friendly, competent mother with a friendly, competent, very warm father appears in six cases. This is obviously not a stereotypical couple in traditional terms, which may in part account for the salience of these features in the daughter's consciousness and in the shared vignettes. The number of such parental couples is larger than for any other relevant pair type I can discern in the data. It occurs to me that this might well be investigated as a possible ideal-type couple for socializing girl children high in the quality Erik Erikson calls "generativity"—mature identity integrity spontaneously employed to assist other humans toward healthy development.

It may be noteworthy that the four informants with the most positive images of early years are in or beyond mid-life. For me this raises a question of age stage effect on the content of memory. I do not doubt the credibility of the data, and I am not suggesting that there is heavy romanticization of memories as a function of aging. The amount of concrete, particularized detail delivered serves to counter such suspicions. Rather, I wonder whether input from childhood experience is less thoroughly evaluated and less salient in human consciousness during early adulthood, and whether it crystallizes later as persons are stimulated repeatedly to interpret their identities and behaviors in various contexts.

Were I to stop here in discussing the clergywomen's early experiences, an impression of unusually strong, positive, rich family environments would result.

The data allow little serious doubt about the validity of such an impression; but the picture is not yet complete. The stories also contain tragedy, pain, and ugliness along with the beauty and supportive strength.

An informant, now in her own second marriage, remembers the shock and confusion she felt as a child when she was caught up in the scandal attending the public revelation of her well-known father's extramarital affair. She describes the abrupt splitting of the household and sudden relocation to other communities. Years later, in the aftermath of her own divorce (which was similar in many respects but lacked the public notoriety), she claims she drew heavily on her mother's example for how to survive and create a new life.

A woman tells of her trauma and bewilderment created by prolonged sexual abuse by her father, a public figure who in many ways was also a good parent. For several years she struggled for sanity as she frequently contemplated suicide and ''wondered where God was in all this.'' Though she often felt severely incapacitated in dealing with life during her teens, she nevertheless continued to function acceptably in school and maintained an ambivalent interest in church, where her father was an active member. She credits her husband with contributing the steady, sensitive caring necessary for finally defusing her residual anger and disorientation from incestuous exploitation.

A recovered alcoholic is among the informants. She says there were also youthful bouts with other drugs, compulsive overeating (her mother's compulsion, too), anorexia, and defiant dating of men calculated to get her father's attention. ''I was staking out my own territory in power games with my father.''

There are memories of protracted illnesses that deeply affected family organization. One woman's mother suffered from multiple sclerosis and died when the future clergy daughter was in high school. Another's grandmother was bedfast for 20 years and cared for in the childhood home. Birth of a sickly younger sister in one household substantially altered the informant's relationship with her parents.

Mythic elements surrounding illness or death are powerful identity anchors in certain of the clergywomen's memories. One informant, who was herself sickly and often in danger of death as a small child, gained robust health through the then newly discovered antibiotics. She recalls her father's oft-repeated comment as important in her self-understanding: ''God has saved you from death for a very special reason. Don't settle for second rate.''

The woman whose mother died when the little girl was two recalls hearing her father tell again and again how he loved his family and struggled to keep them together. In this story, the father preserved a memory of the dead mother and of their early life together. As a consequence, the woman carries a strong mental image of a ''sweet mother . . . who loved her children much . . . and was so happy with her first little girl'' (the informant).

A vivid early memory held by one informant involves playing with fire at the age of four and accidentally igniting a curtain. The family home was destroyed in the ensuing blaze. (She has never forgotten her bitter disappointment that, in the panic to save important belongings, nobody would save her favorite hat!)

An informant's father lost his job soon after her birth. For 14 years after that her mother and the children lived in a house rented for them by a relative. During that period the father had low-pay employment in another city and joined the family only on weekends. At last he was able to get work with substantially improved earnings, and the family began living together throughout the week. The informant remembers a very stressful family adjustment to the altered circumstances.

One father's compulsive drinking focused family tensions and finally became a major factor in the parents' divorce.

Another informant only recently discovered that a longstanding conflict between her father and her oldest brother is rooted in the father's knowledge that this son he reared is not his own biological offspring.

As a teenager, an informant was removed by court order from her parental home to a foster home. This case and two others are the only ones with indications of especially turbulent adolescent rebellions. One of the three declares, "My home was a warm and comfortable home, but I was not warm and comfortable in it." The same informant later comments, "I was gifted with magnificent environments and they have made a difference. I have taken much from them."

A woman describes two isolated experiences of sexual intercourse, as a teenager, with two different men, and a baby was the result in each case. In addition to the problems associated with the pregnancies and early single-parenting, the first sexual experience was "an overwhelming, frightening, fearful thing," and this very religious girl was shunned by the church community during her ordeals.

As the stories move away from childhood and adolescence and into adulthood, there are the five divorces mentioned earlier. Several of these separations ended personally traumatic experiences of marriage, in one case to a child-abusing husband. A different woman (who is now married to someone she describes as loving, supportive, helpful, cooperative) says of her brief early marriage, "I felt dead. I couldn't cope with the lying, cheating, stealing, and extramarital affairs."

Each of two women reports a son imprisoned for a legal offense. Another dealt with the birth and, some years later, the death of a multiply disabled and mentally retarded son.

These are the more dramatic problems that have taxed the coping skills of the 17 women I interviewed. As I presented my findings before a number of groups, listeners expressed little surprise at the family strength found in the backgrounds. After all, these are women selected as professionally successful in a pioneering way. The surprise, rather, is voiced in response to information about the profoundly disturbing events and issues threatening personal stability. Questions are raised about whether the incidence is greater than normal for a group this size. Probably not, I think, but I cannot tell from these data. Given assurances of confidentiality, and other informants with comparable self-awareness and expressive skills, I suspect a similar list of potentially destabilizing personal traumas might emerge. People also wonder whether the negative items are concentrated in just a few of the cases. They are not. In fact, the distribution is broad, and the items mentioned involved 14 of the 17 women.

It seems to me that the recollections of what life was like "at home" can be divided meaningfully, for these women, into four categories:

1. Four informants recall unusually happy childhoods with essentially nonconflictive relationships, and much creative activity stimulating to their intellectual/personal development.

2. Seven put forth pictures of adequately supportive family environments, generally conducive to healthy growth, yet containing a steady low level of conflict, trouble, and tension that sounds fairly usual for our society—that is, aggravating but not absorbing the major portion of family energies.

3. In four cases there is a mixture of traumatic elements and powerfully positive resources that allow these clergywomen to transcend the potentially destructive influences.

4. Finally, two women describe quite uniformly negative family experiences in the kind of relationships often referred to in family sociology as "conflict habituated." For these latter informants, a more positive and satisfying direction for their lives took shape in connection with certain extrafamilial church and school networks. They noted the dramatic contrasts between Christians who, in the words of one, "were shitty and tacky with each other" and those who "were really kind and considerate." These informants devoted considerable energy to putting themselves in contact with the persons they admired. Strong identification with new models and careful observation helped them to set new directions in their lives. They did not want to be like people "who wore large crosses at all times but were Christian creeps with no vision, no imagination," as one puts it.

Some patterns run very strong in the interview data. Apart from the special situation of the Jewish family mentioned above, all the informants were having regular contact with church activities (worship, instructional, social) from childhood. With two or three possible exceptions they had steady, extensive exposure to Biblical literature. Four also mentioned the memorization of Scripture, sometimes connected with organized competitions.

The overall tone of 11 informants describing their early religious experiences is pleasant—generally light, happy, warm, supportive, communal, service-oriented, rich. Six have more negative memories of oppressiveness—fear, guilt, narrowness, restrictions, "awful, long services," ominous "elder visitations," joyless heaviness. Even these six, though, speak of profoundly positive aspects of that early religious formation which, at least in retrospect, are the roots of a more hopeful present outlook. One informant with an especially dark childhood memory of church was allowed to go "just for fun" to another friendly, warm Sunday school in addition to "her own" church activities. She loved the other church and participated enthusiastically, though at that time it remained outside her religious identity as she understood it. Now she identifies strongly with the "just for fun" memories.

The informant with the most fear-filled religious milieu in childhood was presented regularly with vivid images of the hell awaiting unsaved, unrepentent sinners. And the "sins" were always specific acts she was sure she had committed. One sermon, for example, warned against women wearing men's clothes, and she "had just the night before gone out to the barn in the rain with [her] father's old coat [over her]." She always felt she was in danger. This woman, from her late teens, began seeing alternative views of God and faith as she made geographic moves and affiliated with other religious communities. She says each new view of God got better and better. She is not sure whether she would have grown just as she has anyway or whether each group played a necessary role in her spiritual development. At any rate, she says,

• I wouldn't trade that early training . . . though it was an angry God then. I *did* learn to pray and I learned about God . . . and I feel *very* special to God.

An informant, with no inclination whatsoever to minister according to her rigidly fundamentalist early learnings, has a strong recollection of a time at vacation Bible school when she knelt and "became a Christian" at the age of eight. She recalls weeping and feeling a terrible burden of guilt. Though there was little joy and a great deal of pressure to prove herself constantly, it was a profound commitment and "got more positive later." At the same time that the guilt was feeding her feeling of inferiority, she says, the Bible study and memorization was a sturdy source of personal security and pride in accomplishment.

Not one of the 17 clergywomen currently finds a negative, fear-generating proclamation true to her vision of God. This will be apparent to the reader in later chapters. While those with such beginnings are not strongly condemning in their comments about early religious teachers, all of them now consider such judgmental approaches offensive as well as threatening to healthy human development. The most common theme in the more positive childhood religious experiences is the combination of Biblical conservatism with social liberalism. Later on, the reader will see how the clergywomen incorporate this double influence into their present views of life and ministry. For all of the Christian informants church involvement was steady enough, over time, that there was contact with contrasting ministerial approaches, either through changes in local personnel, family moves, or attendance at special events with guest leaders. This provided ample opportunity for considering options in the interpretation of Christianity.

All of the clergywomen point to the following type occurrence as having utmost importance in both their personal development and their religious faith journeys: at some crucial moments in their lives, people from within their religious communities offered the needed support and/or stimulation for the next step in growth. The forms varied: permission and encouragement for serious intellectual questioning of beliefs, sensitive acceptance and help in grief and distress, counseling that took them seriously as responsible moral agents, and offers of opportunities that implied confidence in their abilities. The opening up of responsibly critical thinking as a religiously acceptable pursuit seems to be a turning point of immense significance in many of these biographies. Characteristically it happened in college and seminary experiences, but also at much earlier times for several who credited especially charismatic teachers and pastors with helping them to move out of static views of life and God, into developmental views that are personally freeing.

Before dealing with interview material focused directly on the women as ministers, I want to present a set of findings about how they came to choose ordination. (The *choice* to be a priest is a longstanding one for the Roman Catholic woman, though she is denied the official institutional status of ordination for her priestly functioning.) If I step back from the detailed data about individual situations and take a panoramic look at what the data convey, I am impressed with the almost casual way that actual ordination appears in their biographies.

For the 11 middle-aged and older women, religiously based ministries to human needs were highly developed, as well as extensively recognized and affirmed in their associations, long before they considered, sought, or acquired ordained status. Most of them had no mental niche for an ordained woman; they had developed their spiritual life and commitments as intrinsically meaningful responses to a felt call to be faithful to God. They experienced this God as very real, consummately loving, and central in their existence. However, one states bluntly,

• I am not a spiritual person. I am oriented toward practical social action that directly benefits real people.

Her self-assessment appears to be based on a definition of spirituality that is more devotional and mystical than she senses herself to be.

These eleven experienced from youth (sometimes a datable experience, sometimes not) a call from God to give their lives to God's work among people. They involved themselves in much church activity, but their basic understanding of the call was for a whole-life commitment to help people. The later call to ordination evolved for them as a culminating stage in ministries they see themselves as having entered much earlier.

In religious leadership much is made of the idea of *call*. Traditions vary as to whether one ought be embarrassed by having had some dramatic beckoning vision or by not having had such an experience. In spite of inspiring stories in all traditions about compelling events seen as crisis points from which a person's devotional response springs, contemporary church leaders tend to think of the call to ordained status in more naturalistic, developmental terms. When they attempt to describe abstract ideas or internal states, people normally reach for expressive metaphor from the concrete details of mundane happenings. Many of these women speak of their call in explicitly or implicitly gestational terms:

• Back to the old birthing imagery. . . . It's like when you're pregnant and you first feel the stirrings inside . . . or you begin to feel different and you wonder if you *are* pregnant. . . . For some people like me it started when I was a little girl[2]. . . . For others it starts much later . . . but it begins with just a little faint stirring. . . . You go about and you look at other alternatives and all, but it just keeps growing and growing and growing until pretty soon . . . you have no choice. It begins to take more and more space inside you until it has a life of its own and you recognize that this is not just you; this is something God's put in you and you have to let it come to birth. . . . For some people the birth process is a lot more long and painful than for others . . . The [pregnancy] image has its limits. . . . The way that you begin to feel it [the call], or at least that *I* did, began to be . . . I'm *needed*. . . . The wisdom of the church says . . . [one needs] the confirmation of other Christians, the recognition that this is what I was equipped and gifted to do and the call from them to go do it . . . coming from many different people. . . . I think an authentic call to ministry is sort of like . . . people who paint and compose and write . . . have always said, "Don't do it unless you can't not do it. Don't just choose it as, 'That would be a kind of interesting thing to do; why not?' "

The dual influence of inner impulses on one hand and urgings from associates on the other is noted by all the women who entered professional ministry after young adulthood.

Nine years prior to her ordination a woman decided, in the throes of a critical health problem, to "serve God." She told her pastor that she believed God had called her to "teach the Word," but she did not then understand that call to be to the official leadership of the church. From that point on there were "just many little moves" that led in the direction of ordination. As she was asked to speak in various places and taught numerous classes, people noticed her development and the flourishing, growing ministry that was taking shape in an informal way. There came a time when her pastor witnessed the overwhelmingly positive audience response after her presentation in a huge public auditorium. He confided, "You are ready to be ordained." She says she felt ordained already and questioned whether a paper title was required. He thought she could go further if the church officially recognized her calling. At his suggestion an "irregular" exception was made, and the church ordained her. She is now, after the fact, completing some of the education that usually is a prerequisite.

Ordination, for the oldest informant in the study, caps a lifetime of Christian ministry while changing very little about her actual life circumstances. The following quoted material is excerpted from her ordination essay:

• [As a girl] I felt drawn to things spiritual. I prayed that God would use me in His work. I felt that God wanted me to serve Him in a special way.

[. . .]

• Do I feel that God called me to be a minister? [. . .] All that I can say is that I have tried all my life to minister to people in need in relation to my understanding, ability,

and opportunity. [. . .] I have always participated in church activities wherever I have
lived and worked. [. . .] I have always been at home with God's people and I have
considered myself part of God's church family. . . .

[. . .]

I do not know how much longer I will live nor how much strength I will have to give,
but this I know, I would like to live for Christ and use that strength in His work for as
long as God wills.

[. . .]

This petition for ordination comes near the end rather than at the beginning of a life
of service as a minister for Christ. I retired from government service last year and after
six months of relaxation, meditation, and contemplation on how I would spend my
retirement years, I felt drawn to the decision made many years ago—to dedicate my life
to full-time Christian service. "Full-time" to me means complete dedication to the single
goal of service to Christ. It is not a new goal. It is one which I followed more than 20
years prior to entering public service. After 12 years in "Babylonian Exile" I seek to
return to Jerusalem, "the City of God." While working in government service I remembered the words of Jeremiah to the exiles in Babylon: "Build houses and live in them,
plant gardens and eat their produce. . . . seek the welfare of the city where I have sent
you in exile, for in its welfare you will find your welfare. . . . when seventy years are
completed. . . . I will visit you and I will bring you back to this place. For I know the
plans I have for you, says the Lord, plans for welfare and not for evil, to give you a
future and hope." (Jer. 29:5,7,10,11). Though these words were written to a nation in
exile, they have a deep meaning for me as a person who felt a call to be God's servant
many years ago but whose service was interrupted or directed in some unusual channels.
I seek now to rededicate myself by seeking ordination to the ministry.

Here is a woman who has parlayed the hopeful, personalized approach and
supportive base of a traditional institution into potent opportunities for social
influence, moving across and outside existing role permissions for decades prior
to formal institutional recognition and inclusion of her efforts. She did not wait
for ordination before entering ministry. Nor has the fact of ordination removed
the remaining barriers to full acceptance of her as a minister. It is no small thing,
institutionally and culturally, that she, as a black woman, now has official access
to a leadership role in a largely white denomination. It may represent no huge
change in her life situation at this point, but it may well be one of her most far-
reaching contributions to the life possibilities of others. Precedent by way of
exceptional circumstances is, nonetheless, accessing precedent; it provides leverage for subsequent aspirants to the role. Her life story is not of a "career"
but of a series of associations ranging over the South and North: academic and
social service settings; church and public agencies; international, integrated, and
segregated communities. In spite of her ostensibly oppressed status due to race,
sex, and age, she declares simply, "Life has been good for me."

As early as second grade, one clergywoman remembers being attracted to a
religious vocation. Her family held church workers in high respect, and together
they often listened to the talks of visiting missionaries. Overseas work and
attempts to alleviate the suffering of oppressed and deprived people especially

excited the child's imagination. She once, for a while, took five cents each week from her allowance, taped it to a paper, and sent it to a missionary who worked among very poor people. She maintains she has never been able to forget her call as a child to full-time church service and, she believes, to the priesthood that she is officially denied (while at the same time she is being encouraged in her work by male priest associates). She entered a convent while still in her teens, has studied and taught extensively in her church, and has entered very fully into ministerial roles in several locations. With quiet intensity she reveals that her fondest dream is that God will allow her to celebrate the Eucharist as a church-approved officiant before her death.

Another voice:

• I had a clear call from the [religious] community—not just an individual call where somebody says, "I heard from the Lord and I'm going to get ordained," but the community really saying, "You ought to think about this."

These words come from a woman who was becoming more and more involved in lay ministry. She was primarily a youth leader developing worship through music and dance. After a profound spiritual experience at a retreat, she told her minister about it. He arranged a conversation with a regional clergy supervisor who asked her to consider ordination. This confirmation of parish response by the church hierarchy was a powerful impetus. A year later, after careful information-gathering and consideration of implications for herself and her family, she entered seminary with ordination as a goal.

In response to the question, "How do you think of your call?" several informants indicated that the call may be easier to locate, as a turning point, in retrospect than when it is emerging in one's experience.

• When you've been in church all your life it's hard to say "This is it!"
• The minister, whether ordained or not, goes into action according to the need when something happens.
• If the accomplishment of a goal is evidence of calling to perform it, then I can show the evidence of my call.
• We were there [in Asia] about three years. I was bothered by the poverty and filth and different customs, but I survived culture shock much better than the other military wives. I continued my classical music studies and learned the language. My husband and I were invited to native celebrations and we talked with people about religious faith . . . theirs and ours. . . . The going rate for maids was *so* low; I paid ours more, and I shared clothing, food, and soap. I saw it as ministry. While I was there I began to see a new direction. . . . I could start to feel the ministry growing in me.
• For me "the call" was developmental. There was a growing in conscious awareness . . . a sense of pursuit by God for a special job for which I seemed fitted . . . a sense that I needed to obey this urging that I understood to be God's urging.

At some point the "call to ordination" may be little more than a new clarity about the expanded access to people's needs conferred by professional status, coupled with a personal desire to move in that direction.

One informant speaks of the call to professional ministry in a way that strongly democratizes the concept. She once had a profound life-altering spiritual experience of the datable sort[3] (not the call to ordination), but she hesitates to mention it, except in very special circumstances, because she fears its divisive potential.

• When you talk about *call* it causes people to kind of move away . . . it can somehow sound like it's establishing your direct line to God . . . they feel they don't have that in some sense. . . . I think that's part of why I'm always feeling the need to help people understand *their* calls . . . I would define the church as a place where we can help one another to see and understand and use our gifts and our calls.

She indicates that she felt as *called* to motherhood, at an earlier point in her life, as she does now to her clergy work. She describes it as "a sense that God has hold of your life."

In several cases, husbands were instrumental in planting the actual idea of clergy vocation. One woman with many years of public school teaching and lay leadership in the church was asked by her spouse, "Have you ever considered entering the ministry"? She claims she had not.

• It was like the light bulb in cartoons . . . more like Reagan's "kick in the keester". . . . [The call] had been creeping up for a long time and finally said, "Boo". . . . I filled out a seminary application the next day.

A woman who refers to her call as a compelling urgency to help others that just grew and grew, and who thinks of her ordination from God as antedating the church act, nonetheless speculates that ordination may mean more to women than to men, at least in some ways. She thinks that the official institutional act leads to acceptance of a woman as a pastor, as an authority, and helps people to take her more seriously as a person in a society where women's gifts are often overlooked.

For the six youngest women in the study, lengthy preludes of volunteer or professional nonclerical church service did not precede their decisions to seek ordination, though patterns of youthful religious activity look similar to those of the older women and often include the teaching of younger children. Certain aspects of their perceived calls into the role are very similar to the cases of the others mentioned. There is the same urgency to make their lives useful on behalf of others, the same welcoming of opportunities to increase the range of such human service, the same dawning conviction that a clergical vocation is one for which they are well suited. The major difference seems to be that, as the younger women considered vocational preference, clergy ordination of females was actually happening "out there" among religious institutions. It could be considered as a professional work option beyond a merely personal spiritual commitment.

As they sifted experiences and observations of their social environments, they evaluated the imagined possibilities for themselves in the clerical role, though in most cases they had no female clergy models to observe directly. Sometimes with side trips into other work, sometimes in a straight line from college, they entered seminary at an early age, knowing that ordination could happen, either in their own religious group or some other denomination acceptable to them. Four of the younger informants, like the older ones, indicated that they had received encouragement from certain friends, teachers, and ministers to pursue a clergy calling. The two who noted no suggestions, support, or urging from others through the decision process were influenced profoundly by male pastoral models who ministered sensitively and helpfully to their families in times of crisis and deep need. Both of these latter women exhibited a high degree of independence, assertiveness, and ability to translate or adapt male role performances for use in their own identity development. The career alternative one of them had considered was nuclear physics; the other had begun work as an athletic director.

Given the frequency of male clergy references to pressures toward the ministry from parents, it is noteworthy that none of the informants was alerted to the possibility of a clergy role or pushed toward it by conversation with parents. Family responses to the declaration of intention from a daughter/sister/wife/mother range from evident acceptance and delight through bemusement to some open hostility and contempt. The weighting is heavily toward positive receptions, and all informants report steady progress toward fuller acceptance. Only three women had to deal with significantly alienated attitudes among close relatives.

The following accounts contain interesting details connected with how the six youngest women describe the call to ministry:

As a young girl, an informant noticed a woman's picture in a newspaper. What caught her attention was the title "Rev." attached to the woman's name. Her mother explained that the woman was a minister. The girl mentioned it to her pastor, who commented, "Our church doesn't do that." When she asked, "Why?" he had no answer, and she adds, "Bless his heart, he didn't try to come up with one on the spot." From this moment of awareness that women were actually in professional ministry, she says, work in a religious role had a growing appeal for her, and she gradually increased her knowledge of possibilities for women in church leadership positions. The pastor continued to talk with her about national discussions regarding female clergy. She credits him with keeping her informed of institutional progress in her denomination toward official acceptance of women clergy, which occurred when she was a high school sophomore. She also acknowledges much loving support from other pastors for her vocational objectives.

Another woman remembers that from her childhood she was clear about wanting to be in a "helping profession." Her pastor planted a seed by suggesting that their denomination might "someday" have women as ministers, and by adding playfully, "Maybe you'll come and take my job away from me." Over a number of years she moved toward ordination, mainly because she saw it as offering a wider age range of contacts and a greater task diversity than other human service jobs she was considering. The pastor who originally planted the seed stood by with helpful advice and reassurance about her aptitude. He was instrumental in arranging her seminary financing.

"An overwhelming sense of responsibility that I should be doing just this" is the way one young clergywoman speaks of her call. She continues:

• It's a demanding call. [My ministry] feels like an obedient thing to do. Partly it's a sense that I have been given some talents that are effective in ministry. I fit the job description. The call was like, "Get it in gear and *do* this!"

She had come to know herself as being good at public speaking, knowledgeable about social change needs, and deeply invested in the struggle for a more humane world, all of which seemed congruent with ideals for professional ministry.

An informant whose initial impulse to be a full-time religious worker came in connection with a religious camping experience at about age 12, says the urge persisted and grew in her from that time. It was amplified by what she sees as God's intervention in events that might have been wholly destructive aspects of her early life.

The most apparent conflict about vocational choice occurs in a young woman who is highly intellectual and frankly reformist in her perspective. She feels called "to call the church back to be what it can be," but has some misgivings about her patience for allowing people the necessary time to grow in their faith. She wants to build on traditions while struggling with others in the church to make rational choices relevant to contemporary life.

The rabbi and a Christian both speak passionately of their deep desire to give back in life some of what they so generously have been given. They see God acting in their own histories as hope, even in the lowest moments, and want to bring hope to others. One says:

• I'm here now because I've been given a gift of "advanced grace"—a second chance at living. All I can show people is where I've walked and where some of the strength comes from.

Having now gathered together the biographical items I consider pertinent for characterizing the group of women interviewed, I remind the reader that the data in this chapter indicate the kinds of persons delivering the observations still to be reported. This description of interviewees can*not* serve as trustworthy evidence of what kinds of people become clergywomen or of what demographic factors operate among clergywomen in general. It is primarily helpful in revealing the human resource base for the information in the study. While some commonalities have, indeed, been noted, the clear emphasis here is on the immense variety in biographical particulars among the women.

NOTES

1. In this study I do not make separate designations of "church" and "synagogue" where the reference is a generalized one to the relevant religious communities. Also, the Roman Catholic woman minister will be considered a clergywoman here, except when the material requires greater specification.

2. At age five this woman, who is now close to 50, told her mother that she wanted to be a minister.

3. Many religious groups consider it important to be able to date one's "salvation experience." Others do not. However, those that do not, still recognize that profound spiritual turning points are often remembered in connection with datable events.

Chapter 3

Gender Orientation

In the section on gender differences in Chapter 1 I outlined some of the differences scholars have noted in the modal response patterns of U.S. females and males. The reader is referred to Chapter 1 for a list of salient and well-established contrasts. Jeanne Block (1984) has discussed her reservations about current empirical support for such conclusions. She points out that there are, nevertheless, strong reasons to believe that the burgeoning research now being done in gender behavior will verify the existence of clear life-mode distinctions attached to sex and will show how they are shaped, in part, by the child-rearing milieu normative for U.S. society.

There is little serious scholarly questioning of the premise that both genetic predisposition and interaction with the social environment are important dynamics in the formation of human responses. How this occurs, and how the interactive socialization varies with individuals and categories, according to outcome and critical input, is, at present, only tenuously established in the disciplines concerned with human development. What is more thoroughly confirmed is the existence, for whatever reasons, of life orientations and ego developments that are significantly predictable among humans when their sex is known.

This chapter takes the conclusions of that literature and uses them as a reference base. I am not testing the conclusions of that literature; my work has neither the numbers of cases nor the comparison categories necessary for such testing. I am trying to see whether and how these particular clergywomen, stepping into a traditionally male-shaped role, may reveal a reputedly female orientation toward reality as they talk about themselves and their ministries. Of course, any person may be typical or exceptional. The question here is : Do these clergywomen speak of their lives in ways more usually chosen by men or by women? Imbedded in the simple question is a more complex set of questions having sociological interest: Are selective factors causing the clergywoman's role to be filled by women with primarily male-type life perspectives? Are women conforming to the existing role by adopting essentially male ways of professional thinking and acting? Are U.S. religious institutions now moving into a position where including women serves institutional goals? Is the inclusion of women driving the institutions into a different course? The nature of this study is such that it can provide fascinating glimpses into possible answers to all of these questions, but trustworthy testing of none of them. It is crucial that the reader keep this in mind, understanding that this research does not offer anything more than empirically based suggestions about where the answers to such questions may lie.

An unquestionably female orientation to life emerges from the gathered data. I shall use the general tendencies listed for women in Chapter 1 as a framework for a discussion of these findings, grouping outlooks characteristic of females in our society into these themes: intimacy and identity; personal focus; intrinsic satisfaction; nurturance; integrative thinking and intuition. These terms are by no means equivalencies. Yet there exists an internal logic by which they are developmentally intertwined and imply each other in nontrivial ways. Hence, neat categorical distinctions will continue to be elusive, even as categories are attempted for the sake of deeper insight.

INTIMACY AND IDENTITY

Women commonly report that the clearest and most satisfying sense of who they are occurs within the context of intimacy (from Chapter 1).

In her book, *Intimate Strangers* (1983), Lillian Rubin makes much of this point and offers the following partial definition of adult intimacy: "the wish to know another's inner life along with the ability to share one's own." This implies equalitarian access to both the attention and the cooperative intention of another.

Women seem to seek out the companionship of others for its own sake and to rely on sustained close relationships for personal growth, self-assessment, and a sense of well-being. Freedom to develop the vulnerability of mutual trust depends on confidence not only that such deep communication is intrinsically worthwhile, but also that it will not be used impersonally or adversarially by either person to exploit some strategic advantage external to the relationship— hence the emphasis among women on the status, health, maintenance, and restoration of relationships.

From very early in life, females (compared to males) are observed as more sociable, cooperative, "socially desirable" (i.e., pleasant, compliant), and more given to drawing physically close to persons in their environment (Block 1984). Jeanne Block comments that the developmental context for females in the early years is more strongly focused on feedback about personal acceptability and trust than about objective competence or concrete achievement. She cites earlier work, by Bakan, and uses his terms *agency* and *communion* as polar concepts to help describe gender-specific tendencies in personality development. Bakan's terms are especially interesting for our discussion here. They bear an almost precious coincidence of usage with the traditional polarities of religious institutions. She gives due recognition to Bakan's assertion that the viability of all developing organisms depends on the successful internal integration of agency and communion. She also attends to the evidence that boys/men are encouraged toward agentic development, and girls/women toward interpersonal/communal development (Block 1984: 5–6).

Agency is concerned with the organism as an individual and manifests itself in self-protection, self-assertion, and self-expansion. Communion, according to Bakan, is descriptive of the individual organism as it exists in some larger organism of which it is a part and manifests itself in the sense of being at one with other organisms.

There is an array of paired terms used by scholars when discussing gender differences in ways of dealing with life. Each set is illuminating and limiting in some ways. Taking the first of each as the female, we note: expressive/instrumental; assimilative/accommodative; person-focused/project-focused; concerned with developing inner space/concerned with developing outer space; specializing in primary (holistic, intimate, particular) relationships/specializing in secondary (limited, utilitarian, transferable) relationships.

Gender analysis literature abounds with conclusions that (1) there are differences in cultural norms for males and females; (2) all persons represent something of a mix of the norms; (3) some persons are quite untypical for their sex in their culture; (4) most people lean toward gender-normative development in their culture.

Though my data will also show that the informants express some perspectives more typical of men, there can be no doubt that they exhibit a type of ego organization that is primarily affirmed, according to them, by being "let into" others' lives through mutual openness and trust—intimacy. Over and over I heard something like the following:

• One of the greatest rewards in the ministry is being with people at moments important to them—celebrations, hurtings, times of growth and change.
• Being let into people's lives is such a privilege—the connecting with people and sharing a vision.
• I love it when people open up and share deeply from their lives or when they brighten visibly in my presence.
• Witnessing the "Aha!" moments for others when I'm teaching feeds my hunger for connectedness.

One woman who said, with great passion, "I so like being close, among, with people!" also spoke of her deep frustration that the clergy role, in some ways and with certain people, creates distance and interferes with closeness.

• I don't like being left out of activities because of my being a minister. I want them to feel I'm one of them. I'd hope they could say, "She loved *all* kinds of people—even the ugly ones—those in trouble."

Others reveal similar desires and concerns as they report with clear satisfaction that parishioners say, "She's one of us!"

The redundancy of sentiment alone cannot convey to the reader the depth of feeling that I, as the interviewer, could sense in these declarations. One woman, in a denomination not generally noted for emotional fervor, says that, for her, the highest rewards of ordained status happen when the Church is *really* being the Church. I asked her to explain:

• Sometimes the atmosphere becomes charged with aliveness to the Gospel . . . the "good news" that people can be empowered, refreshed, made new . . . from any point in their experience . . . that God is loving. It can happen in ecumenical settings, at weddings across church lines, through neighborhood outreach, anyplace. I love being with people . . . knowing I'm part of it . . . the closeness, the excitement of people beginning to catch the vision and to think in terms of it. I'm awed that the ministry gives access to such intimate places in people's lives. It's a rare privilege.

Though the above statement exudes a sort of breathless idealism often associated with very young and naive women, it comes from an informant in her middle years—one whose life has contained much struggle in dealing creatively with tragic events. This is also true of the woman who says,

• I want people to be glad that I have been part of their lives. It is a great joy being received into people's lives . . . being able to share at crisis times . . . feeling that my presence may have helped in some way . . . feeling in *partnership* with people.

Some of the statements are so nearly identical to others that to include them would look like editorial carelessness. The different ages do not strike different notes on this theme. A very young woman talks about the mutual growth she senses as her life "touches deeply the lives of others in ways that seem important." She especially mentions talking with the elderly about their hopes and fears as they face sickness or impending death; and she emphasizes the importance to her of "establishing rapport" with those who share their sufferings of any sort. Another of the youngest ones says of her ministry:

• The best part is when people let you in and let you love them and they love you back . . . when people say, "Here's my gut; I'll trust you with it."

The oldest informant, whose communal perspective is globally pan-human, nevertheless fears that the reality of persons can be obscured and neglected all too easily when churches become devoted mainly to the analytical or programmatical engagement with large social issues. She thinks they must not fail to consult persons about what is happening to them as individuals. Personal closeness and compassion are important dimensions of the ministry she sees for herself. She believes that women may bring to institutions the gift of this reminder about where human experience is *truly experienced*.

With only two exceptions, the women spontaneously and explicitly express positive valuing of personal closeness, in and of itself, as a central focus in their lives. This is done with high feeling and a keen sense of the gritty particulars around which such intimacy is developed. The importance of the personal relationship ideal for their ministerial identities is unmistakable. This study, of course, is not designed to produce evidence of the objective realization of such ideals in professional performance. But if we can assume that ideal self-image is to some degree indicative of either existing behavior rationalized, or intended behavior imaged, then it cannot be inconsequential to know that, among these professional influencers of ideals, empathic peer identification with others' experiences is a core commitment with assumed intrinsic rewards. Their stories of vocational "call" contain evidence, as described previously, of others' subjective responses to their presence as "ministerial" and trust-evoking. In many cases these were a greater motivation in job selection than were "objective" assessments of aptitudes and skills.

Clearly, the identity/intimacy connection usually thought of as "womanly" is alive and well among these women. As the data are examined further, especially in Chapters 5 through 8, we can see, in their own words, the profound implications of this basic life orientation for their institutional perspectives and activities. This shows, for example, with regard to issues of authority, morality, and "success." The emphasis on closeness to people does not here represent some retreat from the rigors of evaluative discrimination in relationships; nor does it stand for a romantic preference that authentic confrontations and negotiations among unique individuals be laid aside in favor of glossing exchanges. It simply means that the informants' characteristic ways of perceiving and responding lean strongly toward *communion* (rather than *agency*) as the primary orienting perspective.

PERSONAL FOCUS

The intimate is essentially the personal—a nontransferable, multilevel connection with a unique human responder. These women, most of whom were identified for me as being professionally influential and respected among male associates, express themselves throughout the interview data in thoroughly personalized terms. I would have to resort to considerable fabrication in order to produce anything but arguable instances of emphasis on such agentic goals as organizational expansion, structural elegance, increased budget, or other "concrete results" of ministry. As a matter of fact, those women reputed to be extraordinarily effective in program management, public performance, and intellectual crispness are precisely the ones who most ably articulate their *person-centeredness* in faith and ministry, as well as their dependence for life satisfaction on the internal joys of mutually nurturant personal encounters.

One hears substantial merging of meanings as the women speak of the *spiritual* and the *personal* in human experience. The metaphor of one concept is often used to illuminate the other, as in a woman's description of a retreat center devoted to the "mutual evoking of spiritual gifts." She uses language that easily exchanges the phrases "spiritual gifts" and "personal gifts." All 17 informants evidence a strong sense of the presence they name "God" as infusing the social-existential realm. Their imagery for God varies significantly, but it remains, in all cases, heavy with a sense of the interrelational and the personally imminent.

During the interviews the women all shared their most comfortable terms for discussing the God experience. References to "power," "might," "transcendence," and "instrumentality" were not absent, and talk about terms usually was introduced with a disclaimer pointing to the inadequacy of *any* verbal formulations. Nevertheless, they were overwhelmingly given over to expressions of personal closeness. A telling example is the woman who, after saying, "Words are not fair; He's too great and honorable and full of power," extended her statement:

• He is someone full of love . . . humility . . . mercy . . . kindness . . . truth—the only *real* truth . . . someone I can relate to easily and quickly as with no one else . . . as if I were looking right at Him. I can feel His presence . . . close. I love Him *very* much when I think about what He's done for me to have me with Him.

Similarly, another says:

• I feel very special to God. He's always moving me on to greater awareness . . . helping me grow all the time. He's taken such good care of me; I wouldn't give up on that!

Some of the women speak out of relatively conservative traditions of personal piety and theology. Others have thrived under steady exposure to liberal secular scholarship and sophisticated modern theological dialogue. Yet with regard to personalization of God-metaphor, as such, the groups appear indistinguishable. Among the women with the most abstract and highly intellectualized understandings of God and faith, the medium of personal experience is assumed and remarked and captured in images. A woman who confides that she is constantly struggling for appropriate imagery refers to the Holy Spirit who is "loving, caring, continuously creating, sustaining, redeeming, being . . . and gracious"— which for her implies God's "willingness to keep on keeping on with us."

Nature and movement terms are favored designations for God, as are ideals such as justice, peace, truth, and love. There are references to God as "life itself," "breath," "wind," "light," "fire," "rock," "eagle," "justice rolling down," "a river flowing," "bread," "water," "food," and "wholeness." Yet a woman who is exceedingly wide-ranging in her God imagery ends her free association on the idea by asserting,

• God is *never* "It" to me! That's offensive. God is *always* personal.

The image of God as father, mother, guide, or faithful lover/friend dominates the conceptualizations in the data, even among the women who reject the consideration of God as an entity. I take it as noteworthy that the parental God images, no less than the partner images, are used with implications of both covenantal reciprocity and mutuality of personal devotion. This underlines the intimately personal tone.

Many of the Christian women reveal that Jesus is their primary image of God. For a few, the meanings of God and Jesus are hardly separable. To whatever degree Jesus becomes the picture of God, a radical personalization of divine presence is in effect. One sees a strong emphasis on Jesus' accessibility, vulnerability, compassion, empathy, and revolutionary love. Jesus is seen as both imaging God and imaging possibilities for humans. Relationship terms are the commonest descriptors: He is trusting, caring, healing, helping, serving, giving. A woman speaks of her strong sense that God somehow lives within her in the way that God lived within Jesus. This understanding enters her thinking about prayer:

• When I pray for strength for others I think of it as a way of sending some of God's energy out from me to someone else.

The Jewish informant's discussion of God imagery is scarcely less personalized. Drawing from Jewish thought she offers,

• One without end . . . in warm shades . . . totally transcendent . . . very imminent . . . only understood through people. God looks like the person you love most . . . which proves that God has a sense of humor!

Then she hastens to add,

• Putting a figure on God limits God. That's a problem in talking about God.

Further development of the terminology-imagery theme will appear in Chapter 8. In merely establishing the personal focus of these women clergy, the data here make it clear that (even for the most traditional, and least intentionally feminist, informants) a "feminized" version of the deity is envisioned. That is, the acknowledged tendency of females to emphasize what social scientists call "primary relationships" (holistic, expressive, mutually satisfying, uniquely personal, and intrinsically valuable exchanges) over "secondary" ones (agentic, limited, specified, rule-ordered) shows in their God language.

Such an emphasis is equally apparent attached to various other topics throughout the interview data. But since many of these themes will be dealt with in their own right, I shall at this point merely skim some scattered examples of the pervasive tendency to personalize phenomena:

• I learned in seminary, "Make it yours and pass it on. Don't just quote 'authorities.' " I must speak to *me* in my sermons; and I must turn it to *their* uses. I don't reduce it; but I have to enter their familiar metaphor with it.

Another commented,

• My preaching is more person-centered and life-related than doctrinally oriented.

It should not be surprising, then, that the prevailing view of the biblical content is of people-to-people sharing—of a struggling, then and now, to understand life, God, and human responsibility, in personal relationships at every level.

• I see the Bible as one huge story containing small stories of how people know God . . . of God's relationship with individuals . . . of how God's love and God's choosing becomes personal . . . applicable to me. The Bible gives me insight on how I might reflect God to others.
• The Bible is full of stories of how God has worked with people . . . of the back-and-forth-ness between God and people.

The women talked about ideal believer-members in their religious communities. Often as they described "the faithful ones" they reported having specific persons in mind, who, I think we can safely infer, may embody ideals they hold for themselves. Some said as much. Here are three that capture the personal thrust of the characterizations:

• Faithful believers are caring, sensitive . . . alert to the needs of others and *there* to help. They make room in their lives for loving acts. Faith is not just something that pulls them in and out of church.
• My idea of a faithful Christian is someone who is flexible, pliable . . . still growing and learning . . . not locked into absolutism, yet continuing to struggle with what God is saying to them . . . aware of others and their own responsibility for breaking down walls of personal alienation and enmity.
• A faithful believer would be simple, humble, aware of individual limits . . . totally present to God and to others . . . someone who delights in life . . . feels deeply with and for others . . . is open to love, to giving, to receiving . . . is nonjudgmental . . . not self-righteously or pridefully condemning but courageous in confronting and challenging injustice and evil with justice and good . . . someone who has no personal hostility . . . someone who makes you feel like a great treasure.

INTRINSIC SATISFACTIONS

Listening to the women talk about personal relationships provides insight into the reasons they value personal intimacy so highly. It provides them with the concrete grounding for pondering the whole of reality. It is the textured reference base for detecting what life's most important projects might be; for evaluating what one's most important contributions are; for discovering and pondering the consequences of certain social arrangements and action choices. So the greatest joy in life becomes the sense of being deeply and authentically in touch with others; one's greatest "achievements" become the most fully developed and mutually satisfying personal relationships. The following illustrative sentiment is framed on an informant's office wall (she does not know the source):

Success

To laugh often and love much; to win the respect of intelligent persons and the affection of children; to earn the approbation of honest critics and endure the betrayal of false friends; to appreciate beauty; to find the best in others; to give of one's self; to leave the world a bit better, whether by a healthy child, a garden patch, or a redeemed social condition; to have played and laughed with enthusiasm and sung with exultation; to know even one life has breathed easier because you have lived—this is to have succeeded.

It would take a fairly acrobatic interpretation to wrench from these words a valuing of the items mainly for their strategic utility in acquiring perhaps more desirable benefits such as status, material wealth, or political power. The woman who chooses to hang the message over her desk has a degree from an Ivy League school, and is institutionally recognized as having strong administrative and teaching competencies. So her choice of criteria of success for public display is especially noteworthy.

The communion perspective in no way rules out agentic behavior. These women are up to their ears in programs, projects, clerical details, and organizational problem-solving on many levels. Still, a perspective in which projects are organized within a concern for personal well-being invites very different conceptual and action responses compared with a perspective in which personal relationships are cultivated and valued for goal attainment extrinsic to the relationship. It is easy to see why personal relationships hold such high intrinsic worth in the former orientation; they "contain," from that point of view, the world of meaning by being the priority organizing frame.

• For me the highest reward from my ministry is the supportiveness I get from interaction with people . . . being let into people's lives at important points for them and me.
• I will feel that I got what I wanted out of life if my own family feels they have gained from having me with them . . . if my faith has been a good experience and a ministry for them also . . . if people are glad I have been part of their lives . . . if I've taken part in societal change that has helped people's lives to be better.

A very young clergywoman, not long established in her present parish, responded to my probe about her most satisfying rewards by saying,

• People are so giving toward their ministers. My congregation is a caring family to say "Hello's" and "Goodbye's" and to help celebrate. I am overwhelmed by their generosity, including the material things they've given to show their love. It's a humbling experience; I feel unworthy . . . but I want it [such affirmation] very much!

An older, more experienced informant said,

• My greatest reward is in visiting the sick. So often I come out having heard their testimony . . . having received a message from the Lord . . . and I have been ministered to.

The internal logic of the *communion* orientation for women leads me to draw out a point sometimes ignored in gender analysis discussions. Much attention is directed at the relatively "flat" career trajectories among women and at their causes. Carroll, Hargrove, and Lummis (1983) note that clergywomen now enter their careers with opportunities for status and pay equal to those of clergymen. But over time they do not rise as quickly or as high as their male counterparts, when rated by prestige and pay. Some analysts consider this the direct consequence of sexist values and power distribution. Others suggest an indirect effect from socialization factors that predispose women to prefer low-status affiliative and service roles; to take comfort, for various reasons, in deferring to men in interactive processes; to be docile and adaptive when opposed in life situations; and to have unnecessarily low self-expectations for influence and accomplishment.

I do not intend here to argue that these effects are inconsequential. Many scholars have garnered much evidence to support them. I do want to propose an additional factor for consideration. The normative orientation for women may have been developed so thoroughly among many of them as an ultimate good, and may now receive such strong rational reinforcement from humanistic social science, dialectical theology, and speculative futurism, that some of the most self-confident, most assertive, and most institutionally promising women may actually be committed to *revaluing the traditional values*—to challenging built-in organizational assumptions about what constitutes social efficacy—to balancing more equally the public honors conferred on personal roles that show no "product," and instrumental roles that do.

Some of the women seem prepared to sacrifice opportunities for "advancement" in order to model and articulate convincingly ministries that offer few public rewards but much intrinsic satisfaction. Even the women who exhibit high levels of talent for administration indicate that, should they be selected for prestigious executive slots, they intend to use their influence to promote a greater institutional recognition of the value of the humbler pastoral skills.

A woman who has already received impressive denominational and regional recognition in her brief career countered my question, "What do you most want to get out of life?" by responding,

• I somehow find that question offensive. If you were to ask "What's most important to you?" I could answer better. It's most important to me to know that *in everything* there is an approach to God—which is a very freeing thought. If I believe that, and if I *desire* to approach God, all of life is its own reward.

Such beliefs and attitudes may encourage the emergence of unconventional (as regards prestige) person/position unions.

A young woman has a congregational charge that is marginally viable by denominational standards. She has been in this location several years. She is very excited about the intra-parish and community service activities currently in progress. She returns frequently, during the interview, to the theme of satisfaction in her work:

• What I want most in life is what I have right now. I tell my husband I feel "in sync" with him, my parents, my congregation, God. This place is very fulfilling. I'd be happy to spend my whole ministry here. I think this place is what churches are about. I'm not into visions but I feel directed by God to be here right now. I feel like I've *arrived* where I want to be. Maybe my doctorate [which she's working on] will gain me the status and credence with church officials to take me seriously when I say I want to make use of it *in this place*. I wouldn't look at a move to a "better" church as a reward. It would feel more like a condemnation if they tried to take me away from here because I've done well. I'm uncomfortable with all the talk among ministers about money and promotion. I don't hear much talk about the *meaning* of ministry in special situations.

A considerably older woman (also at an inner-city parish in a decaying neighborhood, and also enthusiastic about the possibilities for personal and community service) says of her satisfaction with her present location:

• It's almost like being in heaven! I'm excited by the ministry here. I feel the Lord is really using me. Surely I was just as committed . . . surely I was just as devout, or whatever, in the other parishes I served . . . but in this place my preaching is different. Maybe I'm having to rise to the responsibility of pulling a heavier load. The people say "Thank God that the Lord sent us a Holy Ghost filled preacher!" They say that they feel fed by my sermons.

When I asked this same woman what she most wanted in life she said,

• Just to help people. I want a closer walk with the Lord. Always there are things that aren't right yet. Sometimes life is full of distractions. I need more time to work on my relationship with God. That goes with serving people. I have a strong commitment but sometimes it lacks the joy that was there at first in my faith and ministry. I want to be *singing inside*! I don't want a busy career to interfere with my personal devotion.

Women with demonstrated managerial skills regularly receive suggestions and predictions from family and professional associates that they will one day occupy prestigious administrative positions. None admits to, or otherwise shows signs of, a driving ambition toward this end. Several, though, voice sentiments similar to this statement from a woman already being tapped for regional executive tasks:

• I do feel responsibility as a woman, to other women, in opening up areas that have been slow in opening to us. Senior pastor status is the hardest status to crack. If I get an opportunity for that, or judicatory work, I think I should be prepared to do it. . . . But there would be some personal loss in that . . . a multiple staff church or administrative post would not provide the satisfying sense of closeness.

One of the others who also speaks in this vein adds:

• I hope I won't feel compelled to higher office for validation of my ministry. I like where I am now; I feel very blessed.

As I listen to these high-energy, high-ability women with good-to-superb track records in public assertiveness and effective leadership, I note little reluctance to employ their skills managerially, but considerable reluctance to rate such skills higher than the democratic interpersonal skills of pastoral nurturance. One says, point-blank:

• I'm not glory-bound. I'm not looking to rise to the top. I see work as intrinsically valuable—nice to do—not for competition or status or achievement. I love the job and I love what I do, but it's secondary to personal life. I may not stay in a congregation. Parish expectations are not always healthy. I'm much more interested in alternative social structures, feminist issues, social work. . . . What I'm becoming is very unfinished. Each morning I start, "Reporting for duty, God; where do you want me?"

A woman currently established in a high-status position points out,

• Women are very ambivalent about the distance that status, privilege—even ordination itself—create. We want solidarity with people.

NURTURANCE

In pulling out sayings about nurturance, I am aware of the signs of nurturance in the material I earlier chose for demonstrating, for example, "intimacy" or "intrinsic rewards"; and I see in those I select for this section the clear implications for my later discussion of, for example, "integrative thinking" or "ethical stance." This overlap itself spotlights the mental/personal organization patterns dominant among women in our culture.

In spite of the blurred boundaries, nurturance (to which I now want to attend) is not *the same as*, for example, intimacy or personal focus. Lillian Rubin (1983: 90) "disentangles" two of these terms for us with characteristic insight:

> Nurturance is not intimacy. It may be connected to intimacy, may even sometimes be the result of it, but the two are distinct and separate phenomena. Nurturance is caretaking. Intimacy is some kind of reciprocal expression of feeling and thought, not out of fear or dependent need, but out of a wish to know another's inner life and to be able to share one's own.

If there is one word that captures what these women see God doing and what they feel called to be doing as ministers, it is *caring*. So it is crucial, in understanding them and their ministerial intentions, to look at their words about personal nurture. They think about *caring* most commonly in terms of *nurture*— fostering healthy developmental freedom for others and self—helping to maximize human well-being. This is what Erik Erikson calls *generativity*; it is parental caretaking in a broad sense.

• A faithful Christian responds to God's word and acts it out . . . not just in belief . . . or in support of an institution. . . . There is a use of self and possessions busily, in love . . . caring, service, doing things for others . . . perhaps volunteering at a hospital . . . marching on behalf of welfare recipients . . . caring for the environment.

Many of the women express not only the *desire* to care for people in a sensitive and helpful way, professionally and personally, but also the belief that being female may be an advantage in pastoral nurturance. It's not just that women are seen socially by others as more interruptable, available persons who can be approached with less urgent concerns and less deference to their involvements; women frequently cultivate such accessibility as part of what they assume caring entails:

• I have learned the importance of availability and interruptability at need points for parishioners.
• I want to emphasize accessibility rather than distance and awe . . . openness, rather than closedness . . . vulnerability rather than self-protection.

One woman makes a distinction between being "always available to persons" and "always available to the job." The latter she sees as a familiar male pattern and mentions it in connection with her fears of falling into that way of life.

There are several references to caring persons as "always right there for you when you need them." Quite obviously, this cannot be taken literally in a physical/spatial sense; but there is throughout the data a clear tenor that to care means seriously and intentionally staying in touch with someone's needs in order to foster well-being.

Both the imposed and chosen psychological vulnerabilities of women serve, in the estimation of some, to enhance interpersonal accessibility. There are also strong cultural expectations for women to be caretakers. While this admittedly presents some special problems to women, informants note that people may be considerably less hesitant to express need, expose weakness, or voice a request to a woman.

Lillian Rubin addresses this point in her study of working-class marriages, *Worlds of Pain* (1976: 20–21). Specifically, she talks about men's willingness to confide in a woman:

> I had been warned that I might be able to reach the women, but never the men.
> [. . .]
> I was surprised by the openness with which most of the men tried to talk about difficult and delicate subjects. So much so that I asked several about it. "Would it have been easier to talk about these personal issues with a man rather than a woman?" The answer required little thought: "No." And it was best explained by a thirty-one-year-old heavy-equipment mechanic as he walked me to my car very late one night:
> "Guys don't talk about things like that to each other. Me, I'm used to talking to women. I talked to my mother when I was a kid, not my father. When I got older, I talked to girls, not to guys. And now I have my wife to talk to."
> Of course, it makes sense, doesn't it? It is women, not men, who nurture, who comfort, who teach young boys. It is to women they run with their earliest pains and triumphs; it is to women they first confide their fears and fantasies. And to the degree that the American culture approves male expression of closeness or intimacy, it is between a man and a woman, not between two men.

In the presence of a clergywoman, a distressed man may not feel so burdened by the conventional cultural constraints to appear calm, self-sufficient, in control, strong, or unemotional.

• Women and men both confide in a woman more easily. When I hear, "No minister has done this before" or "I've never been able to do this with a minister before," I have to assume that there may be something attached to gender, because almost all ministers in the past have been male. I can cry with people and it makes a bond in some experiences—like in grief over a death. I think sometimes people are afraid that a man won't be sympathetic.
• Somehow, because you are a woman, amazing spiritual openness comes from men . . . the feeling flow is freed . . . the emotional side of spirituality can be expressed.
• Women don't "lose face" for doing things that might threaten traditional males as looking soft or weak.

One can easily sense the delight in these women that the nurturance they desire to give and are experienced in giving is, in the ministerial role, professionally validated and officially required, as well as personally needed. Their talk about caring is often couched in terms of "help to people in trouble." At least as often it comes as "supportiveness to personal growth."

• I believe in helping people to be all they can be.
• I want to emphasize a positive Christianity . . . empowerment rather than restriction or commands. I prefer to minimize prohibitions and maximize possibilities for creative living.
• I suspect I'm a "run-of-the-mill" pastor when it comes to leading and serving and caring—not so different from ordinary male ministers. Maybe I take more adult responsibility for nourishing each relationship as far as possible.
• It's so rewarding to see a person grow and unfold and share the experience of God. People say I'm warm and compassionate and humorous and lively. My hope is to reach out to help change people's lives. I find it rewarding to see people growing and moving and improving in all ways . . . I like picking up and hugging the children. One little girl waits each week for my hug before she will leave to go home after the worship service. Her grandma teases her by trying to take her out another door, but she insists on coming by me . . . so I make a big deal and sweep her up in my arms.

Organizational structure characteristically is judged by the women as worthy of maintaining if it is conducive to *personal* development, over time. This view will be developed more fully in Chapter 6.

The women do not fail to note the similarities to parenting.

• Being a pastor is so much like being a mother. When I first came, the older men and women had misgivings; but they have loved the caring. The early issue, as they now talk about it, seems to have been that they could not *defend* the choice of a woman minister to challengers. They still want help from me about what to say in response to questions. My own motherhood has been very important in my faith development; it has given me the patience to talk things through . . . to wait . . . to hear all sides . . . attempting to draw out the best expressions from others—their truest thoughts and feelings. It's ministry from the bottom up instead of the top down. I felt motherhood was a calling, too. In some early career counseling I rated highest in aptitudes for motherhood and religious ministry!
• Women have a sensitivity to children and how institutions and services affect children. . . . They're less organization- and task-centered . . . more person-centered.
• I think women are more in touch with earth, gut, feelings, cuddling, sheltering. . . . There's a tension in me between the desire to protect and the desire to push people out into the world.

This classic "parental" dilemma is mentioned by others:

• Women sometimes are *too* concerned about hurting feelings . . . wanting everyone to be comfortable.
• I'm always trying to weigh the needs for the prophetic[1] and the pastoral—which one would better facilitate the development toward human wholeness. I try to be perceptive about people's needs and their openness to hear and their readiness to move.

The emphasis on nurturance is abundantly clear in the clergywomen's talk about religious ritual occasions. They often see their officiating as *inviting* or *serving* in an intensely personal way. Two informants are explicit in equating this function with that of the gracious hostess—welcoming, setting at ease, introducing into the gathered community, fostering social/spiritual solidarity:

• I become hospitable in demeanor when I preside at liturgy . . . my voice . . . my gestures . . . the spatial arrangements I set up.

Consistent with this view, they almost all speak of great satisfaction in creatively customizing ritual celebrations for maximum personal impact in special situations.

It is precisely at this place that the Roman Catholic woman feels the highest frustration. In most ways she is free to minister according to perceived congregational needs. She preaches, teaches, and pastors without barriers, though the labels attached to these activities may be different from those for ordained men. However, when a moment in ministry would be captured best in Eucharistic embodiment—when, in her opinion, people require care in this traditional way— the natural flow into the ritual of ultimate nurture is aborted; as a woman, she is denied official permission to preside. Since, as a Catholic, she is imbued with the significance of the Eucharist as spiritual feeding, this is a particularly poignant denial. Her mediating gifts seem needed, but official rules block their delivery.

Funerals and weddings are most often mentioned by the informants as opportunities for inventive, personalized, nurturant, ceremonial attention.

• One of my earliest pastoral responsibilities was to a clergyman approaching death. I was able to assist in arrangements for a brief "return to work" at his church during his final days—an experience which was immensely gratifying to him and his family. For his congregation it was a dramatic demonstration of coping courage. There was a triumphant funeral in which many discovered the power of religious ritual in expressing deep, unarticulated meaning.
• People say, "She does a marvelous funeral . . . a marvelous wedding." Most of what the people see in this community is very traditional. Although some of the stuff I do is kind of traditional, too, I don't use traditional wording. I guess I have a sense of being *with* people in those functions . . . *with* a bride and groom . . . and feeling good *with* them. I take a great deal of trouble getting to know the people for whom I'm performing a wedding. . . . Therefore, a lot of my counseling is premarital counseling. . . . And there's pre-funeral and post-funeral counseling, too. That gives me a sense of where the person was important to those experiencing the loss.
• I've come to be something of a wedding specialist. I have a liturgical bent and I like creating innovative ceremonies that fit people's situations.

Caring is frequently seen as sensitivity and alertness to what people feel in concrete life situations and to their needs for ego support.

• At first people may think I'm too simplistic [with the personal focus] . . . but I think I'm just realistic about people's responses . . . alert to the complexities and actualities of where people are.
• I see people with such low self-esteem from the weight of sin. They're so quick to list

their failings . . . not so quick to celebrate redemption and grace. I want to release more joy, celebration, happiness in my ministry . . . help people be more relaxed, more expressive.

• One of my greatest frustrations is people's inability to *hear* that they are *good people*, worthy of love . . . their unwillingness to risk . . . to *fly* . . . to see the action demands of faith.

• I often see myself as protecting the laity and exercising a dampening effect [on ideas for big projects]. I can visualize the necessary effort involved and identify with the lay response in being given more jobs to do. I tend to form a ministry around the laity . . . as an enabler. I'm not a marshaller of the troops.

• I don't assume cooperation from others without regard for where that person is. I try to be respectful of the office staff and their time schedules . . . and the impact of my requests.

When calling on persons who are ill, the clergywomen check on the needs beyond the immediate physical problems: such as child care; food; financial worries; the specific griefs and fears attending losses of particular organs, limbs, sight; attendant marital insecurities; or the profound need just to share crystallized wisdom from a life story.

The awareness that self-nurture is an important dimension of love for others keeps the ideal of pastoral accessibility from degenerating into obligatory self-denial. A sturdy sense of self-respecting self-care emerges from the interview findings. Not all of the women speak to this point, but there does seem to be a good understanding among many of them that care for people requires care for self.

• I'm not a workaholic. I guard my time. I've always been a person who needed my space. Sometime during every day I have to have time for me. I'm not rigid with the schedule but I do need it at some point. I'm an avid reader; I read professional journals, historical novels, trashy novels, theology, magazines, newspapers . . . And for me, that's relaxing.

Another clergywoman says both she and her husband *are* workaholics. But they manage to make time for participating in events and activities of common interest: watching movies, reading, and long-distance driving (to professional and social gatherings of various sorts). Much of their "recreation" comes from meetings and programs that are simultaneously professional and pleasurable for them in a relaxing way.

Recreational interests mentioned by clergywomen include socializing with intimates, musical performance, physical exercise (skiing, martial arts, skating, dancing), creative arts (poetry writing, painting, needlework), spectator entertainment and a heavy component of wide-ranging reading. Time for devotional/meditational thought is there, too.

• I don't have what I would call a set devotional life but sometime each day I read material that is spiritually helpful. I use an assortment of biblical and contemporary writings.
• Most days I'm up by five. I make coffee and turn on the radio. Sometimes I listen to gospel music or a church service and come into the presence of the Lord. I intend to read every day but sometimes I don't. I like to sing and listen to others' sermons. Often I think about my own sermon ideas.

For those with husbands and/or children in their households, family time tends to be zealously guarded as precious and restorative.

• Dinnertime from six to seven-thirty or eight with my husband is very important to us. It's *our* time. I disconnect the phone and my congregation knows this. We eat our dinner, we watch the news, we talk about what's happened to each other during the day; then we feel comfortable to go off and do whatever else we need to do in the evening. Most often I go to the church for a meeting and my husband watches a movie on TV.
• I *reserve* family time. Our family talks well. I see evening meal time at home as family time and I look forward to it—*never* just as a service my husband performs [he is the primary cook] . . . that I can take or leave or push around, timewise, at my work convenience. I see my male associates doing that sort of thing. Their wives feel supported, in their persons and their marriages, by my habits. I won't use up our dinnertime for little extra staff meetings.

Almost everyone in the study mentions the constant struggle to preserve some personal time and privacy, and no one reports having enough. Yet there are strong indications of disciplined attention to their own need for time alone and family enjoyment. Their experience of family responsibilities as intrinsically recreational can be a tremendous benefit in their hectic and substantially unpredictable work agendas. While they are obviously under great strain to "get it all accomplished," their viewing of their families as essential areas of ministry and their generally keen pleasure in family associations does compensate a great deal for the pressures. Mothers of young children face a different order of pressure in this respect. Mothers of adolescent or adult children, though, sometimes describe an exhilarating counterpoint between "churchwork" and "homework." I don't want to discount the research findings indicating that "working women" just come home to a different "front" of production and performance demands. But it is significant to realize also that women frequently find spending time with family members and even some household tasks relaxing and replenishing for them.

• I cook. I learned to cook and bake at an early age and I love it. There are some quite poor people in our neighborhood, so I share with them as an excuse for cooking and baking more than my husband and I can eat up. I like sewing. I made all my clothes until recently, but now I do decorative needlework—more things like crocheting and counted cross-stitch. I wonder if my congregation doesn't tend to protect me more [regarding time] because I'm a woman. If I take a day off, I suspect they may think . . .

well . . . I've got cleaning and shopping and things to do at home . . . where for a man they'd tend to wonder what he's doing . . . and maybe imagine he's playing golf or something. I haven't really thought this through, but it's something I sense.

Insofar as conventional stereotypes are operating, it is possible that the popular image of a man's time off from labor is "leisure" or "play," and the image for a woman's time-out from the public work world is "personal attentions" and "domestic service"; the latter are more easily rationalized as ministerially admirable.

The women tend to view caring as a commitment to life itself, or a dimension of all life relationships, rather than as a compilation of charitable acts and worthy projects.

• I find myself very involved in the area of peace and seeking out ways to have some kind of influence in that area . . . but it's a part of everything I do. . . . It's not like it's set apart in some way as an all-consuming thing. . . . It has just become a part of my thinking . . . in *all* areas of my thinking.

As I sat and listened for hours to women who, on the surface, are very different from each other and who represent very different realms of social influence and religious thought, I was struck by a common thread that I only dimly perceive, but shall try to articulate, because it seems to me worthy of the attempt.

Some of them refer to God in traditional ways as a spirit entity "out there." This God draws close and deals with persons according to need and readiness. Others are more given to talking about God who is seen as spirit-constituent of all coherent life, movement, meaning, and relationships. This God emerges within all experience and confronts any person ready to get in touch with the ultimate core of reality. But regardless of how the dialogue is envisioned and experienced, God seems to signify both ultimate model as love/care and ultimate imperative to love/care for all that is.

Let me try to reduce what I see in the data to a fantasy soliloquy:

God and I are intimates. It is safe to show myself, in any way that I am, to God. God opens to me, too, and shows me as much as I am ready to see at any time. We know each other and really get into each other. That is, God is devoted to my well-being; God cares. I am devoted to showing forth God. I care. Now all of this happens in ordinary daily life. I care for God as I care for real people according to their real needs. I get God's care as people touch me in my needs. I specially treasure and develop a few close relationships as ways of knowing my closeness with God along the same lines. But in the universe of caring there is seldom a guarantee of full reciprocity between individuals. That's okay. I'm free to care unconditionally, or receive unearned caring from others, because God sees that, over time, I get what I need and am ready to accept. It's enough. It works out well for me. I feel tended by God. I can tend others out of my fullness. I feel intimate with the universe.

I'll make no case for how this all works out in the lives and ministries of these women. I have no systematic evidence in this study for that. I have tried to use only my intuition and the evidence at hand to weave a fantasy statement that I believe to be true, both to what I heard while I was with them, and to what I sensed from the feelings displayed as they spoke of their relationships with God and with people.

INTEGRATIVE THINKING AND INTUITION

At present, being female is firmly associated in our culture with the high probability of thinking and acting in an integrative way. That is, occurrences in life, aspects of phenomena, and levels of experience or persons are understood ecologically—in terms of each other's existence, in terms of interrelatedness and interaction consequences. So when women respond to the question, "What's *that* got to do with *this*?" (which may imply "You're off the track again!"), they are apt to offer explanations that take the question seriously as a straightforward request for information. Women are given to the assimilative organization of knowledge, feeling response, and intentionality. This is neither necessarily nor ideally their exclusive province, but is widely recognized as a socialized disposition in the United States more strongly evident in females than in males. In *The Turning Point*, Fritjof Capra (1982: 38) says:

The rational and the intuitive are complementary modes of functioning of the human mind. Rational thinking is linear, focused, and analytic. It belongs to the realm of the intellect, whose function it is to discriminate, measure, and categorize. Thus rational knowledge tends to be fragmented. Intuitive knowledge, on the other hand, is based on a direct, nonintellectual experience of reality arising in an expanded state of awareness. It tends to be synthesizing, holistic, and nonlinear.

These forms of knowledge coincide with Bakan's *agency* and *communion* orientations to life. I shall reserve for a later chapter the more complete discussion of how each human unit (person, institution, society) seems to require integration of the orientations within each organism if the perspective is not to prove self-limiting and destructive. Here I want to document, with regard to my informants, the tendency to view life as a *whole*—assimilating, integrating, "taking in" new experiences—making sense of them in terms of *everything*.

Psychoanalysts and clinical psychologists, among others, frequently observe dramatic correlations between persons' ways of orienting to life and their ideas about its governing dynamics, whether or not these are cast in traditional God-terms. For example, the person who says in a self-convinced way, "It's a dog-eat-dog world!" is very likely on the prowl for a vulnerable canine, so to speak. There is a longstanding debate between scholars who conclude that action is motivated by ideals and those who see ideals as rational defenses for self-interested action. What is quite unarguable is the connection itself.

It is reasonable to expect that women would either co-opt those facets of traditional theology that emphasize the God characteristics they themselves display, or would attempt to develop those qualities thought to be God's, or both.

An informant states her outlook:

• Action is primary. If you think right, you don't necessarily act right. If you *do* right, you understand.

These women are agentic to a degree untypical for women, and they sometimes speak of God in strongly agentic terms. They have, in the main, received professional training in seminaries emphasizing the highly rational and analytical, and they have performed well (in some cases outstandingly) in those places.

Rational scholarship seems to have been, for most of those exposed to it, a thoroughgoing delight and satisfaction—a ''next step'' in thinking about their faith positions. The newer dialectical theologies offered fresh ways of integrating the rational with the experiential; the intellectual with the devotional; the traditional with the contemporary; the male with the female; the professional with the personal; the administrative with the pastoral; the ethical with the responsible.

Those who are lacking the prestige preparation, it must be said, in no way lack high instrumental/rational development in leadership skills. Nonetheless, the thrust of the interview material is overwhelmingly skewed toward a vision of God as wanting a close relationship with individual persons—caring, compassionate, just (most often seen as a way of caring), bending, accessible— always moving toward a wholeness and fullness of life. And the data show this to be the women's model for themselves as people and as ministers. Wholeness and integration are important themes among them:

• I see God's presence and activity as a constant call to move along into personal wholeness, into communal sharing of resources. I don't need to name ''Jesus'' or ''Christ'' to do Christian things.
• I need always to ask, ''What would facilitate development toward human wholeness?'' I read the Bible in terms of the God seen among us as justice and liberation. My feminist stuff dates long before its clear articulation in my life.
• A lot of my images for God fit with my image of a broken, fragmented world . . . comforter, healer, harmonizer. I see the ''good news'' of a new creation in Jesus as making us complete persons, bringing us into wholeness, love. A person would not be compartmentalized. Faith and life would be joined in simple living and sharing of resources. My central sermon themes are wholeness, love, and reconciliation.
• I want to live in my *full* vision of ministry. My high moments come when the gifts that are needed from me can be used freely in the occasion without official restraints.
• I have a desire for the unity of the church . . . and all the cross-fertilization of the different flowerings of traditions from the common roots.

The woman with the childhood experience of incest found seminary the place where she was helped to get her life together:

• I started seminary saying, "I'm not a 'women's libber.' " Male language didn't bother me. I thought people were making problems that weren't there. At that time I was pretty much a Biblical conservative and a social liberal. But my senior year at seminary really got me to thinking about what we do to other people with our language and how subliminal it is in continually feeding our understandings. I took some women's courses—some gender role stuff—and they changed my perspective and awareness. It was my first chance to integrate my past experience, my sexuality, and my theology. I saw God acting in my own history as hope, even in my lowest moments. I felt tended by God and helped to get my life together.

The faith and life integration also shows in the following statements:

• I loved seminary. I simply ate it up! The seminary provided the setting for a spiritual journey for my husband [not a clergyman], too. He has become an avid feminist and a faithful Christian.
• My four years at seminary were exciting and difficult. I worked in a prison for a while ...my eyes were opened to the world....I had long held a preference for male authority—doctors, teachers, ministers. Now I saw greater competency in female students, in a woman gynecologist...I started questioning authority. Everything was crashing. It was a rebellious time. I had to learn to make my own judgments...to deal with my roots in [a fundamentalist] tradition...to sort out what could be retained and valued from the intense, early religious experience.

In two cases, however, the reintegration of life, after exposure to academic segmenting, presented serious identity problems. The woman whose childhood was an almost perfect fusion of Jewishness with reality itself found her seminary experience alienating and conflictive. It was precisely because of its tendency, for her, to break integrative wholeness and to compartmentalize life that she remembers it as something she "had to transcend."

• There was such a masculine split between body and mind...spirituality and scholarship. The seminary was caught between rabbinical and professional goals. I learned what the authorities said...not what we believed. I think the really faithful Jew is knowledgeable and kind...lives what he preaches...walks what he talks.

Whether by way of traditional, devotional, or intellectual connections, God Herself/Himself is looked upon as a consummately integrative unus of all life, whole humanness, all relationship, all meaning...all! Sin or evil is most frequently seen as a breakup of this unity.

• God is life; God is reality; God is experience; we cannot separate God from creation. He is life in us. *Life* does not die. God is absolute good; *we* cause evil.... We can utilize power to destroy or build; so *we* can be the devil. The Devil uses God's power...to destroy.
• I have a gut feeling within myself that morality is more than individual decisions; it is a social fabric. I have a conviction that there is a moral sense to the whole of life and

part of my calling is to say "No!" to injustice and immorality. I think it's very hard for Christians to act responsibly toward justice. I see injustice as a negation of God. People's need to be free of caring for the brother is sin. I *am* my brother's keeper! The Devil is people saying they don't need God in actions or words.

Nowhere in the interview data do I detect the perception of religious or human phenomena as self-contained in their significance. Such a perspective is foreign to the thinking I have documented. In personal histories the past and present are known and described in terms of each other.

Unique biographical items, especially the traumatic, are looked upon as important developmental reference points that enrich possibilities of ministry. They invite empathy with others facing similar problems and objectify the hope that even tragedy can bring a stronger, wiser personal position.

• I think my husband and I have been successful [their children are now adult] in breaking generational chains of abusive parenting in both of our families. The growth process has continued for us. We now have a grandson. These are the *best times* in our marriage.
• The traumas of the past have brought growth that might not have happened otherwise. I draw on *all* of it for my ministry.

In Chapter 2 I described the dreary judgmental religion that colored the childhood experiences of some of the informants. A positive influence brought forward from the, in some ways, gloomy early learnings is the intertwining of faith and life events. Certain disciplines are pointed to as having been established at an early age and continued, though content and style may have undergone much change. These include devotional routines (e.g., prayer, meditational reading, group worship) and involvements of various sorts with an array of organizations and human welfare services.

So also, in church life, assimilation of the past into the present is taken for granted. I asked the women if they saw themselves more as preservers, refiners, or reformers of tradition in their institutional roles. Here are some typical responses:

• I see myself as preserver, refiner, reformer, and replacer of traditions—all at different times. I have never been one to throw out tradition. It seems to be that there's a great deal to be gained that keeps us linked with our heritage. Whether it's *all* applicable or appropriate now, it's had its reason for developing. I think we need to know that we are writing tradition for the next generation. At no point along the way can we stop and say, "Tradition is *it*; we stop here." That doesn't work. We're the link. I would see myself as refining and reforming and doing those kinds of things that keep the tradition, change it where it's needed, and add to it in ways that make it effective.
• I see myself as "conservative liberal." Tradition should be honed to its living core. I am thoroughly excited and refreshed by new theological insights. Truth is far more exciting and alive than traditional teachings. The past doesn't have it all. My most positive responses come from people who are open to change . . . living . . . growing.

• I am preserver, refiner, reformer. . . . I see myself as a "breaker-outer" into new forms . . . new ways . . . based on tradition but pushing it along.
• *Reformer* is more my self-image, but I realize more and more how much I'm into preserving tradition . . . helping it live anew as a heritage . . . refining, honing images.
• Part of me wants to preserve tradition, but the tradition blatantly excludes me; so, in a literal sense I *can't* preserve tradition. Women now need a ritual that affirms them as women, using the same kind of "fleshly" imagery. We must create what can be lived in. It's a problem for me in Judaism that what's inside now used to be on the outside.

Another woman echoes this observation:

• The only thing reformist about me is my being a woman . . . which is, of course, a *big* important change.

She sees her ministry in traditional terms as "God calling." She knows, though, that many women in her congregation see her ministry as "making history."
From a woman who fully embraces a reformist identity:

• In my ministry I emphasize reforming the church . . . building on traditions but making rational choices relevant to the present.

The perspectives are hardly different; each takes the received forms and their current experiences very seriously and holds them in creative tension.
God as integrating, unifying spirit is seen as constituting fruitful dialectics between not only such polarities as past and present, traditional and contemporary, but also such closely related ones as scholarly and mundane, institutional and personal, administrative and pastoral, professional and intimate, structural and existential. Illustrations, already given, of the informants' tendency to submit belief and organizational structures to the tests of personal nurture and existential authenticity are also illustrations of the tendency to integrate the above polarities. Every one of the women gives clear indications that her own witness to what is true must be a felt, known, lived perspective coming from the depths of her own being, not just an official doctrine transmitted by authorities. (Chapter 8 extends this discussion of "doing theology.") There is among the informants a thoroughgoing insistence on the ideal of total accountability for expressive behavior, an honest, nondefensive sharing springing from who we are and where we are.

• To me you have to have a living dialogue between an abstract principle and a concrete situation. I make judgments only within such a dialogue. You may or may not come out, in a given case, where you would if you just imposed the abstract principle, in itself. I might be against abortion in principle but for it in a given situation, and I wouldn't even be prepared to predict what the situation might be. Imposing principles, like the "just war" theory, tends to encourage casuistry rather than healthy spirituality and responsible decisions.

• Preaching is so much a part of who I am. It's such a joy to share faith and insights regarding Scripture with people who are thereby helped. I feel most truly myself leading liturgy, preaching, joining in devotions. I feel the giftedness of it. A sermon has never once been a chore. Sermons are always simply *there* ready to be preached. Preaching demands honesty . . . sharing my struggle with people . . . facing myself in a way that otherwise might be avoided.

• Scholarly theology gets into my sermon preparation and teaching. I'm a channel from scholarly traditions to my parish . . . but it must be translated into *their* images. It must come out in my *decisions* more than in technical terms. The jargon and disciplinary vocabularies must be reduced to essentials and expressed in the vernacular. *Doing theology* is a powerful phrase. Theology must be *lived*. My sermons tend to end always in the here and now . . . in our situation . . . what we can do right now. This is a known reputation. People talk about it.

As mentioned in Chapter 2, several of the clergywomen were ordained without being required to study scholarly traditions beyond their own denominations. The training within their denominations was a highly personal passing-on-of-faith from functioning pastors designated by the church bodies. Yet, in spite of their more literal and traditional approaches to Scriptural interpretation, their free-flowing devotional, personal, and allegorical renditions of Scripture work against rigidity and end up sounding much like the dialectical approaches of the more academically sophisticated, although not rationally articulated in the same way. They are engaged actively in trying to work out a dynamic faith/life congruence. They are in the position described by an earlier quoted informant, who said of her pre-college life, "I was a biblical conservative and a social liberal." You will remember that, for her, *intellectual* reconciliation of the two occurred as she got her personal life together under the influence of seminary study in academic theology. But prior to that time, and without the academic conceptual tools, she already felt an impulse toward personal integration, and reported the experience of God holding it all together for her and making some overall sense on her behalf. It was she who said about that earlier time, "I felt tended by God and helped to get life together."

Though some may lean toward the language of contemporary theologies and some more toward the language of inner mystical dialogue with God about what certain life-happenings mean, overall there appears to be the same drive to reconcile aspects of experience.

• I did an awful lot of studying. Scriptures seemed to be running through my head all the time. The Word [meaning Bible, here] seemed so vivid to me . . . so revealing . . . and that was another miraculous thing to me: I could read the Scriptures and get the meaning . . . I would go and check with the commentaries and it seemed as though the theologians and I had the same understanding. That was thrilling. I'm not a theologian, and these are people of authority. The good feeling was that *God* had revealed this to me. I didn't have the scholarly authority, so it couldn't have come to me that way . . . People say the Bible is so confusing . . . but it really isn't. There are many different interpretations . . . but much agreement, too. The Bible is my life, my bread, my food

... You can always find something for everyday living ... guidance ... wisdom. It gives deeper insight on life itself ... information ... the attitudes required for living happily. The Bible is a character builder ... a lot of questions are answered if you search with the right attitude ... There is a *real* right and wrong. The true believer, tempered with the Spirit of the Lord, does the right thing. Oh, you might do or say something wrong, but the Bible will let you know you're wrong, too. My own help comes mostly from the Bible, but you can't start there with the unchurched. You must establish confidence with love and care and openness; then, after that, work on spiritual growth possibilities and offer strength from the Lord.

The integration of the personal with the institutional is never in question among these women. Mostly they speak of this in positive terms, as we have seen, but there are also indications, especially for young mothers, that role integration can be a source of considerable conflict, especially over responsible use of time.

• I have a working image of relationship between ministry and family life. I have to give in to time demands of the ministry more than I would like, but family time is a priority item for me and my husband. It's a very intentional discipline ... days off together, et cetera. ... It *has* to be ... so that the ministry doesn't eat up the family.

A single mother, facing a severe crisis with one of her sons, took the matter to a personal consulting group she had already carefully developed as part of the congregational structure. She observes:

• Parenting and ministry used to interfere with each other. There was a lot of guilt stuff for me on both sides for a while. Now I am able to ask the church to minister to *me* and it's a whole new ballgame. There's a real outpouring of empathy from the congregation ... a needed opening to more closeness. They are very careful not to intrude on my family time.

Others say:

• I interpolate mothering into ministry. As a woman, women's concerns are very apparent to me. I can empathize with those who "work" and those who do household tasks and parenting. Illustrations from female experience also emerge in my sermons.
• I see my family as my most important parishioners.

The integration of ministerial and family concerns sometimes extends to colleagues' families as well.

• Before accepting this call I checked with my partner's wife to be sure my working with him would be no issue with her.

Later in the interview, this clergywoman listed among her "major support sources" her own family and her co-pastor's family.

In a few cases there remain some problem areas in achieving relatively full integration of the professional role with the personal identity; but in all of these cases, it is a desired goal.

• One of my former professors talked seriously with me about "accepting my ordination." I had to grow into the idea of accepting "professional minister" as my identity. It seemed to me like the "priesthood of all believers" idea worked against superior status. All the good models I had were aggressive, take-charge men. I didn't feel negative or terribly critical, but I didn't identify. The pattern doesn't fit who I am. I function a lot in low-key, low-visibility ways; but I do understand people want to know what they're paying for. PR aspects of the role just go against my grain [though people say she's a good preacher]. I'm now trying harder to plan further ahead, make more proposals, and show my ideas more as a leader.
• When I visit someone sick I want to relate as a caring person . . . but I want just the role itself, symbolically, to convey meaning without its being either personally aggrandizing or discounted and trivialized. I want to be accepted as legitimate in my role without grasping at the role for status or having to prove myself all the time.

The main sticking point in the above cases seems to be a desire to distance self-images from a role image so frequently stereotyped as authoritarian. Already, in this discomfort, we can see the desire to be, or at least to be thought of as, equalitarian in social relationships.

The integrative perspective has implications for a wide range of polarities beyond those noted: "top-down" philosophical ethics and "bottom-up" situational ethics; the intellectual realm and the emotional realm; "high church" ceremonialism and "low church" fervency or informality. Perhaps most importantly for this study, male and female dispositions themselves are seen as requiring both personal and institutional integration for full-flowering human development. If the clergywomen do think in terms of women's ways being superior, it is either repressed or suppressed; because what I *heard* was undeniable gender inclusiveness—the ideal of gender integration.

No one proposed traditionally feminine orientation as ideally normative for all humans, and I suspect that a large part of the initial discomfort some had with speaking to this question rested in the fear that their words could be construed as saying something like that. They seem to want a sustained dialectical balance of the perspectives traditionally assigned to the sexes, in both personal and societal realms.

This is so keenly felt, and so earnest is the desire to bring it about, that I experienced noticeable resistance from the women in response to my question about how they see their ministries differing from those of most male clergy. They signaled reluctance to list differences, lest it seem to be divisive, compartmentalizing, adversarial, or arrogant to be saying something like, "I'd like to do my ministry thus and so, and I think that may be different from what's mostly been done by men."

I want to deal with one additional aspect of integrative orientation: the genre of insights and judgments called *intuitive*. Intuition implies some order of subconscious developmental integration—of many carefully thought-out positions—now delivered up to consciousness in response to a unique stimulus. It constitutes a unified composite of conclusions, which may be separable again into rational components only upon lengthy disciplined reflection, if at all.

Checking out the content of intuitive knowledge is a standard part of informal, personal trust-building conversations. An illustration of an intuitive response is the human ability to recognize a given face, though one may not have been able consciously to remember the hairline, nose shape, eye color, mouth size, or skin texture.

It has been said, "Men win arguments; women win friends." At least some part of what is revealed in this saying is the recognized tendency of men to orient toward logical-empirical clarity in limited arenas of discourse, and the tendency of women to orient toward ecological coherence in an arena of discourse limited only by experience itself. This means that even the most analytically sharp woman may be expected to employ her logical-empirical skills in the interest of total coherence; and the most intuitive of men may characteristically use insight to enhance his rational problem-solving force. We should expect the normative orientation of women, then, to foster and include *intuition* precisely because of the integrative, holistic, how-does-this-all-make-sense focus.

Some of the women note the disparity of conversational styles flowing from gender-distinctive perspectives on life:

• When my colleagues [men] argue, they go point-for-point like a sport. They have an unspoken set of rules that I don't understand.

An Ivy League graduate mentions her more ecological form of rationality (as contrasted with linear rationality) almost apologetically, or at least as something she will be called on to correct if she is to converse credibly with men.

• I am very vulnerable in arguments with men. They bring out concrete statistical information and make points with *facts*; I remember my overall conclusions but may have lost details. In order to get their attention to communicate with them I have to shift to talk their language. They won't talk mine. They may not even know it exists. They are so much in the corporate business world.

Intuitive judgments abound in the interview data, as can be seen in the quotations already used to buttress other factors under consideration. As the women describe their models of "faithful believers," there are many references to people who have what might be called good intuition about human need at many levels. Moral decisions are largely envisioned as intuitive perceptions based on extensive weighing of information and clarifying of intention. The sense that "I am where I am supposed to be" is an intuition, though, of course, it is not necessarily lacking objective input of various sorts. Objectives and goals are often stated in intuitive/subjective terms, which, to people oriented differently, may appear insubstantial, vague, and unevaluable. The whole realm of mystical apprehension (a personal God experience) is, in itself, the realm of the intuitive; although, again, it is not necessarily without concrete referents. An existential perspective assumes the validity of the intuitive. Empathic knowledge is intuitive knowledge. The artistic imaging of beliefs and capturing of collective experience in evocative ceremonies are intuitive exercises.

I have drawn from the collected material some passages reflecting matter-of-fact acceptance of intuitive perception:

• [As a preacher] people say I give them fresh connections to ponder. I don't have a high awareness of methodology. I'm more intuitive in my approach. Standard commentaries haven't been very helpful. I use Bible stories of how God has worked with people—stories of struggle. The patriarchy there is strong, but liberation and justice images are clear, too.

• The Bible is a communicating tool for speaking about God and for struggling to understand in a disciplined way. It's not a dead rulebook. It's always communicating to a new people who hear it in a new way. I do scholarly exegesis [scientific critical interpretation] and use "higher criticism," but also I do simple reading and seeing what it reveals now. It's a living reservoir of stories that carry messages into each person's historic time. God speaks profoundly in changing ways to people who see new revelations out of their different situations.

• The teachings are time- and culture-bound, but they still speak to us—not literal truth, not concrete. It's a guide in the *spirit* of faith. . . . This is a real reversal from ten years ago, when I was into proof-texting.

Much intuitional content appears in the accounts of transitions to feminist thinking. (Few use the latter phrase to describe their position.)

• I was sent on to study French. I really wanted to study theology instead. I was becoming more conscious of "woman's place," but there was not much real feminism yet. Those were years of transition for me, for the church. The dialectic between change and traditions resulted in a lot of *healthy* change but also in a lot of confusion. My imagery for God has changed in the last five years. I have very positive feelings about God as father, but now as mother, too, especially in my personal life. I often feel a restraint on talking about God in the parish: It's easy in teaching to say, "God is neither male nor female . . . but all that is male and all that is female . . . and beyond. When I preach I can do some of that, but I find myself in a community where that is *very* innovative . . . and, knowing that my own theology is different from the traditional, I try to be open to where people are and not offend them. . . . I freely choose to put constraints on myself, and so I often find myself using some traditional language that is now uncomfortable for me. That's really difficult . . . dealing with maintaining my own integrity and communicating effectively in ways that are familiar to them.

• [On the foreign mission field, and prior to her ordination] I encountered ordained native women in my own denomination. This didn't seem to be any issue at all for them, though the native culture strongly supported male domination. Women were accepted as equals in church leadership. I refused to help serve communion, though I was expected to do so; at the time, it was against my ideas of propriety. But internal changes were taking

place in my views on women in ministry. I experienced much cultural prejudice as a *foreigner*, but not as a *woman*. The full respect given me as a woman was savored and noted and valued.
• When I was in the tenth grade we were in the U.S. again. It was a hard year. The narrowness of Christians here bothered me from the beginning. Indian Christians seemed *real* to me. U.S. Christians didn't. The downgrading and exclusion of women was a new experience for me among *my* people.

Moral decision-making is a theme that brings out much evidence of reliance on essentially intuitive, integrative judgments.

• I draw on traditional, contemporary, religious, and secular sources, without any hierarchy of finality for moral truth. I have an initial gut understanding of the situation and then I continually review and evaluate my opinions and responses. I get information on the subject . . . I consider the theological context . . . I tend to pull others into the evaluation of opinions, but I tend to think things through very independently. I am *most* uneasy about the breaking of covenanted relationships . . . more judgmental about the hurt and disorder coming from broken promises. I feel that the restoration of relationships often requires submission to some degree of injustice. . . . In interventions, I weigh strategies . . . what will be most effective . . . and also I weigh alienation factors all around. I draw on the reservoir of commitments and insights within myself . . . and then continually, continually review all the factors.

What may seem, on the face of it, like a radically different approach to moral dilemmas is the following one, frequently employed and recommended by a clergywoman who refers to the discipline as "transcendent treatment." While the procedure is unlike the one just described, the dependence on intuition, rather than strict adherence to rules, is again unmistakable. Here, however, the belief system of the woman contains the implication of direct intervention by God.

• The discipline starts with a prayer every hour on the hour, from six to one o'clock, and then three times a day for seven days. Every time the thought [of the moral issue with its impending decision] comes up, you just say to it, "I'm not ready yet to make a decision; I release you in the name of God." At the end of the seven days a solution will be apparent to you.

Notice in these next selections the implied high confidence and comfort in using intuitive knowledge:

• Someone who has faith in God can be calm. There is an inner center that the person is able to draw from at all times. Faith is held in the face of questions . . . not blindly. This is someone who knows and assumes responsibility for freedom . . . whose autonomous spiritual development is apparent . . . who is called by God to act . . . who hears . . . who responds . . . who is not just passive in faith explained as "God's will" . . . not just a receiver and doer of church expressions.
• I have many friendly associations but no continuing companionship. Maybe it's my

own fault. I'm always busy with helping others and I may seem self-sufficient . . . so possibly that discourages people from thinking of me as needy or feeling that I have any time to spend.
• I was weighing [at age eighteen] marriage with my "steady." I prayed a lot and asked God for a sign. It was a time of inner darkness. One day I got a call from an old family friend asking if I wanted to go to Africa on an assignment. My decision to go included a decision to split with my boyfriend. I felt "on track" again!

In arriving at conclusions in many areas, various women talk about starting with a "gut understanding" and/or ending with a "gut feeling" that leads to some decision, some action. Logical-empirical analysis seems to be used by them for, among other functions, ongoing critical assessment of any and all components of integrative "gut knowledge."

ROLE FIT

In this chapter I have presented passages from the interview data to indicate the normative female orientation of these women. Since normative gender orientation connotes *primary* orientation, not *exclusive* orientation, it is not contradictory that the informants are also high in self-assertiveness, have instrumental efficiency with task-organization, and possess other agentic characteristics. The critical observation is that there exists among them an overwhelming tendency to talk about themselves and their ministries out of a communal orientation. I have gathered and displayed evidence according to five dimensional criteria: intimacy and identity; personal focus; intrinsic satisfactions; nurturance; integrative thinking and intuition. While these are not exhaustive, they should be adequate to show sufficient support in the data for the communion view.

Before proceeding to discuss the clergywomen's approach to ministerial tasks, as such, I want to review briefly why I consider these women to be suited to their clergy and gender roles, when looked at both subjectively and objectively.

With few exceptions there is high and unambivalent satisfaction with the work of professional ministry. Even the exceptions are undecided only about the *type* of ministerial functions for which they are best suited.

• I have *no* ambivalence about my choice for the ministry. It's been frustrating and joyful. I may be crazy, but I would do it again!
• I'm not one bit ambivalent about my decision to be a minister. The denomination is a good fit with my personal faith. I'm very comfortable about my work.
• Sometimes I do wonder whether God really wants me here—when I hear people say, "Women shouldn't be doing such things," . . . but He just keeps making opportunities; I believe I'm where I should be.
• Ambivalence? No. My commitment to the ministry role is comfortable. My denomination is a good fit. I'm Catholic "in the bones," so I'll stay and fight for justice. But there *is* true oppression. It's frustrating to be treated as a second-class citizen because I'm a woman.

• The bedrock of my faith is that I am where I'm supposed to be. Sometimes it wavers, but it's pretty solid.

Subjective satisfaction in the gender role also emerges. Though many express dissatisfaction at social arrangements that deny barrier-free access to full functioning for women, still no one speaks enviously of the male position in society, and most declare themselves glad to be women. This seemed apparent to me in their demeanor as I talked with them; they are self-confident, and comfortable with themselves.

• I don't want to do things like a man. I *like* being a woman. I have come to learn and appreciate the directness of approach that is more characteristic of men, but that's also appropriate for women. I don't want to hold on to any passive-aggressive "tact" that defers coyly to males and manipulates. Actually I learned the directness from women, but it's a mode that seems more natural for men.
• I'm aware of the excitement that my status has as a model for women. What's sad is that it's needed, but I'm joyful that it's happening. I don't feel any pressure to become more like males. On the contrary, more the reverse . . . I feel a lot of support for my womanness.
• I feel a lot of pressure to be more like a man—to wear subdued clothing, to cover emotion, to compartmentalize life, to always show strength. I don't want things to change for me. I think showing weakness is valuable. The ministry shouldn't be just a "tower of strength" role. When I've had a "heavy duty" weekend there's no way I can put it behind and separate the personal sphere. I believe in "women's spirit" as different. I'm not sure what it is, but I know it's there.

Few of the women show any substantial knowledge of the scientific literature of gender differentiation. Yet it is clear from their words that they are tuned in to the social expectations for women *as women* and men *as men*, and that they have done considerable thinking about these expectations in relation to themselves.

In addition to their allusions to subjective feelings about their ministerial and gender statuses, they also report, on the "objective" side, some responses from parishioners.

• They say, "She's great!" . . . "It works fine." . . . "She's brought a lot we didn't have." . . . "She 'fills the shoes' well." They seem awed that a woman can handle it. [Women ministers are rare in her denomination.]
• People look for a role model in a woman minister—not just for how to be a minister or a Christian woman, but for how to be a woman in a new role. It goes beyond religious interests. They seem most grateful when they find that *womanhood* has not been lost in an authority role. I'm not sure what exactly they call "feminine," but anyway, they affirm me as being "feminine" and liking it.
• I'm not conscious in the ministry, most of the time, of being a *woman* minister, but sometimes . . . now I hear great pride in the congregation that I can "handle things so well without becoming like a man." I really don't feel pressures to become "like a man" in order to succeed.

Also, in the selection process, I had information from denominational officials and colleagues about the institutional acceptability and/or ministerial "success" of most of the informants, which adds some objective weight to conclusions on professional role fit.

I conclude that these particular women clearly do not represent the primary orientation typical in our culture for males. They fit well within the primary orientation expected for females; they are not "nontypical" in this respect. However, they incorporate numerous agentic qualities and skills into their ego structures and thus might be called "epi-typical," in that they have developed through and beyond the narrowly normative, transcending certain of the distortions and constraints of relatively exclusive female orientation. They are highly androgynous persons, without exception; that is, they have developed a personal approach to life that freely draws on both female and male norms, as appropriate. Yet they all maintain a fundamental perspective that is, unquestionably, normatively female.

NOTE

1. As clergy these women do not tend to use the word "prophecy" in the popular sense of "foretelling the future," but in the more biblical sense of "crying out the truth of the moment," penetrating so profoundly into the heart of social meaning that one can lift out the implications for the future as an essence to behold, and as a call to action.

Chapter 4

A Sociological Digression

The women in this study have taken on a clergy role that already exists culturally, for them and for others, as a cluster of social expectations. It is a role with a history, until very recently, of almost exclusively male occupancy. A number of U.S. mainstream denominations are drawing near to the end of their first decade with women in ordained status. A few groups have a longer history of sexual inclusiveness in leadership, and others continue to reserve professional ordained ministry for males only. Regardless of the group and the pace of change, clergywomen still represent some degree of social deviance in U.S. society, both as women and as clergy.

• At weddings and funerals I wear the signs of the office: robe, collar, cross. I did a wedding last weekend. At the reception a woman came up to me and said she had talked several days earlier with a friend who had gone to a funeral I conducted. She asked the friend, "Who was the minister at the funeral?" and the friend replied, "Well, there really wasn't a minister. Some woman got up and did it."

Not infrequently, as people inquire about my research and I describe the focus, they register surprise and say things like, "I didn't know that was happening in churches," or "How far are you having to travel to find people like that?" Repeatedly, people misunderstand "clergywomen" to mean "preachers' wives." Perhaps a student or teacher in a seminary where women have been studying for a long period of time could imagine that gender-inclusive clergy norms are fully accepted and operational in religious institutions; but "out in society" clergywomen often draw the curiosity attached to strange phenomena. This provides unique opportunities for attracting attention to the role performance. It also means that women in the role dare not assume that the traditional authority residual in the role is necessarily transferring to them.

Before talking about what women are intending and attempting as leaders in a major institutional sector, I shall digress at some length and say something about key concepts being employed here.

Since I cannot assume a sociology background among all interested readers, I should make clear how I am understanding certain terms: namely, *role*, *institution*, *stratification*, *authority*, and *social change*. But perhaps even more importantly, in a discussion of religious professionals, I should explain what I understand to be the nature of *religion*. I have not taken the time in all cases to enter this kind of semantic exercise, nor shall I try to remedy the possible deficiency in an exhaustive way. Yet, in a few instances, it may be time well spent if it helps shed light on the implications of the data.

RELIGION

All cultures manifest religion; though not all people are conventionally or even consciously religious. Religions consist of shared systems of (1) beliefs about what is ultimately real and true; (2) feelings and sentiments that, among other things, signify the value of the beliefs to persons; (3) rituals and other tangible symbolic referents that evoke the beliefs and feelings; and (4) social organization that systematizes the impression/expression flow over time, maintaining social solidarity and the personal identity orientation of individuals.[1]

A religion may or may not have holy writings, visions of supernatural presences, or even a separate, specialized institutional structure. A religion certainly will have (according to Paul Tillich) ideas of transcendency, ultimate concern, and a fundamental version of reality (i.e., a "point of view"). In Tillich's sense, all persons are religious in that they honor, celebrate, sacrifice for, and speak in terms of that which seems to them consummately important. And they develop shared explanations for central human issues: for example, the meanings of life, death, good, evil, hope, despair, love, hate, suffering, tragedy, irony.

We all seem to have some experiences of awe, some experiences of communion, some experiences of dramatic breakthrough into new insight or new comprehension in life. Often we desire to tell others, to "witness" to the experience. If we discover that others recognize it as something they know, too, we may find such mutual awareness exhilarating, affirming, and uniting. We are likely to share the details spontaneously and desire to meet again over this bond. Symbolic items (settings, tokens of friendship, artistic renditions, literary expressions) tend to emerge as carriers of ineffable dimensions of the Absolute, the "I," and the "we" sensed. The group comes to rely on this symbol-fabric to remind, to evoke anew, and to teach the central experience to the "children" literally or figuratively born into it. Of such stuff religions come to be.[2]

The shared religious heritage, then, offers a transcendent, orientating vision of reality and ties it to earthly existence. In offering adherents a way to make sense of life, and a way to arrive at acceptance of one's situation or even hopefulness in it, a relatively stabilized belief system characteristically implies a set of attitudes about social change. Whether God requires individuals to influence world events actively, adapt to world events through internal discipline, or make some other ideal response, is a crucial distinguishing factor in religious positions.

Some contradiction inevitably exists between correct, obedient conformity in religious traditions and authentic, spontaneous spiritual experience. The former emphasizes authoritarian knowledge passed to persons through officially legiti- mated channels; and the latter emphasizes fresh and direct spiritual infusion of experience. Traditionalism risks idolatry—mistaking the symbolic form for the lively spirit essence; existentialism risks destructive separations from life-giving rootedness in culturally evolved meanings.

In Judaism and Christianity there is a peculiar centrality to this dialectical tension between spirit and form, meaning and structure. It stems from the ex- periencing of God as acting, or coming, or showing *in* history, *in* the world, *in* culture, *in* flesh and substance, and yet as somehow very separate and exalted *over* it all, at the pinnacle of hierarchical control. Some of this can be seen in the prevalence of sacramental acts that remind people of human dependency on the graciousness of a high God, even as they remind them of the enfleshedness of all human spirituality and the need for direct God encounters. Throughout the stories from Jewish and Christian literature there runs the counterpoint be- tween two kinds of faithfulness in ministry: priestly mediation of God to people through traditional roles and procedures performed correctly; and prophetic me- diation of God through spontaneous testimony about God "caught in the act," revealed and identified anew in a particular time and place.

An ongoing critical question in Western religion is how to assess the truth value of the God vision developed among ordinary believers, compared with the God vision handed down through culturally legitimated hierarchies of "experts." Since religious faith and social structure are as interpenetrated as heredity and environment, religious communities have a constant need for trustworthy "God- watchers" who say what God means in the present moment. Denominations, theologies, and pieties split on the question of whether the faithful believer primarily obeys the demands of orthodox correctness interpreted in official pron- ouncements or of prophetic witness validated experientially by charismatic in- terpersonal credibility.

In the former outlook, believers view faith as involving acceptance of precisely formulated, institutionally interpreted statements based on Scriptural truths and handed down through time as eternal standards for right thinking and right living. In the latter outlook, believers embrace the proposal that God is encountered in human experience as people, alerted by honored traditions, are (1) radically opened to new possibilities of ways to see and ways to be; (2) courageously committed to action benefiting humankind and based on the broadest possible knowledge; and (3) given to awe and humility in the face of limitations of time, space, and biographical particularity.

The views are not neatly divided according to persons or groups. They represent poles of a continuum and often there is as much range *within* religious denominations as *among* them. Interesting blends occur in contemporary scholarship where both theology and science have used scientific research methodologies (in biblical, historical, anthropological, sociological, psychological, biological, and ecological studies) to illuminate the nature of God talk, religious experience, and institutionalized religion.

This study examines the viewpoint of women who have assumed a leadership role in an institutional sector heavy with traditional meanings. Among those meanings is the longstanding assumption that women do not do such things because women are not fit by God to do such things. Yet here they are, carrying institutionally legitimated religious knowledge, from the society and to the society.

I am hopeful that the above discussion will be helpful in analyzing the women's words about how they do their ministries—where their intentions are rooted and what those intentions are. They are entrusted with identifying a God who is perceived, met, described, and served within a sociocultural situation but not necessarily reducible to it. Our objective is to see how they are dealing with the trust.

ROLES AND INSTITUTIONS

Cultural patterns (norms) develop in all societies as blueprints for how to face life. They are exhibited and intuited through social interaction, largely at a subconscious level, while ordinary people are making ordinary decisions about ordinary problems arising in ordinary situations. Norms *hold* individuals in an environmental web of efficiently repeated social responses, a web that takes on the force of *reality itself* in the developing person. It is the way things *are*. Norms are also *held by* individuals in whom they reside as readily available ideas for how to see, think, and act.

Cultural patterns touch every aspect of social existence: religious beliefs, mating techniques, perceptions of time and space, expressions of sudden pain, and so on. It would be impossible for a human to respond with freedom, originality, and rationality to every received stimulus at every moment in life. The complexity of human experience requires reduction of conscious choice to manageable proportions through socially shared procedures that can be adopted, taken for granted, and not even realized as *alternatives*. Sanity itself, let alone coping confidence and the perception of what humans know as *freedom*, is dependent on such reduction. Thus each maturing individual in a culture is being given an amazingly sophisticated "tool" (culture) for dealing with the environment.

Roles and institutions are types of cultural patterns. A *role* is a coherent accumulation of familiar behavior expectations associated with some social location (say, "waitress," "uncle," or "pupil"). Roles can be considered in terms of the self-expectations of their occupants or the expectations of observers. Role performances and the responses evoked are all relative to some internalized standards of anticipation. Known expectations form both a foundation for effective role functioning (including a departure point for innovation) and a limitation on that functioning (including the socially negotiated boundary beyond which the occupant is not understood to be "in" the role). The available margin for significant creative shaping by the occupant varies greatly, according to role and situation, but it is frequently substantial. Roles are always in the making through the impact of particular role performances. Occupants in *new* social roles, such as the clergywomen studied here, are especially influential in shaping the social expectations for their role.

Of course, people occupy many roles simultaneously (e.g., woman, daughter, wife, sister, mother, neighbor, minister, dancer). A given role may also contain subroles—a minister may be expected to be a public speaker, a counselor, an administrator, a singer, or a fundraiser. Thus, complex prioritizing of demands from multiple roles is a personal consideration in most role performances.

Part of social change is the shift in social expectations normatively attached to role behaviors. New roles may emerge in a society (such as that of computer programmer); new categories of persons may be admitted to a certain social status (such as black senator, blind physical therapist); new role functions may demand new adaptive skills. Even in the average, conventional role, the uniqueness of occupants is such that some degree of role modification is inevitable. This study focuses squarely on role performance, role taking, role creation, role integrity, role satisfaction, role conflict, and other aspects of social role significance. Role change is indication of institutional change.

On a different scale of social organization, an *institution* is a macro-system of social interactions that has its own specialized role functions in the society as a whole. It is a comparatively stable and formal union of subsidiary norms, values, roles, and procedures that arises and is maintained in a society because, with fairly dependable efficiency, it serves some deeply felt, ongoing social need. "Religion," "the family," and "the economy" are examples of such institutional sectors.

In contemporary societies large-scale institutions tend to be organized bureaucratically. This is not merely an escalation of scale but is a qualitatively different type of social coordination, gaining a prodigious power and efficiency advantage from abstract, impersonal rationalization of procedures. It is a goal- and objective-oriented arena *par excellence*. The competitive edge conferred by bureaucratic structuring is not lost on institutional planners, even those traditionally devoted to personal development and expressiveness (namely, in religion and education). The reader may recognize the bureaucratic approach as an elaborate case of the agency orientation encouraged socially among males.

This discussion suggests the possibility of important social implications when female role status combines with ministerial role status in a bureaucratized institution whose idealized function is the articulation of human meaning and the service of human needs. Such rather tortuous descriptions are an appropriate sign of the complicated significance of the ordination of females.

POWER AND AUTHORITY

The way power is gained, held, and exercised in a social milieu—the way it emerges in the system, resides in the "rules," and controls the moves in the "life-game"—determines to a large extent how truth, goodness, and social order are viewed. The relationship between social power and prevailing point of view about reality is so strong over time that Edwin Schur (1980) suggests we have only to know the ideology and determine its chief beneficiaries to locate the real power in a social order.

Decades of debate have not laid to rest finally the question of whether successful people are "blessed by God" for coming so close to what "He" is and wants, or whether the image of God is created according to what successful people understand themselves, ideally, to be. We shall not settle that debate here either, but alertness to the connection can shed much light on the view of ministry these women tend to develop in the nexus of a traditionally de-powered status (woman) and a traditionally empowered status (clergy). The one woman not yet ordained speaks:

• What if the church says it will ordain? Can I buy into the hierarchical power system as it exists? People need continuity with the past, and I don't think I can start a church on my own. Sometimes I think it's good that we didn't get in sooner; we could easily have entered with the same power-based role as men. Sensitivity to alternative modes is increasing in powerlessness. There is strong identification with the laity.

At least since Max Weber, social thinkers have distinguished several quite different ways of exerting influence over others in social situations. Raw physical force is one way, and it obviously does not require any social legitimacy or authority to prevail. In general, though, throughout human history, social influence has been wielded by those thought by others to have some right to that influence. They are honored, obeyed, and attended because somehow they seem to most others worthy of such regard. The source of their power tends to be traditional types of assignment, rational types of selection, or personal charm.

Certain people arrive at leadership roles because, according to long usage, leadership is expected from the person(s) in the social position they represent (the oldest male, the particular tribe or family, the skill group, etc.). Theirs is *traditional* authority.

Others are identified and selected through rational group processes deemed best for securing suitable persons to wield power in specified ways. This is *legal-rational* or bureaucratic authority—an authority vested in carefully defined abstract roles and, derivatively, in persons officially chosen for their abilities to fill the roles adequately.

But sometimes individuals come into substantial social power merely, or primarily, on the basis of their personal appeal—their charisma, their extraordinary social magnetism.

The first two types may, of course, be held by charming persons; but their essence is in *correctness* of power location (i.e., persons rightfully in the right places have a right and obligation to say what's right and to exert control over others). The third type depends on believability and admirable qualities that are noticed in social exchanges. The first is based on entitlement according to social position of the person; the second, on entitlement according to social definition of the role (and by personal qualifications to fill it); the third, on personal appeal.

Charismatic authority sometimes commands more than its share of attention because, even in renditions of history, it retains the potential to fascinate, to inspire loyalty, to activate personal fantasies and aspirations, to invite awe and emulation. A large part of the excitement about charismatic persons and their stories may lie in an illusion. In spite of the fact that in the public arena such authority is *more* unusual than other kinds, it implies access to power from any life status and a direct connection between personal superiority and social reward.

It should be obvious that one form of power can be brokered into another and that they often are combined in particular roles or persons. For example, the traditional power of the throne in England is now dependent for maintenance on the legal-rational power of Parliament. A charismatic leader may use power to secure a succession of that power to descendents. Traditional or charismatic authority may be used to construct a democratic bureaucracy. Legal-rational authority may be augmented through charismatic influence.

Traditional religious authority has been assigned to an elite of males. Over time, *charismatic* leadership by non-elites and their sympathizers has influenced *legal-rational* policies that now include the sharing of official power with those formerly shut out. Of course, this is by no means the whole story.

Already we have seen the strong emphasis among my informants on charismatic ministerial influence (though their ordination was by legal-rational permission). As women, they are *oriented* toward this type of influence; they believe in it as a way of life. This raises an interesting question for them and for religious institutions: Will the immediacy of authentic faith and interpersonal influence idealized among women enter increasingly into the *official* interpretations of institutional authority?

As yet the leadership incidence of women is such that they mostly feel they are "on stage," to some degree, establishing their qualifications for the ministerial role. Charismatic appeal has special impact right now in role shaping and in ministerial effectiveness. When they can relax from the rigors of establishing a social role, will they continue to regard charismatic credibility as the primary professional religious authority?

STRATIFICATION

Human societies all come to have preferences for certain kinds of people, whom they then reward more highly than others by giving them greater material benefits, greater honor, and greater control over their own and others' life circumstances. The preferences are broadly based, and they are held by those who are not "preferred types" as well as by those who are. Some anthropologists think that the first people to be honored and excused from subsistence labor in order to devote themselves to a specialty were religious leaders. Whatever the origins, a dimension of all complex social organization is some degree of layering of classes of people, according to the level of importance they come to have for the group. Whether their excellence is judged in terms of beauty, athletic prowess, negotiating skill, or intelligence, the extra benefits they are permitted not only signal their influence but increase it. The mutual reinforcement of social esteem and social reward (whether it be relatively low or high) means that there is a marked tendency for a category to maintain its rank, over time, in a system of status positions.

Personal identities are oriented from social positions, each of which has characteristic life styles with accompanying hopes, fears, language idioms, opinions, tastes, moral judgments, and pastimes. Those who share a similar social position are therefore apt to share among themselves a similar personal orientation— similar expectations for the roles they and others occupy.

Part of what we learn as we mature in our native social stratum is how much authority is intrinsic to our public status. Must I learn the nuances of polite deference to almost no one, to almost everyone, or to certain select types of people in order to stay out of trouble and be generally approved or, at least, unnoticed? These are complex subtleties of learning, usually absorbed into ego structure without high awareness of what is happening. Whether I must back out of a conversational stance in order not to rile my partner, or whether I may be outrageous without consequence (or with specific desired consequence) are matters choreographed according to an understanding of what authority my position carries in my social surroundings.

Just as I occupy many role statuses as an individual (and they may cause considerable richness and/or conflict for me as the compounded expectations create great complexity), so I may occupy discrepant strata of society. When crossed status communication is part of one's *inner* dialogue, as well as of external communications, very complicated disciplines of self-presentation are necessary. For example, a black concert pianist, a physically disabled Nobel laureate, or a female physicist must all devise sophisticated signals, while initiating and maintaining comfortable communication, for acknowledging a high-status position in a low-status category.

Higher consciousness of role performances and strata entitlements are developed as a strategic necessity under such circumstances. Being different from the norm stimulates consciousness of the norm. ("If water is discovered, it won't be by a fish!") Living in the stratum of society conventionally accorded the highest authority for imposing one's ideals as *the* ideals tends to blunt the ability to imagine views from other strata as worthy interpretations of reality, or, for that matter, as even making sense.

So non-elites come to be "double-socialized"—socialized simultaneously into elite ideals (for approaching elites to get benefits, or to avoid negative sanctions), and also into ideals that fit their "place" in the prevailing stratification system. In giving preparation for life "in the real world," a non-elite child's parents and mentors offer pointers on how to juggle the ploys of cross-status communication for responding "appropriately" (perhaps with maximum exploitative effectiveness) in life situations.

Women, as a class, form a particularly interesting case of crossed statuses because, though low in authority as a sex class they are intimately integrated and identified with their family men according to other criteria (e.g., economic, racial, educational).

The women in this study mostly learned at an early age to incorporate into their ideas of femaleness their extraordinarily high achievement goals and performances. Such integration of mildly discrepant status correlates, at an early age, provides preparation for later, more dramatically discrepant status (in this case, "female" and "religious authority," now officially empowered by the latter role to discuss the nature of reality).

The data show a strong disposition among the informants to resolve conflicts and discrepancies assimilatively. They speak in terms of conflicting realities that must continually inform and correct and complete each other in a finely tuned synergetic tension.

It would seem, from the data, that they are using the intellectual skills developed in double socialization and exploiting the potential of those skills to meet demands of role innovation, modern theological thought, and moral leadership. That is, a salient status correlate for non-elites (dialectical consciousness) may be turning for many of them into a central asset in role performance and in status mobility.

SOCIAL CHANGE

No more than with the other terms will I attempt a thorough, let alone exhaustive, discussion of social change. I shall raise only a few points that I consider most relevant to this study; first, social change as a complex process.

The normative systems of societies or of their subgroups consist of exquisitely intercalibrated responses, techniques, and values. They are clustered as institutions, ideologies, statuses or roles, around social functions of various sorts. The interconnectedness is never fully articulated and remains recognized only at the tacit level, if at all, by most members of a social order, unless a significant disruption occurs in the familiar ways and an acceptable way of dealing with it from familiar approaches is not immediately apparent.

Interdependent systems elements are so delicately adjusted and so elaborate that introducing an innovative factor throws many other components into system-threatening trauma, pending some ''shakedown'' process in which relevant modifications bring about reorganization on a new basis.

Certain eagerly embraced technological advances have increased life expectancy, improved conception control, and relieved household maintenance of much manual labor. These and other factors have coalesced to increase the likelihood that women will seek social legitimation in statuses formerly unavailable to them apart from exceptional circumstance.

Whatever the particular factors that have allowed their entry into ordained status, the clergywomen's functional presence *within* the institutionalized expressions of religion in the United States means that the institution will henceforth somehow reflect their point of view along with that of men from the past and present.

The sex ratio of clergy rosters will continue to be a critical predictor of institutional ideology, insofar as women and men, as categories, represent life orientations that are more than trivially distinctive. If the ratio is not so lopsided, or a category so overwhelming, that one group's influence can be functionally ignored, the groups will need to take each other into consideration as contributing partners. Some overall ideological coherence can be expected from their shared authority. Glimpses into the possible forms of such coherence are available here and there in the data.

Other principles of social change will be considered as they fit the discussion in the final chapters. For now, I'll bring one other set to attention: the acceleration of the pace of social change and the expansion of its scale, attached to the technological impetus of ''world modernization'' in recent history. This mind-boggling explosion of culture movement, especially in knowledge and industry, so escalates the impact of social inventions that individuals and institutions require a qualitatively different repertoire of adjustment responses to preserve both sufficient identity stability and sufficient adaptive flexibility. Viability of persons and groups can no longer be imaged helpfully in static terms. People must understand their security developmentally, in terms of dependable, evolving approaches to social existence. Since time to ''grow together'' into effective social rules is collapsed in the modern world, a much better articulated set of everyday communication techniques is a pressing need in cultural systems.

Efficient and intuitively operating conflict resolution skills are demanded by the conditions of contemporary existence at all levels of social organization, from intimacy to international relations. Communications between mates or work buddies, let alone at United Nations debates, nowadays cannot assume similarities of background or perspective, as once was commonly possible in private and public discussions. The more self-contained, slow-changing communities of the past often held their membership in life-long, face-to-face relationships with little entry or exit except by birth and death. That kind of social stability is becoming rare in our highly mobile, electronically wired modern connectedness. Innumerable books and speeches, as well as coffee conversations, deplore the cultural integration deficiencies signaled by societal drift and personal pathology, as groups and individuals lose their way amid transient meanings. For a sense of well-being, humans need a relatively high level of confidence in coping with the environment they (in the species sense) have brought about and in whose terms they know themselves.

A major function of religion, historically, has been to interpret people to themselves in terms of a worldview that is credible and recognizable in experience. Contemporary religious groups and leaders struggle to perform this task today in a setting generally understood in secular, scientific, and technological terms. Often "eternal truth" has been interpreted with socially static rigidity. Modern religionists search for ways to be faithful to received traditions and relevant to contemporary experience as the normative system shifts. Many deplore a stance of religious reaction to secular social forces; they advocate religious participation in the direction of social change. Nostalgic appeals from illusions of stability and stimulating appeals from avant-garde innovations combine in myriad ways.

Whatever the women in this study say they are about in their ministries, in later chapters we will want to compare this with what social analysts say is now needed for humane consequences in culture development.

NOTES

1. Adapted from several sources.
2. Max Weber elaborated on the fact that, as a precious, capturing vision ebbs in immediacy and the preservation of its essence becomes an absorbing project, religious groups increasingly formalize their procedures and move toward greater rigidity about correctness.

Chapter 5

Authority and "Struggle"

ESTABLISHING AUTHORITY

I have already cited material indicating that women tend to image leadership as a central enabling position in a peer network. I have no empirical evidence for how the informants actually exercise authority or for how others understand the clergywomen's authority ideals. I do have clear evidence for how the women view authority and how they think it is best used in religious ministry.

I previously mentioned the hesitancy the women show about discussing gender differences. Most of them remain very cautious about generalizations according to category, even though in each case I said, "I know you cannot represent clergywomen in general, and you haven't known all clergymen, but I'd just like to know how you might see your ministry to be different, if at all, from that of the male ministers you've known." Sometimes the comparisons came more spontaneously in other parts of the interview, where they inadvertently crept in as illustrations or were simply implied. An example is the statement, "Women are allowed to be more feeling in life"—an obvious use of men as referents while the informant talks about pastoral care.

However, the women refer to power and its use explicitly in terms of gender. They all recognize the systematic social differentiation between females and males with regard to the acceptability of assertiveness and domination. They know that they will not be widely approved as women if they handle authority "like a man." Not unexpectedly, they have developed points of view that idealize the kinds of authority more accessible to women and more socially acceptable in their self-presentation.

• Men live in social expectations that get them locked into power. Women can be more free from a power stance. We can more easily develop governance that embodies collegiality . . . that is enabling rather than dominating.
• I think women have different rationales for their actions. Their expectations are different. Women back off from power and want to share it. We don't tend to think of it as an end in itself. I see things differently from men and I use words differently . . . but I work within a very male-oriented authority. I operate as a whole and don't really understand concentrated use of power. I don't know how to wield it. I think men know how better, rightly or wrongly. I haven't found the codebook to the male world. When I argue it doesn't work the same; they come down as the final word . . . a very different mode . . . and don't consider my points. They can and do get angry. They always show strength. Anger is a big issue. . . . Women can't get angry . . . don't know how. . . . People can't deal with it when they do. . . . It's important to me to be sensitive and attuned to problems; I'm just not tuned in right now to career . . . power . . . money. In some ways there are fewer societal strictures for me and it makes a big difference.
• I can be stubborn when principles are involved. But I value others' ideas and often change in response. I believe in a shared ministry. I want to work cooperatively toward consensual action rather than imposing order and projects on groups. I don't feel like I have to have the last word. People should be together in life's struggles and puzzles . . . with equalitarian sharing . . . and their own integrity.
• People who respond positively to me like it that I open issues for struggle and consideration rather than just making specific solution proposals. People who want clear-cut, firm leadership decisions and strategies, in a concrete political sense, might be uncomfortable with my approach. I'm anti-hierarchical. That principle can't be absolutized, but it's a major commitment for me.
• I'm more an enabler in a team—drawing people out toward self-expression rather than assigning responsibilities.
• I dream of a church that is a circle rather than a pyramid . . . where there is mutuality of ministering . . . with diversity of gifts recognized. Ordination should mean a special professional role, but side by side with the laity . . . not high and low. I want to be an enabler of people . . . a nurturer of spiritual community.

Social thinkers have turned out many versions of the observation that socialization into cultural patterns leads people to "prefer their fate as a matter of choice." It is certainly not surprising, then, to see these women largely rejecting a type of power use that has routinely been denied them, and embracing a more personal, charismatic type of influence that they have been encouraged socially to perfect. The intrinsic authority of face to face authenticity, integrity, respect, and helpful intentions is valued by these women, across the board, as the ultimately humane social power.

Many of the informants' hopeful expectations for the "opportunities God keeps providing" show (but are not necessarily reduced to) the inventiveness of women and/or blacks who face limited social opportunities and invent personal responses.

They often bypass institutional structures to exert social influence that may be validated institutionally later on. From the interviews, I see almost no indication of impulse to enter power issues through counter-mobilization of strategic power.

One woman, after successfully handling an interim between senior pastorates, was closed out of most of her public ministerial functions by the new minister (who, during his employment interview, said he had no objection to working with a clergywoman).

• I just left quietly. I thought God wouldn't want trouble. I knew my ministry was from God and couldn't be taken away. I can carry it with me wherever I go. My husband was angry. He thought I should fight. He's a real advocate for me and respects God's call for me. I was invited right away to another church where the pastor already knew me. I have to fight in the Bible way. I must stand up for what's right even against ridicule . . . and pray! . . . and move as God gives opportunity. There are many opportunities in ministry to interpret through speaking. I'm reluctant to strike out against people. God may be giving direction through them. I can accept . . . and leave as a peacemaker. It opens the chance for reconciliation. I admire Mother Teresa . . . she's so strong. Often women have to take so much ridicule to do their ministries. Men probably couldn't put up with so much.

Three very young women represent a wide variation in personal style, and in how they juggle sex role and authority role implications. The first quoted below is able and self-confident but *very* low-key. Her friendly, nonconfrontational approach to relationships makes for comfort on both sides with many types of people. Conventional "womanly" demeanor coupled with high competency in church leadership drew attention from clergy while she was still in high school. She was guided toward ordination by numerous helpful clergymen in a denomination not notably congenial to women.

• I had very good male ministry models as a young person, but they were all commanding presences. I feel understanding of them and I don't actively reject that *in them*. I feel called to ministry primarily to help people . . . to share . . . to model . . . to care . . . to assist. I'm not much for putting on a show; I'm more of a teacher-preacher. I go more for eye contact and person-to-person talk from the center of my being. I don't push myself forward into the driver's seat. I work more effectively behind the scenes. A few parishioners think I should be more assertive . . . more visible as a leader. I like the parish ministry, but I really don't want a church alone. I've never had models for how to be "in charge" and "low-key" at the same time.
• I'm young and I look young. [She's also very attractive.] No one would ever mistake me for a pastor! That can be refreshing and freeing, but it can also be a handicap in that I'm not taken seriously without a clerical collar. If I don't wear it—to hospitals and such places—I'm not believable as a professional. If I do, I'm such a novelty. At first I felt some pressures to be more like a man. More often I've felt internal and external pressures to be more "professional" . . . in dress, for instance. Mostly, I've come to be accepted pretty much on my own terms. My parishioners see me as never "down" or discouraged— always on top of things. Sometimes that feels burdensome. I'm a very organized person—

I usually have situations under control when I'm the one responsible. It would be good if they saw my goofs more. They seem surprised in Bible study that I'm so well versed. A local newspaper article mentioned that I've studied ten languages and that really surprised them. They see me as a loving, affectionate wife. They wonder if I want to become a mother.

In telling this, the above woman interpreted her church members' surprise at the newspaper information as approval that she did not flaunt her erudition!

The third young informant I want to describe here shows fairly high distress and indecision about how to integrate social expectations associated with gender and professional authority. In appearance she is close to American ideals for women; her initial self-presentation is reserved; she is very intelligent and insightful, unusually so about her own ambivalence in authority. She was socialized in authoritarian values that she came to question and then reject through an intellectual route. A respected teacher was instrumental in encouraging her growth and easing her guilt as she brought her reason to bear on her rigid, rule-based faith:

• I was a very self-righteous kid. I went to church, I didn't drink, I didn't smoke. Later I came to see self-righteousness itself as a sin.

A big theme for this woman's ministry is fostering human development—intellectual, social, and personal. But she is clear-headed about her own conflicts in encouraging such growth in others.

• I see myself as a controlling person, given to perfectionist extremes. Also I sometimes want to be an earth mother, caning chairs and canning fruit, taking care of people. Sometimes I feel pressures to be more like a traditional woman—while doing a traditionally male role. I've always been quite assertive. Sometimes I've been more assertive than the male clergy around me. I want people to just take my word for something that I've come to see as right after a long process. It's frustrating not finding people who see things my way—[with a rueful laugh] the right way! Given my take-charge personality and need to see things happen quickly, maybe I should be in a secular occupation. I don't like to wait for people to grow into ideas as I had to. I want to help people search and learn and expand their views. I need to learn to give them time to grow in their faith rather than wanting to give them answers. I have difficulty separating negative things directed at the *role* from personal attacks. I'm so super-sensitive to people's complaints; I feel targeted by their criticisms.

The need here for the "right to be right" in an authoritarian way is pitted painfully against developmental ideals that are incompatible. This woman's struggle is of special interest, not only because of her acute awareness of inner value inconsistencies and her astonishing forthrightness on the subject. It also appears to be rather exceptional among these informants. The others quite clearly reject as undesirable the position of authoritarian solution-giver/truth-teller, preferring to abdicate control over others' views and decisions in favor of influence by authentic, open-ended interpersonal dialogue. It would be possible to suspect that these others are simply less honest. In listening to them, though, I am convinced that, in this small group of women, she is uniquely troubled by her role integration project.

I am inclined to think that age is a contributing factor of considerable significance in this matter. Many of the older women report youthful ego and relational conflicts involving issues of power. Most such issues were resolved as the informants abandoned more controlling modes of influence that were at war with their major value commitments, and learned what to them were more satisfactory modes of assertion that protected freedom for healthy growth all around.

The young woman mentioned above talks freely about her personal need to draw credibility from the ministerial office itself, even though she would prefer not to have such a need. She seems fearful that there will be no clergy/laity distinctions, yet uncomfortable about hierarchical arrangements, as she recalls her own rebellions.

• Elderly people have more respect for the office. People my age—who are so active and involved—challenge the authority of the role and rebel against elevated status for the pastor. Perhaps there are some special problems with authority in my denomination's traditions. I have trouble saying comfortably "God is working in me" without implying conceit. I think my congregation's lay leaders will force me to define my ministry role better. My hope is for mutuality in the definition.

Her sex and her strong predisposition toward conventionally male expressions of authority set up identity issues she knows she needs to transcend for her own well-being and for her ministry's sake. Though her anxiety level and ambivalence about authority are unusual for this particular set of clergywomen (only one other comes close), I suspect they could well be repeated more frequently among clergywomen at large. After all, my selection process disposes toward especially successful or promising professional women. Such a criterion could be expected to yield informants who have resolved fairly well crucial issues about how to represent public authority in a way that fits them.

The three young women above offer informative contrasts in personal role integration. None was exposed early to ministerial women or even much at all to women exercising public authority. Newness in an ill-defined professional role, youth, and femaleness converge to stimulate high consciousness of intentions and tensions. Two have arrived at comfortable resolutions in their complex personal roles. One has not. She is the only informant who admits to a yearning for unquestioned acceptance of her teachings. The rest have generally adopted a view of challenges that sees them as opportunities to interpret and to gain face-to-face authority through convincing people rather than through imposing views on them. The latter position is well represented by the woman who says,

• I'm not ambivalent about my choice [of the ministry]; I feel *good* in the role. I don't go into places with a feeling that people *should* accept me . . . So maybe they are reassured that they can take their good old time to observe and form opinions. Sometimes in marital counseling a woman will be doing all the talking and then it will come out that the husband doesn't want to talk with a woman pastor; he agreed he'd come "just one time to see." . . . But it works out okay, because it's no issue for me. I get a chance to show them how I can understand and help . . . and usually the men come back with their wives, over and over. Some of them seem surprised that I can understand their situation.

Whether as adjustment to social inevitability or as development of authentic self-expression (or both), the 17 clergywomen tend to assume that they are called upon to wield authority primarily from a stance of charismatic credibility and trust. For most of them this is raised to a point of faith; they are openly suspicious of authority that exists only in terms of traditions or official role qualifications. They seem grateful that legal-rational authority now grants them permission to occupy institutional platforms. But it remains the existential performance on that platform that is the *real* authority for them. With few exceptions they welcome such a test of their ministerial calling. In most cases I thought I detected even a desire or *need* for such testing as a means of continual self-assessment, that is, as a way of "hearing God" and keeping "on track" in ministerial effectiveness. It seems crucial to them that their authority as ministers not rest merely on their official claim to that status.

Perhaps I should explain that when I talk about charismatic authority as a socially legitimated type of power, I am *not* implying either dramatic manifestations of God's indwelling (such as "speaking in tongues") or stunningly attractive personal styles. I am simply referring to the authority of personal influence, intrinsic to interactions, claimed and maintained as it is spontaneously recognized. It is a type of authority conventionally accessible to females. The women in this study seem to feel that they must "earn" their authority firsthand, even when "rights" have been conferred through legitimate channels. As many women become both traditional and official occupants of the clergy role over time, will clergywomen remain as focused on authoritative *enactment* as they now are? It is clear that many of the informants were experienced in charismatic ministerial authoritativeness prior to ordination.

They talk much of reliance on interpretive words and demonstrative acts as expressions of personal integrity, demanding thoroughgoing developmental congruence for establishing authority in spiritual matters. They say that God constantly provides them with opportunities to discuss meanings of events and processes to convince, to display integrity, to care, to engender trust. Even their hopes for their lives tend to be stated in personal influence terms:

• I would like people to see me as making sense . . . as wise . . . a good counselor . . . using good judgment . . . communicating well. In college I could begin to tell I was effective in public speaking. I saw it as a way to participate in social change.

The informants refer to at least three types of interpretive speaking that have potential for evoking trust: preaching, informal exchanges, and responses to critical or adversarial approaches.

By and large they report enthusiastic feedback from parishioners about their preaching:

• They say I'm a good preacher. I'm short and to the point and my ideas are very accessible to them. I speak as one of them. There's a community feeling.
• Sometimes people introduce me as "a real go-getter." They say, "You ought to hear her preach! She's a super preacher. She always rises to the occasion when needed." They seem to feel that the quality and helpfulness of my teaching is more than they had a right to expect . . . and they express surprise at my plainness about reporting congregational business matters. They tell me they're very pleased at the amount of attention and caring they're getting from me.
• People say my sermons are plain and simple. I must speak to Ph.D.'s as well as to the uneducated. I mustn't talk over the heads of my people. I have to know the theology but I must put it in their terms; it must be workable for them.
• I use less traditional verbal formulas of the faith. . . . I say things in more situation-tied terms that are easier for the people to understand.

I have two other sources of evidence for the verbal effectiveness of these and other women clergy. While gathering data I listened to sermons delivered by five of the informants as well as by numerous other clergywomen. They are, indeed, superior communicators, in my estimation. None had affected pulpit voices; none used stilted religious language; all maintained direct eye contact with the audience and seemed either to use no notes at all or to be exceptionally free of dependency on written materials. Additionally, I have talked formally and informally with numerous seminary and regional church administrators (with one exception, all men) about my research. Many of them volunteered their judgments that women seminarians and ministers, in the past decade, generally display high levels of preaching skill. They warn against understanding this change too simply in terms of gender alone. There are indications that, for men with high ability, other career possibilities are currently more exciting, lucrative, prestigious, and hence more attractive. So women in seminaries may be coming initially from a higher-ability stratum than male students. But the seminary personnel do not think the group differences in ability are the whole story either. They surmise that the ways women characteristically orient to life and express themselves are peculiarly compatible with a synthesizing discipline such as theology and with the interpersonal caring ideals of professional ministry. Two men shared their relief that the presence of women had moved their class discussions away from tedious debates about correct religious thinking and toward consideration of alternative views of truth, spiritual growth, and ways of being responsible believers.

The view of critical challenge as opportunity to build trust is implied in the following statements:

• Critical questions are more welcomed by me as an opportunity to interpret than feared as an attack. My responses come out of a deep sense of need to remain true to myself. I confront issues rather than avoid them and occasionally that gets me into trouble, but I'm respectful of members' sometimes defensive, fearful testing of my ideas. The dialogue is more a sharing . . . an exchange . . . than a debate. It doesn't require some final resolution.

• One becomes spokesperson, as minister, in ways one is not always prepared for. Recently, with the big press publicity about the new nonsexist translation of the Bible, male pastors and parishioners expected me to interpret the effort as if I were somehow responsible. Some are judgmental, some are just inquisitive, and some are supportive. I'm not resentful of being put in that position; it's a chance to interpret.

EQUALITARIAN IDEALS

Charismatic authority, established mainly by way of personal credibility in ably guiding and interpreting human experience, fits the informants' equalitarian values and "peer leadership" ideals. Charismatic authority is not necessarily equalitarian, but among these women there are no noticeable exceptions to the rule that "first among equals" leadership is the conscious aspiration. It is rooted in the theological position that persons are of equal worth to God, and that true authority must be recognized experientially rather than imposed hierarchically. For the Christians it is attached to images of Jesus' ministry as a continuing exercise in giving full respect to all persons he encountered. The preferred community-building stance is as "central struggler" toward consensus in faith rather than as official repository of absolute religious correctness. There is conscious avoidance of the role of the authoritarian religious expert dishing up correct answers and fixing people.

I jotted down a few summarizing points, while one of my informants preached her first sermon as newly installed senior pastor in a large congregation. Here is the gist of what she said:

• There are no important distinctions between the ministries of preachers and of laity. We are all here to focus attention on what God is doing among us; to make visible God's love by *doing* the Lord's loving; and to enable each other to be and do our best, humbly and hopefully. As God's instruments of ministry, we find God's mercy in giving it to each other.

This equalitarian theme of mutual ministering occurs again and again in the interview data.

• Last week a man had a stroke during the worship service and was taken directly to the hospital. Later I stopped by the hospital to see how he was doing. He was still in the emergency room. He wanted to talk about the miracle of birth and the hope of rebirth. *He* became *my* minister.

• I'm aware of my limited knowledge and experience. I want to be open to people and ideas and give the Holy Spirit a chance.

• My idea of a faithful Christian is somebody who "deals justly, loves mercy, and walks humbly with God" . . . who listens actively and responds out of the center of being . . . to persons who need not just answers but reassurances of support. I'm so aware of the help I've received . . . it's a real compulsion with me to help others. I know few folks who can't at some level understand the need to be "family" to each other. . . . I have a special congregational committee that I formed as a "listening group" for me and the parishioners. Such a committee might scare some parishes. Their role is to keep tuned in to complaints and concerns from people who don't bring them directly to me . . . and to call me to account if necessary. We're still in the long, long process of learning to trust each other, but I think they're learning how to deal with that kind of vulnerability. A new role for them now is to be my personal family of support . . . my counsel. They function well . . . as a good liaison. People who just want a firm, "right" answer might not find me appealing as a minister; they might be threatened by an authority figure who *searches*.

• In my ministering I want to be respected as a professional, but I don't need last-word infallibility to be maintained. I go for friendship, togetherness, community, mutuality . . . rather than authoritarian deference in a hierarchical structure. We're on a journey together to discover "the answers."

• My favorite image of ministry now is as "a covenanted friend." I find it hard to connect with openly racist or sexist people, but I am committed to taking them and all people seriously as persons and trying to minister. I think a leader must be accountable simultaneously as leader and follower. There is no way to short-cut democratic trust-building. It's a frustrating, slow process. As I ask people to be flexible and to accept my nontraditional ways, I have to show flexibility, too, in using the traditional ways they find comfortable.

Part of the informants' emphasis on democratic relationships is the clear preference for being addressed by their first names. Only a few say that, in some situations, the title of Pastor or Rabbi is acceptable because it may help others to take them seriously as professionals. But "Reverend" is disliked actively by almost all of them. The distance and deference it implies are discomfiting.

Whether or not they are consciously feminist, these women are strongly drawn to equalitarian values and their logical extension into discourse techniques. As women, socially accustomed to a status subordinate to that of men, there is substantial appeal for them in the idea of peer networks in social organization, compared with hierarchies. Peer negotiation principles combine ideological defensibility as a single, universal standard with the psychological freedom of mutual respect, an important step up for women as a group. They seem neither psychologically nor ideologically prepared to lead from a high position of dominance and control over others. Ambivalence on this score is exceptional among the informants. Most of them are notably at ease approaching both men and women with an almost identical repertoire of responses: straightforward, flexible, and slanted systematically neither up nor down. I make this statement from my own observations of exchanges peripheral to interview sessions, as well as from their stated ideals.

The informants seem to accept the inevitability of some sorts of status structure in social organization. But generally they do not find it acceptable to relate to others *in terms of* the hierarchical entitlements of office. In their families and their ministries they therefore espouse the rationales and techniques of equalitarian community-building, which they put forth as God's way, based on biblical and theological study. Few of them even acknowledge a wish for top-down control over others' decisions, let alone justify such a wish as a religious position. Again, nothing is being said here about the extent to which the women are consistently able to embody their views. It is the views themselves that concern us in this study.

The strong skew toward nonhierarchical, equalitarian, single-standard values is understandable in a group whose traditional place in society is a relatively de-powered status. For these particular women to grasp the conventional male orientation, formerly associated with the clergy role, would amount to self-alienation from their developed identities. It would also open them to considerable hostility that, from an unfamiliar stance, they would be ill-equipped to handle confidently. They are convinced, in the main, that their equalitarian stance fits traditional religious ideals of liberation, if not always institutional ideals of order.

"STRUGGLE": IN-PROCESS HUMANITY

The theme of *struggle* is dramatically evident and central throughout the interview data. If there is little appetite among the informants for traditional authoritarian power struggles, there *is* a type of struggle they do appear to engage in continuously. It is not just the biographical stories of tragedy and pain to which I refer. I have no intention to minimize the heroic battles represented in transcending the consequences of alcoholism, incest, and destructive marriages. Still, the more significant lesson here is that *personal growth through struggle* has model-for-life status in the ministries of most of these women. Awareness of the growth potential arising from their own distress comes into their professional work as a learning that encourages flexibility, patience, and hopefulness in dealing with problem situations or puzzling ideological tangles.

They look at struggle (attempting to resolve social, personal, moral, and intellectual conflicts) as the ongoing basis for building personal integrity, understanding, and trust among people. It is taken to be the living core of human communion. Never is struggle in life interpreted by the informants as mere "trouble" or aggravation.

They speak of the Bible as a struggle story; biblical study and theology as struggle to understand and enliven the traditions in our own time; moral rigor, language use, and religious administration as struggle for appropriate expressions of the faith. Struggle has a positive tone in the data beyond the distress aspect that is also there and not ignored. A number of the women talk about revealing their own struggles purposefully as an invitation to others to join in a never-ending community struggle for insight.

The approach is creative and growth-focused. Social solidarity among the authentic participants is an expected outcome. There is expressed willingness to live with necessarily incomplete views, developmental ambiguities and ironies, partially accomplished agendas, and shifting programs. One does not have to be or know the "final word." Issues need to be always *in progress* and on top of the table. There is a keen sense of movement and direction, in a known spirit, but toward an end not wholly defined or definable in concrete terms.

All this does not feel like terrible disorder to them, or out of control in some crucial way. It is rather seen as the required condition for the healthy, complex, and sometimes discrepant growth of persons and groups. In a nutshell, the message is, "Let's discover the truth together. *I* am not the voice of God. *We* listen *together* for the voice and tell each other what we hear. When the pieces don't fit, we listen harder, but we know we'll never get it all straightened out. Still, we'll get it clear enough for living a good life now."

The theme of struggle is coupled with the imaging of faith and salvation as *process*, not destination.

• My emphasis is on wholeness. Belief encompasses everything, including your ethical decisions. Your life actions have to be congruent with your belief system to model your faith, in the congregation and in the rest of the world. Creative stewardship is a life process.
• The pain of having children makes available to me the image of all God's children as "in process" humans.
• Faith is not necessarily lived out within the boundaries of the organized church. A faithful Christian is always trying to grow in doing God's will. It's a never-ending journey—a never-ending growth in faith.

Many of the Christian clergywomen take their images of faithful spiritual growth directly from their understanding of the Jesus stories.

• God is life. God is reality. God is experience. Jesus is the "way-shower." He showed us every facet of what we would go through—even in death, where his spirit could not be destroyed. I find help in the stories of Jesus on the Cross.
• With Jesus you see the God/human tension . . . the struggle. People use excuses to get off on both sides and remove that tension. He was loving, compassionate, harsh with injustice, clear about truth, "Lord," "Savior," friend, teacher, guide. He seemed to grow into the role. Perhaps he was unclear, at points, about what was ahead. But when it became clear he chose for love, for life through death, and for salvation possibilities. I don't understand the time-framing some people do with the idea of the Second Coming. I think our salvation joins us to eternity when it happens, not at some future time. A faithful Christian stays flexible, pliable, able to move and bend with varying ideas and ideologies, growing, learning . . . never locked into absolutism . . . aware of others . . .

aware of their own responsibility. They continue to struggle with what the faith is saying to them.
• Action-oriented people respond positively to me . . . strugglers . . . honest strugglers . . . people who have experienced their own struggles and are aware of them and are willing to look at themselves . . . "rebels" who sense in me something of themselves, desiring to change traditional social systems. Status quo lovers, those who need not to be stirred, respond more negatively.

One woman is especially eloquent on this subject of struggle, of wrestling with truth. I will quote her and some others more extensively later, as we pick up the theme again in connection with existential theologizing. She comments:

•You've got to be a little cracked to take Abraham seriously at first. You look at Isaac, Jacob, Moses and say, "Why are *they* in the Bible? They could have come up with better people." They're there because they were human. I wonder, "What am *I* supposed to learn?" I have to wrestle. There's a wonderful set of questions there. So much is non-sensical, it really makes you work. Guidance only comes from wrestling with what's there. It comes. Hang out a while; the answer will come when it's supposed to.

Others add:

• You mustn't violate another's personhood and say, "You must believe [this]," but support them in the struggle to live a good life.
• Moral decisions are often a struggle. You have to act with a keen sense of being "in process." You need to say, "I could be wrong, but this is the best light I have so far."

Living in a prejudiced and discriminatory society, the black women have doubtless faced more than their share of human struggle. Though they do not depart from the general tendency among the informants to interpret life and faith in process and growth terms, it is from them that I hear more reservations, more awareness of the need for being *selective* about entering struggle.

• I have mixed feelings about avoiding conflicts or using them for growth. Conflict makes me feel so burdened down.

One informant interprets her whole life and her whole ministry primarily in terms of the struggle to make room for the full expression of women in her denomination. As a minister she is far from a "one-string fiddle"; it is unlikely that her parishioners would even recognize or label her a feminist by their understanding of that term. Yet institutional inclusion of both sexes is her basic ministerial project, and to her way of thinking, this project will be a struggle.

• I have low moments when I feel there is such lack of understanding, lack of openness, and resistance to change! In all my parish situations I've worked with the *most* open men . . . the best! They're modern, cooperative, sensitive . . . and they respond to challenges with positive, helpful attitudes. But still there are *huge* problems. There is no understanding of the pain and frustration of women, especially women in the church . . . such unawareness of sexist comments, blindness to women's issues, fear of my full involvement, surprise at my distress. *I have to bring up all the problems; as long as I just cooperate they don't notice anything wrong.* Yet they all have really tried. Consciousness-raising is slow and hard!

One woman, after talking about the value in struggling, said,

• It isn't that you get so good at struggling; it's that you come to know struggle as producing very valuable insights.

These 17 informants are strikingly positive, hopeful, confident women. I see no tendency whatsoever among them to embrace struggle or suffering, *per se*, at any level as some heroic display or proof of virtue. But they see the ongoing struggle to resolve both intrapersonal and interpersonal conflict as essential to healthy identity and community for humans.

Chapter 6

Doing Administration

In this section on classic ministerial tasks we look first at the administrative function—the management of the religious organizational unit—the presiding over concrete religious community.

I have relatively few quotations to offer here that exhibit specifically the women's ideas about executive leadership. The more meager material could mean lower interest in this area among the women in the study, a lower sense of competence, a failure to identify with this aspect of the role, or, as I think is more likely, the women group administrative concerns under another rubric, such as ''development of spiritual community'' or ''responsibility for mutual caring.'' It is clear that, for most, the administrative focus is on democratically building trust.

• If a rule doesn't work, throw it out! . . . If a structure doesn't work, bag it! . . . Let's not think that everything has been settled because we have this nice neat structure that looks so good on paper. Let's see how *people* are faring in this structure and not hang on to the structure if it doesn't help the *people* flourish, even if it might be efficient in terms of getting some task done. . . . Women are much less wedded to structure . . . period . . . partially because they don't have that much invested in it like men do.

Four of the women are relatively quiet about executive aspects of ministry. They are in specialized ministries or assistantships that require little special administrative skill, and they say little about church management. Those who speak about organizational ideals and procedures tend to illustrate and amplify the now familiar themes of charismatic authority; equalitarianism; responsible caring; communal, dialectical growth in faith; and unification of life experience. For light in new areas we thus continue to spiral back over previously noted tendencies in ministerial/personal viewpoint.

Since the informants appear very close to the understanding Hans Küng represents as "the church from 'below,' " I shall quote from his work:

The first thing we have to tell ourselves again and again is that we are the People of God. And the Church at its origin for all its weaknesses and defects regards itself essentially as God's community, God's people.

[. . .]

So I think it is illegitimate to separate church from laity—although the attempt has always been made again and again. I think this is really a hierarchistic, clericalistic misunderstanding of the church. And we must just not follow this but we have to protest against this use of the word. As women have quite often protested against sexist language, I think we also have to protest against this hierarchistic language.

[. . .]

And so any cult of personalities, any buildup of an individual who alone is empowered to speak while all the others are condemned to hear and applaud, that is inconceivable according to the New Testament. That is the first point, the theological point. The church is essentially in principle "below."

The second point is that we are a charismatic movement. [. . .] It is already clear that the charisms are not given only to certain office holders but are given to the whole people of God and often in a very ordinary way. [. . .] Everybody has a gift, as Paul says, maybe of consoling, of advising, of helping, of administering and (coming very late in Paul's list of charisms) the gift of governing. You see, God's activity within the church has its effect not only on the people but also on the individual. And so the whole church is a pneumatic reality with a charismatic dimension.

And we are not to forget this when we only see the big machinery.

[. . .]

So I think we have to insist that everybody who has a charism has, according to Paul, his or her own authority. And he or she has to be heard. Even if he or she has no official position, a charism gives authority. And we have to say that nobody in the church has any right to suppress charisms and nobody has the right to say that certain charisms may not come up. And nobody has to say, according to Paul, that he has all charisms. L'Eglise—c'est moi!

[. . .]

I must insist here that all this also gives us an order—that where the Spirit is working we have no disorder. And we do not speak here for a wild, undisciplined enthusiasm— the degenerating into anarchy, knowing no limits, with everybody doing what he or she wants. That is not the image of the church in the New Testament, and that is certainly not what we want here. But on the other side, it is not possible to have order manifested in conformism, where all have to do what one person wants. The Christian order must be an order in freedom. Because if it is only order and no freedom, it is not a Christian order.[1]

The difference between thinking in hierarchical or communitarian categories is not simply a matter of rearranging mental furniture. Deep primal needs and feelings at the core of identity tend to hold the mental categories in place for shoring up personal safety in well-known ways. Carol Gilligan has some helpful insights, here attached to gender differences.

The reason women's experience has been so difficult to decipher or even discern is that a shift in the imagery of relationships gives rise to a problem of interpretation. The images of hierarchy and web, drawn from the texts of men's and women's fantasies and thoughts, convey different ways of structuring relationships and are associated with different views of morality and self. But these images create a problem in understanding because each distorts the other's representation. As the top of the hierarchy becomes the edge of the web and as the center of a network of connection becomes the middle of a hierarchical progression, each image marks as dangerous the place which the other defines as safe. Thus the images of hierarchy and web inform different modes of assertion and response: the wish to be alone at the top and the consequent fear that others will get too close; the wish to be at the center of connection and the consequent fear of being too far out on the edge. These disparate fears of being stranded and being caught give rise to different portrayals of achievement and affiliation, leading to different modes of action and different ways of assessing the consequences of choice.

The reinterpretation of women's experience in terms of their own imagery of relationships thus clarifies that experience and also provides a nonhierarchical vision of human connection. Since relationships, when cast in the image of hierarchy, appear inherently unstable and morally problematic, their transposition into the image of web changes an order of inequality into a structure of interconnection. But the power of the images of hierarchy and web, their evocation of feelings and their recurrence in thought, signifies the embeddedness of both of these images in the cycle of human life. The experience of inequality and interconnection, inherent in the relation of parent and child, then gives rise to the ethics of justice and care, the ideals of human relationship—the vision that self and other will be treated as of equal worth, that despite differences in power, things will be fair; the vision that everyone will be responded to and included, that no one will be left alone or hurt. These disparate visions in their tension reflect the paradoxical truths of human experience—that we know ourselves as separate only insofar as we live in connection with others, and that we experience relationship only insofar as we differentiate other from self. (1982: 62–63).

As Gilligan points out in this last sentence and as my use of male citations further illustrates, the gender-specific tendencies in life orientation are intrinsic to each other's development (in individuals as well as in social groups) and not at all exclusive to a sex category. Yet, in understanding self, others, and society, it is crucial that we know and carefully consider the fact that the predominating tendencies are, indeed, gender-specific.

It may be helpful to review informant quotations in other sections at this point, especially those on authority, equalitarian ideals, and nurturance. The women really seem to recoil from a self-image as director or "boss" of a congregation or region. Critical comments are directed by some of them toward ministers who interpret their calling, or authority, as placing them "in charge" of laity who do the hands-on ministering under professional management. The women see their own administrative leadership much more comfortably in catalytic, charismatic, enabling, coordinating, negotiating terms. Truth-telling, pastoral care, and institutional management are not so much discrete categories of activity in their ministerial functioning as they are recognizable dimensions of a unified leadership. From this one might anticipate a certain sloppiness in administrative detail. Indeed, traditionally, women have been deemed deficient in imaging and imposing institutional order. Such a suspicion would be inconsistent, however, with information I have about the particular women who speak most eloquently about structure emerging out of communal growth in faith (versus structure imposed as a template for religious activities). In the initial referrals several were described as fine administrators; but also the incidence of their involvement with building programs, supervision of regional matters, and lengthy solo parish administration goes beyond what might reasonably be expected apart from recognition of special competency.

Computer expert Sherry Turkle, from MIT, recently lectured on our campus. She talked about how people's relationships to computers over time reflect their own style of thinking and their own ways of being human (unless they are intimidated and incapacitated by the imposition of rigidly doctrinaire ideas of programming). She says that persons working as "planners" (modal for males) organize projects from a formal outline which they devise at the outset; those working as "negotiators" (modal for females) let the outline emerge at the end from the operational relationships. She maintains that both men and women work in both ways, but that since the "planning" way is modal for males, and males have dominated computer technology, the "outline first" approach to information processing usually has been considered normative and prescriptive in computer use. Often this has resulted in persons who "watch it emerge" being judged—and judging themselves—incompetent with computers.

Church administration poses parallel possibilities for "engineering" and "farming" approaches to ministry—for setting up drafting shops designing blueprints for building or marketplaces distributing fruits that have been cultivated. In a society such as ours where executive standards are defined relative to the styles of male executives, the more typically female management styles may appear chaotic, irrational, underarticulated, or inept. As with moral perspectives, the historic tendency to treat male reality as *reality* stifles appropriate critiquing among women and men of women's characteristic ways of doing things. The intrinsic integrity and worth of women's lives and expressive contributions are often not just unnoticed but unnotice*able*, according to traditional norms for public accomplishments. Even customary technical language is awkward for persons whose lives are not lived according to the dynamics that language expresses.

Modern religious bureaucracies share the essential organizational characteristics of other corporate bureaucracies: Budgetary procedures, flow charts, chains of command, job descriptions, five-year plans, split labor policies, perquisites, personnel guidelines, constitutions, policy statements, and on and on. Hierarchical rational coordination of specialized tasks gives bureaucratic organization amazing competitive strength (and some characteristic problems) in ordering human affairs. However, just as parenting is often understood only or primarily in mothering terms, so institutional management is often popularly equated with bureaucratic management, which is a projected distillation of male cognitive style, the disposition to impose a procedural outline on human activity toward some specified end. And, just as we are learning that fathering is a parenting paradigm that is distinctive and valuable, so we are learning that nonhierarchical networks contribute a distinctive and valuable organizational paradigm for the various institutional sectors to consider. Moreover, the most fruitful contributions of the alternative paradigms to human well-being, in each case, can be made only if the polar tendencies are well integrated *within* concrete operations.

Understandably, the most extensive comments on church organization come from women with major commitments and involvements in administrative aspects of ministry. The first woman quoted has done the initial organizing of one congregation and now serves as senior pastor of another. Before her ordination she and her husband joined with other couples to create an ''alternative spiritual community'' outside the auspices of incorporated denominations. She comments on that early experimental group,

• It was a pivotal experience for me . . . that four or five years . . . lots of folks . . . lots of creativity.

Of her professional ministry since her ordination she goes on to say,

• I didn't feel pressures to do things like a man nearly so much in the new church I began, where we were doing things from the ground up, as in a church like this one where there's a long tradition which has been established mostly by males. You don't want to make changes too fast too soon and the ways things are when you come feels alien to you because they are, in fact, not created by women and so you feel pressure, like with the budget business. . . . I just personally don't worry about that. I feel that it's a spiritual matter and if I work with the spiritual part there will be no problem. . . . But they want a stewardship campaign and all that kind of stuff and they get all tied in knots about it . . . or approach it by trying to browbeat people into giving more . . . rather than saying the reason they're not giving more is because they need some spiritual nourishment in life. . . . Let's work on *that*. It may take a little longer, but it's going to pay off more richly in the end. . . . The way the churches are organized . . . they're all like the local businesses, which are male structures, too. You've got committees and subcommittees and task forces. . . . Elders and deacons, instead of taking care of people, are running committees and then everyone wonders why people are not feeling cared for. . . . There's parliamentary procedure and voting on everything . . . and to change that whole thing around after it's started . . . I have this image of getting a *huge* ocean liner turned around. . . . The structures don't help the people think of the church *as church*; it imposes an alien model on the church. . . . I have such a deep-seated down-in-my-guts gratitude that I'm not a man that I don't experience trying to be more like men. . . . I don't even like wearing suits. . . . I suppose I do try to follow a male model of running meetings efficiently and getting them over with quickly. . . . I'm not the least bit wishy-washy; I have strong opinions on things but people seem to feel I'm flexible and listen well. . . . I don't like confrontation but, generally speaking, I can't let things lie . . . I mean, if I sense that someone's upset with me or I'm upset with somebody and we're in an ongoing relationship in the congregation, I'll make sure that we sit down and talk about it. . . . I'll take the initiative. . . . I'll say, "Hey, you know, what's wrong? Have I done something to offend you? Please let me know. . . . If there's anything I can do to rectify it I will. . . . Let's talk it out. Let's not just let it sit there." . . . Also, if there's a conflict in a group you have to give people the time and opportunity to air their feelings and not crush them down for the sake of making a decision . . . and bury all the doubts and fears and questions people have. I believe in getting them out on the table. I'm willing to negotiate and sit down and say, "I could be wrong," or, "Tell me what I've done," or, "Tell me how you're feeling," . . . because I think that often it's just a misunderstanding. . . . I very intentionally create an atmosphere in what I do and say from the pulpit and in personal relationships that encourages a community where people can disagree with each other deeply and still love each other. . . . There are people who know very well that I don't agree with an opinion they have or even a thing that they may be doing . . . but I still demonstrate that I care for them . . . and they're still a friend. . . . I respect them and support them as persons. They're still my brother and sister in Christ, after all. I've always tried to do everything I could to articulate that and let the church be the kind of atmosphere in which there's that kind of freedom. I've said, "Don't think that every time the church says something everyone's gotta get on the bandwagon. Let's not have a convoy mentality; let's have a smorgasbord mentality where there are many ways of serving and of articulating the Gospel." Give people the credit for doing what they feel called and led to do. . . . Even though you may not understand it you're willing to be supportive because you trust the Holy Spirit to lead in their life. . . . I think women tend to be much more keyed in to the effect of structures or rules or policies on individuals and tend to be much more "make it up as you go along" rather than fitting into some preconceived "come hell or high water it's got to be this way" kind of thing. There's more of a personal touch. . . . For example, just with the thing of membership . . . every church wants to "clean its rolls" . . . and so they make up their rules: . . . If somebody hasn't been to church for two years you write them a letter and if they don't respond in another six months you wipe them off the roll and inform them in a letter. . . . Well, I don't do things that way and I just don't think that's a human way to treat people. . . . I think that the least you should do is make a phone call or see them personally and talk about it . . . explore where they are and then make a decision about whether they belong on the inactive list or not. . . . Don't try to fit people into categories! . . . For another example . . . membership class . . . okay, so there's this policy someone made up that all people who want to join this church should have to go through six weeks of a class in which they cover the following materials. . . . I say, "Let's look at who we've got here." Maybe some have hardly any Christian background and ought to be linked up with someone in the church for a one-on-one induction into Christian life and thought for a couple of years. . . . Maybe someone else is switching from the church down the road and they know as much or more than I do. . . . It's ridiculous for them to come to class. . . . Just give them a little booklet on this particular church's history and be done with it.

She has served in two denominations as a professional minister and names a third where the polity might be more in line with her ministerial ideals. Still she expresses high satisfaction with ministry in her present denominational niche.

• In some ways I feel like a good fit in my denomination; in some ways I don't. I might fit somewhere else more comfortably . . . but then I wouldn't be part of the larger picture of what God is doing . . . of cross-fertilization of denominations . . . toward erosion of walls until the time when people will say, "'What is this nonsense! Let's start sitting at table together and recognizing each other's ministries and quit all this folderol!'" . . . It's better that I do that rather than just leave for where I might personally feel more at home.
• The church was badly split at the time of my arrival. They had literally driven the last pastor out; but I have not had problems. I said to them, "I only know one way to function: I lay everything out on the table and deal with things as they happen. I'm no good at playing games and party politics and talking behind backs. I take it as it comes . . . deal with it . . . and move on." That's scary to some, especially some women . . . but now they support me strongly. One woman on the call committee said, "That sounds too harsh for a woman." She has come to see that it isn't a harsh way at all It's quite like how she conducts her own life; she just never thought of it in those terms. . . . I teach a seminar on conflict management. My first two loves in ministry are preaching and administration. I want a ministry from the bottom up instead of the top down. I think men sometimes have more sense of the structure of an organization than of the people involved. The corporate image is emphasized more than the persons, as such. Men pastors more bring up the thing, "Well, maybe you can do this or that better because you're a woman." Maybe there's a little envy . . . a little wish to be in my skin . . . because they feel I don't have the pressures and expectations they do . . . within themselves and from other people. I think, in one case at least, a man felt that I could pull things off that would make him lose face with other men . . . if he attempted. I feel there's a great deal to be gained from vulnerability. I mean, you have to be aware from Scripture that we're not talking about ignorance. . . . People put up walls because they're scared to death. . . . At the regional level I sense that I may constitute a threat to some. . . . It hasn't surfaced as a significant problem but it comes out subtly from a small minority of persons very grounded in administration. . . . Also outside the congregation I sometimes feel a little resistance from women my own age. I'm not sure. . . . Are they jealous? . . . Are they threatened? . . . by someone living out dreams they gave up? . . . In my own congregation people of all types seem to respond positively now. . . . There are more women than men in churches. . . . Affinity and empathy are perhaps easier with a woman pastor—even with those women who were resistant to the idea of a woman pastor. Women tell on themselves. . . . One said, "I jumped out of my chair to say 'Absolutely not!' when they asked if we'd take a woman pastor. I didn't want her thinking about the roast while she preached the sermon. Now I love it!" . . . This is a good congregation. The people are much involved; they take a lot of initiative. In my first year the desk work interfered with pastoral calling. Now I take two afternoons a week—one for shut-ins and one for membership calls. Mornings are in the office and most evenings are filled with meetings or counseling. . . . Counseling and education are my third- and fourth-place loves.
• I didn't go into the ministry to bring something different as a woman, though I think that's a legitimate call for some. But I find it being noted by others. . . . Maybe it's a willingness to be more personal, more vulnerable. . . . I work easily with the team. I tend

to fill in information about the congregation to the other pastors. Often men don't take seriously who a person is "off the job." I'm a caretaker of team relationships and carry out the kind of communications that enhance the ministry. . . . I think my central approach may be different. I don't need to be thought necessary to every operation. Clergy-lay communication in this parish is excellent, but I think clergy should be less involved, timewise. It's too demanding. . . . The built-in rigidity of parish life could be freed up by the minister in charge. I would want to free the congregation more to visit around and feed themselves. I'd have laypeople more involved in leading the liturgy. . . . Integrity and direction and flexibility can be better organized for optimal satisfaction among staff personnel.
• I emphasize collegiality and mutuality rather than deference and reverence. I urge lay leadership and involvement of the people in the liturgy. It's rewarding to see some of my goals happening . . . others coming to share the vision I have.
• My congregation was not prepared for a woman minister. I think they wanted middle-aged, experienced, authoritarian leadership. I haven't encountered a great deal of neg-ativism. I'm not much different from men in basic theology or congregational polity; but in relating to people the culture-bound ways show up. . . . I'm personally and spiritually more nurturing . . . more concerned with wholeness. . . . Also the ways people relate to me are different. I think it's easier for women to relate to women as pastors. My greatest source of support is older women . . . above fifty.

Quite a few of the informants talk appreciatively about the spiritual and ad-ministrative supportiveness of women in their congregations. Sometimes there has been initial opposition or coolness, after which solid rapport has been built. The younger women, especially, refer to the almost doting affection they often receive from old women in the parishes.

• At first I thought older women were shying away and skeptical, but they've turned out to be supportive and admiring.
• The really excited gushy-positive response is from older women . . . roughly sixty-five and up . . . but also many my own age. The older women seem to experience me as a sort of daughter-teacher.

Some criticize the use of administrative procedures for impersonal control of community relationships.

• I feel low consciousness of restrictions from femaleness. I recognize differences in the *ways* women perform. Women will offer different options in administration, for example. They are sensitized to different issues. Women are allowed to show more vulnerability, caring, mercy, warmth. Chains of command seem obstructive in a work environment. Delegation is a cop-out: "You do this and get back to me." It creates extra work and loses focus.
• I'm infuriated when I see bureaucratic efficiency used to squash people—to short-circuit the building of relationships. . . . I hate placation and patronizing responses that smooth things without dealing with the real issues. . . . Ministers often distance themselves through having an approach to members of a *category* . . . like "older women" or "business men."

The above clergywoman seems to arrive at a judgment similar to John Stuart Mill's when he observes that "all silencing of discussion is an assumption of infallibility," and then points out that there is a great and moral difference between opinion whose certitude is based on the welcoming of every opportunity for testing it and opinion whose certitude is based on stifling the opposition.

• There are no big issues in the congregation. It has a history of being a "tough church." I have not found it so. Some of the "old cusses" the people tell about are dead . . . but I think my approach may be different, too. . . . I have insisted on full responsibility for acting committees. . . . They don't have to get permission to act . . . but they report back to the board what they have done. I have insisted on clear decisions of the board and I respect those decisions even if I disagree. . . . We have a large board [thirty]. It meets four times a year. I usually go home satisfied. I'm seldom upset with how things stand in the congregation. . . . I do the secretarial chores so the congregation can afford a community worker instead. Other ministers say, "You should demand a secretary." They want to get ideas for how other people can help other people . . . and they remain "above all this" in a fantasy world.   Jesus is an example for me of a shepherd and a revolutionary . . . who cares intimately but overturns things because love demands it in shepherd roles. . . . I feel that what this congregation is about is what the church is about. . . . I like the heavy use of the building. It's open seven days a week and 1500 people move through each week for meals, services, etc. . . . I feel ill-equipped for the fund-raising aspects of the program and budgetary things . . . running the soup kitchen, keeping the community center open, getting foundation grants. . . . I get positive responses from people who already have been itching for a social response ministry . . . liberals disillusioned with church conservatism . . . the elderly . . . people hurting. For some people in their fifties and sixties . . . scared . . . losing power . . . wanting security . . . maybe taking early retirement . . . they may feel their pastor is taking away even more of their familiar signs in life.

Three things the above woman mentions recur in other interviews: dislike for money management or lack of confidence in fund raising; absence of back-up staff, imposing limitations on how they must organize their ministries; and the importance of managing routine business or conflict openly, with respect for all concerned.

• I'm pretty reserved, though I try to be genuine and open. I aspire to dealing "on the table" with issues.
• Financial support is more difficult for women. There's not enough money to fill the needs of people . . . hunger . . . housing . . .
• Women do not concern themselves so much with money. Men expect a lot more of their congregations . . . money and assistance. I've heard them say, "Don't go over there and spoil those people!"

Absence of back-up persons in or around the ministerial role takes several forms: no "pastor's wife" to fill in at church and at home, no other minister to be on call for emergencies in pastoral care, and no office staff to help with clerical chores. For those women who do not have a spouse or office help or clergy partners (three informants), efficient communication in unscheduled matters as well as administrative scheduling flexibility can be problematic. This concerns them, since they aspire to accessibility as pastors (and phone machines are only partially satisfactory as a solution).

• One of my biggest frustrations is the organization of time in my ministry with *no* help.
• My daughter and son-in-law lived here for a while and joined this church. She said, "It's a really neat church but you know what's missing? . . . A minister's wife . . . somebody aware of what's going on behind the scenes . . . working to smooth ruffled feathers . . . buffering . . . interpreting . . . advocating."
• Since there's no secretary, people find me hard to get hold of. They feel I'm too busy, Part of that comes from my brisk body style . . . I make lots of quick moves. . . . But when they do stop me . . . and stop themselves! . . . they find me able to listen . . . to tune in actively. . . . I'm sometimes made to feel comparison with males who don't take so much time for ministry to their own families. But I think this aspect of ministry is important for congregations to learn. . . . I don't like the secretarial and maintenance stuff and sewed-up weekends. . . . I get bogged down in detail and paperwork. . . . Maybe a man would just say, "I can't function without a secretary." I have a tendency, for efficiency, to do things myself rather than try to organize and train and coordinate volunteers.

It is interesting to note that this woman is willing to devote much time to development and coordination of the group of volunteer consultants on parish relations. She is unwilling to devote time to development and coordination of volunteer clerical assistants.

Lack of full back-up services in child care limits the career options for women who have both young children and talent for administration.

• I had to turn down a regional traveling job because I couldn't see how it would fit with my marriage [and joint parenting of a small child].

Beyond the few very complete descriptions of administrative style, I am able to show only fragments referring to management perspective and authority ideals. yet the unmistakable bias is toward personal need priorities and communal solidarity rather than structural or material priorities and hierarchical control.

• I want to offer people a chance to look freshly at their lives . . . to see a freedom and support coming from the church in ways they hadn't expected.
• I lot of what the clergy position is, is giving people permission to do the things that they like best to do within the work of a parish . . . wherever their gifts are.
• I value personal relationships and get along well with a whole range of parishioners. I went into this work because of the diversity of people I'd meet. I never have much difficulty making conversation with almost anyone. I have friends and supporters in all the groups. I treat people and understand them as individual persons. . . . Behind everyone's profession or job is just another real person. . . . I'm considered well organized but

I don't like the administrative aspects of ministry especially. I'm not interested in administrative climbing. The parish is more appealing than administrative responsibilities.

It is clear that the young woman above mentally separates organizing parish activities (which she is said to do well) and "administration." She continues:

• I do presentations and teaching usually by enabling interactions . . . small group stuff. I tend to keep control of a group by being personal with them, so kids look to me for discipline and justice even in the presence of male ministers. I work well with youth and children, but my disciplinary stances are different from men's. They clown around till the kids are almost out of control. The guys are always stimulating competition among classes of youth. They seem to go more for popularity. They're apt to wait until the kids have crossed some boundary of behavior far beyond mine and then come down hard in an almost angry way.
• Sometimes I realize that others' attitudes are being directed just by my sharing my attitudes plainly.
• I want to recapture the richness of traditions, but I want innovation, too, especially in communication . . . people talking *with* each other, not *at* each other. Innovation moves *so* slowly because people have to *own* the changes themselves. I want them to *be* the church . . . not just have me as "professional believer."
• Some pastors handle the flock too much like a ruler instead of a servant . . . not a shepherd inviter, but a driving force, pushing people and ordering people to serve them. It ought to be the other way around. There shouldn't be so much pomp and circumstance and regal style and show and pride. I'm concerned about spiritual depth. I would want more faith criteria for membership. People want easy access to membership for the social activity. They should be more eager to develop as Christians.
• Issues of authority are difficult . . . how to influence without being authoritarian. The achievement pressures I feel to change the whole world may be like some men. . . . I struggle with when to speak and when not to speak.

There is conceivably a connection between this struggle to choose appropriate moments for sharing views (mentioned by several clergywomen) and the almost gleeful enjoyment many of them find in the preaching function.

The informants are skilled in communication. They have strong urges to make a difference in the world, strong convictions about better ways of life for people. Their preferred way of establishing authority is to demonstrate personal integrity, caring flexibility, and imaginative strategies in community organization while being very clear about where they stand. So verbal interpretation is critical. Yet they are inevitably affected to some degree, throughout informal exchanges, by recognized conventions of social deference. If attraction to their influence is to be maintained, the women must not trigger opposition and repulsion by dramatically defying intuited rules for when a person has "gone too far" in trying to influence others by speaking.

Recent social psychology research establishes that in mixed gender conversations both males and females tend to conform to expectations that females will defer to males, males will control the direction of the conversations, males will have entitlement to interrupt females more than the reverse, and males will dominate the time used by various speakers. It logically follows that assertive, articulate women, if dependent on personal magnetism for influence, must develop high consciousness of the precarious balance between stating oneself clearly/completely and losing appeal. The discomfort and alertness may be exacerbated by the contrasting dispositions of male and female conversationalists, toward debating contest style and added insight style, respectively.

In most cases these particular women exercise leadership among heavily male parish councils and colleague groups. Thus the pulpit may provide them with an officially bounded and protected opportunity for revealing their ideas and clarifying their intentions with unself-consciousness and freedom not as available in other circumstances. This may be why they say things like, "I am most truly myself when I'm preaching"; "A sermon has never once been a chore. Sermons are always simply *there*, ready to be preached."

It is not that the clergywomen cannot express themselves adequately in spontaneous exchanges. I merely point to the possibility that sermonizing may be an expressive release and may encourage optimal spontaneity in them, providing the exhilaration they report, in that they are not required to monitor their speech entrances and exits with such conventional vigilance. So it is not surprising to hear the one woman earlier in this chapter describe her administrative use of sermons to encourage an atmosphere in which the low structure leadership she envisions can emerge to support parish spirituality.

The ordination essay, from which we have seen other excerpts, provides the following view of church organization. Though it has little to say about administration as such, it is worthy of inclusion for the overall perspective it contributes.

• The church as a building has meaning only if it symbolizes the presence of the church, a fellowship of Christ's followers at worship and at work at a particular location. The congregation which carries on its services to God and to mankind in that building is the church in microcosm. The denomination with which the churches affiliate becomes a broader expression of the Body of Christ bringing together their spiritual, mental, and material resources to increase the impact of their common mission to a needy world. The Church Universal . . . is the church in macrocosm . . . a spiritual fellowship, not easily identified by human beings but known to God, because God knows what is in our hearts. . . . The most meaningful and satisfying experiences that I have had in the church have been in the face-to-face encounters with fellow Christians in services shared at the local level. The most spiritually moving experiences that I have had have been in worldwide ecumenical encounters where the universality of the church was graphically portrayed.

Membership numbers, money matters, and formal organizational structure do not emerge as central concerns in the administration of religious groups among the informants. Except incidentally, such things hardly enter into their descriptions of rewarding and frustrating aspects of their work, preoccupying interests, personal strengths, overall goals, or characteristics of their congregations. Where they talk about finance at all, it is usually either in connection with involvement in community welfare assistance or for purposes of distancing themselves from ministry images with which they don't wish to identify.

I really cannot present a comprehensive picture of how the informants handle administrative specifics. Apart from the small number who volunteer quite a bit of information, there are shreds and oblique references, at best; and many of these are about authority perspectives and evaluative criteria rather than executive procedures as such.

Still, drawing on silences, asides, inferences, and the lengthier statements from the research data, some tentative hypotheses emerge from the evidence at hand:

1. Membership, money, and organizational structure are conceptualized more as indicators of spiritual vigor in the community than as discrete management sectors or goals.
2. Membership, money, and structure are conceptualized more as resources for caring than as parameters of the congregation.
3. By current professional assessment standards in bureaucratic management, the informants likely appear somewhat incompetent or inefficient, or substantially unevaluable, in spite of the fact that some have reputations as extraordinarily good managers.

In other words, with respect to the organizational administration task, also, these ministers' primary orientation is epi-normatively female. Most of them tend to articulate the explicitly agentic ministry function in communion terms. The focus is on how the spiritual community orders most efficiently its caring for persons.

NOTE

1. The Church from Above and the Church from Below," a talk given by Fr. Hans Küng at the Fifth Anniversary Celebration of Chicago Call to Action, November 7, 1981, McCormick Place.

Chapter 7

Doing Ethics: Moral Leadership as Responsible Caring

Shortly before I set up the data-gathering interviews, an informant had a cross-cultural experience that was very important to her. She was in charge of extensive arrangements, including the engagement agenda, for a visiting African clergyman. During his stay in the United States, she spent much time with him, exchanging information, opinions, and insights. The association became the basis for a close friendship.

Near his departure, at one of several farewell occasions, he was asked by someone to tell what had surprised him most in the United States. He talked about two things: the amazing color change of tree leaves in the fall, a phenomenon he had never before witnessed; and a woman functioning as a pastor. He declared to the assembly that he thought she did a good job and had a good relationship with the congregation, so he wanted to carry this idea back home to see what could be done about women in ministry there.

Throughout their conversations, over the period of his visit, moral choices were a central concern. His native church was clear about moral rules and strict in excluding persons who did not conform. Divorce, smoking, drinking, and so on were simply not permitted within the church community there.

• He struggled so with our "loose morals" in the U.S. We talked and thought a lot about what obedience to God and witness imply . . . about responsibility for life and decisions, on the one hand, and on the other hand, rules that say "this is it and when you've done this, everything will be fine."

The woman used the above story to introduce her own position, which she went on to expand:

• Some code is necessary . . . some structure . . . but the encoded must be broken immediately. As soon as you put something into absolute form you can easily see the instances where you have to break that absolute. In our church now we have an adult class, "Ten Commandments for Modern Living." One commandment says simply, "Thou shalt not kill." That's very clear, but we're going to be talking seven weeks about abortion, war, capital punishment, euthanasia and all kinds of things that are involved there that suddenly make that a very complicated thing to understand. Individual cases don't fit the package neatly. How do you make your decision? How do you decide where that's right and where that's wrong? What do you do about capital punishment? You can make a very good case from the Bible for holy war. Jesus himself struggled with the law and there were times he broke the law. I find much help in Scripture . . . in the broad sense . . . the justice sense . . . guides for how to break the rules, so to speak . . . ways we're to treat one another . . . ways to make decisions. I'm aware of my personal heritage growing up and being aware of society and seeing the way decision making was done in a very practical way . . . then making my own decisions as I grew and matured . . . what ways I would choose to use . . . what ways wouldn't be appropriate for me. We don't always have the assurance that a decision we make is right. We pray for forgiveness through the decision. People often want firm rules but we have to help them make their own decisions and be accountable—alert to intentions and consequences. We need to help people see the issues and make good decisions rather than dishing up answers for them. At intense decision-making times hopefully you have a clear head and can think ahead of where they are . . . look at all sides . . . and bring in some kind of perspective in a situation. My own moral base has changed from biblical rules to personal responsibility based on sensitivity to the community of persons . . . consultation with the community . . . testing in the community.

The ultimate moral criterion represented by all 17 women as their own is authentic love—responsible caring for others and self. They are not disposed to talk in terms of compliance with a formal "goodness code'" (whether modern or biblical). A few of the informants talk a language of personal/situational exceptions to *rules*, but they, too, exhibit a care ethic orientation as they make references to moral rules.

A responsibility ethic or care ethic is keyed to a radically unified intentionality, within and among persons, to the bringing about of the greatest developmental good in human experience. All systems or principles of evaluative choice must finally come under judgment and revision from such a commitment, according to its logic. Thus the system must be judged by the needs of the person rather than the reverse.

Yet, as with the twin shoals of pure *agency* and pure *communion* in identity orientation, moral *order* and moral *response* as ultimates are each deadly dangerous to the healthy moral development of persons and societies, if they are not held jointly as crucial referents in moral integrity.

The opening account of the clergywoman and her African guest serves to dramatize conventional differences in gender orientation to moral issues, as well as cultural differences. In recent years Carol Gilligan, developing her thought out of earlier work with Lawrence Kohlberg on the stages of moral development among humans,[1] has made important contributions to the understanding of characteristic differences between the sexes in developmental paths and typical perspectives.

Her curiosity was piqued by females' widespread failure to show moral maturation according to the standard of the original Kohlberg model. She went on to develop an impressive body of research data and theory indicating nontrivial differences between men and women in the area of moral sensitivity and criteria for moral decisions. I rely heavily on her work and that of Jean Baker Miller for my own awareness here, and I shall quote substantial portions of the Gilligan (1982) material, which in the first paragraph reflects Miller's (1976) ideas:

[W]omen not only define themselves in a context of human relationship but also judge themselves in terms of their ability to care. Women's place in man's life cycle has been that of nurturer, caretaker, and helpmate, the weaver of those networks of relationships on which she in turn relies. But while women have thus taken care of men, men have, in their theories of psychological development, as in their economic arrangements, tended to assume or devalue care. When the focus on individuation and individual achievement extends into adulthood, and maturity is equated with personal autonomy, concern with relationships appears as a weakness of women rather than as a human strength.

[. . .]

[M]ale and female voices typically speak of the importance of different truths, the former of the role of separation as it defines and empowers the self, the latter of the ongoing process of attachment that creates and sustains the human community.

[. . .]

[I]n the transition from adolescence to adulthood, the dilemma itself is the same for both sexes, a conflict between integrity and care. But approached from different perspectives, this dilemma generates the recognition of opposite truths. These different perspectives are reflected in two different moral ideologies, since separation is justified by an ethic of rights while attachment is supported by an ethic of care.

[. . :]

For both sexes the existence of two contexts for moral decision makes judgment by definition contextually relative and leads to a new understanding of responsibility and choice.

[. . .]

As we have listened for centuries to the voices of men and the theories of development that their experience informs, so we have come more recently to notice not only the silence of women but the difficulty in hearing what they say when they speak. Yet in the different voice of women lies the truth of an ethic of care, the tie between relationship and responsibility, and the origins of aggression in the failure of connection. The failure to see the different reality of women's lives and to hear the differences in their voices stems in part from the assumption that there is a single mode of social experience and interpretation. By positing instead two different modes, we arrive at a more complex rendition of human experience which sees the truth of separation and attachment in the lives of women and men and recognizes how these truths are carried by different modes of language and thought.

To understand how the tensions between responsibilities and rights sustains the dialectic of human development is to see the integrity of two disparate modes of experience that are in the end connected. While an ethic of justice proceeds from the premise of equality— that everyone should be treated the same—an ethic of care rests on the premise of nonviolence—that no one should be hurt. In the representation of maturity, both perspectives converge in the realization that just as inequality adversely affects both parties in an unequal relationship, so too violence is destructive for everyone involved. This dialogue between fairness and care not only provides a better understanding of relations between the sexes but also gives rise to a more comprehensive portrayal of adult work and family relationships. (pp. 17, 156–74)

It is likely that the formal requirements of the clergy office are such that a woman, starting from an early developmental stage of affiliation responsibility, ordinarily must move well into a flowering of autonomous integrity in order to qualify for the official clergy role. Thus we are apt to be studying a group selected out from among women partly on the basis of having achieved a relatively "mature," "epi-conventional" merger of self-empowerment and community nurture.

The centering moral concept that emerges from the informant data is responsible caring. Caring is by no means limited in these interview findings to helping, comforting, and supporting individuals. It is expressed also with regard to societal issues, institutional problems, international concerns, human rights, social change movements, and other macro-personal interests. The point to be made here is that these represent escalation in scale of what is still considered a personal concern—a species level of caring for the universe, because it matters for individual well-being.

I wrote the following words in the margin on a page of interview notes while listening to the quiet, rich voice of a middle-aged clergywoman: "Tender, caring, personal, sentimental words—mixed with courageous reformist activities— couched in mundane kindliness that belies the radicality. A warm mother who does not need babies to prove her essential motherhood. A revolutionary imagination and intention in a well-mannered civilized exterior."

At least four of the women serve churches that are heavily involved in major programs of relief provision for needy persons in surrounding severely depressed urban areas. These churches supervise a steady flow of services, including meals, overnight shelter, help with medical prescriptions, and clothing distribution. Several others describe their sustained involvement in projects and politics organized for engineering more humane social arrangements in their communities.

Most of the clergywomen say they work very intentionally to elevate awareness and knowledgeability about the consequences for individuals of certain social beliefs, attitudes, or action patterns imbedded in institutional processes. They also talk of systematically sharing their concerns about what they judge to be harmful choices in world order and in resource consumption.

• Individual and social problems of the day challenge the church to "stay in the world" and meet these problems with the impact of God's redemptive plan for mankind. Many in the country, black and white, have championed the cause of political, social, and economic rights as well as religious rights. They follow in the footsteps of their Master [Jesus], who went about doing good and bringing abundant life to people from all walks of life.

• They [her congregation] mostly say they're not "women's libbers" and they'd probably say that I'm not a "women's libber." But they tell people that "women's libbers" would like me! This is their way of showing their approval. They don't see me as a "ranting, raving feminist"—like I see myself. They like my inclusive, nonalienating approach. I try to avoid polarization without avoiding the issues. In a liberal/conservative split I'd be more liberal than most of my congregation . . . on issues of peace and justice, nuclear power, militarism, abortion, homosexuality.

• The true believer has to be willing to take the necessary risks of faith . . . to be justice and peace comprehensively in society . . . among persons . . . sensitive to the need for the "cup of water" . . . the "visit in jail."

• Many people have grown up in authoritarian solution-giving. I want them to know things have changed, and I help them see what issues are involved

• Christians need to create and model a community where it is safe to disagree or disapprove with brothers and sisters and still love and support and respect each other. . . . Willingness to admit error creates comfort in negotiating new understandings. It's important to preach about such freedom and such an atmosphere . . . about mutual support.

• Currently I'm trying to be more sensitive to the integrity of Jewish faith and distortions from anti-Semitism. I want to be very sure I can affirm the Gospel without in any way putting down Jews. I see Jesus' model of willingness to give up securities for the needs of others . . . being more open and vulnerable . . . to allow healing to take place in broken relationships. It's not an easy life style. It's a "journey" for persons seeking wholeness through lives of obedience [to God].

• I relate across racial lines because no one is better than anyone else. . . . I don't have to right all evil; God will straighten the crooked places. . . . I can love and not divide groups with hate because of Jesus' pattern. You can't love God and hate people.

• For me the key Gospel values are love, nonviolence, the real power in "powerlessness."

• There's a weekday service for street people. . . . It's all right if they're nonreading and bad-smelling. . . . They can get food here and clothing . . . and shelter overnight. . . . The church pays for prescriptions not covered by Medicare and Medicaid. . . . The doors are not barred. . . . The church is not vandalized. . . . God protects. . . . Individuals in the community know the church is theirs and are trying to help.

• My absorbing interests now are human justice issues: anti-Semitism, sexism, racism, war, militarism. What's behind all these? Can they in some way be seen as all *one* problem? I'm working hard on this now—how we treat our world—other people and all our earthy resources. The givenness of God's creation is for me an understanding that underlies how we treat others and our world.

I have concentrated, as my informants did, on the way they made moral choices. It may also be revealing to include at the outset a "laundry list" of projects, concerns, and services mentioned by the clergywomen, at various points in the interviews, as absorbing their attention and energy: world peace; war and militarism; adversarial nationalism; liberation from oppression, racism, sexism, anti-Semitism, gay/lesbian discrimination, and economic injustice; more humane institutions; church reform; environmental responsibility; anti-materialism; simple living; conflict resolution development; health care; death and dying issues; genetic issues; abortion; capital punishment; starvation; personal problems; spouse and child abuse; chemical, food, and gambling compulsions; food and shelter for the poor; lunch programs; distribution of government welfare commodities; criminal justice; and help for the seeking, the hurting, the rejected. This is not an exhaustive list. Other concerns are implied or named in the data exhibits. And, of course, the concerns altogether are not necessarily held or emphasized by any one informant.

Ideas of goodness and truth, the caring for the world and the reality of the world, are thoroughly integrated in the thinking of the informants. The women imply that thought, word, and deed must cohere developmentally over time if true good is to result. Exhibits in Chapters 3, 5, and 8 provide additional data bearing on moral stance, along with what is presented here. In general, these data require little commentary about context in order to carry the force of their meaning. Only one woman's voice is absent from this sequence, and hers is heard on this subject in another place.

• I am not a legalist . . . not rule-oriented. Instead I am person-oriented. I want people to make free choices rather than compulsive choices. I want to get people to see and think through all sides of a question and to make thoughtful, responsible decisions, which may be different for different people and circumstances. I'll tell my own beliefs but I want people to come to their own authentic faith stands. I would try to draw out the opposite sides of any question regardless of my preferences. If a pregnant girl came to me and said, "What shall I do? I can't have an abortion," I'd probably ask, "Why?" I'm pretty Rogerian in trying to get people to identify their experiences and ideas and think about them in connection with their faith. A nonjudgmental approach doesn't mean standardlessness. I'm concerned to weigh competing goods and the maximization of good in a situation. Intentions are important as well as outcomes. Love, mutual support, fellowship, stewardship of talents are important emphases with me, along with peace and justice, simple life style, and anti-materialism. I am concerned about and interested in national and international issues like militarism, but I find them hard to identify with or feel competent to judge. I try to think more in personal terms than in statistical or power terms. I think persons are the center of God's concerns. My moral preoccupations are mainly the preoccupations people bring to me to share and sort out with them. I want to help protect people's chances to live a good life. If Scripture speaks to a moral question I try to find out what it's saying. But the Bible must be understood as a whole. The culture context must be considered, too, with its human element. There must be an informed approach to moral questions. We must be open to the Holy Spirit both with Scripture and beyond. I think the Savior idea is about salvation from the cumulative weight of accountability. It offers freedom from guilt . . . freedom to be . . . freedom to proceed. The companion image for Jesus is uppermost for me; in God's presence I feel safe with my doubts.
• Attitudes are important as moral decision resources. Motivation for action comes from

attitudes. Many issues of "right" or "wrong" are more personality clashes—not decided on the basis of actual issues. Sometimes an issue is used as an opportunity for a personal war. I think when a person comes into church they're saying they need help. There's something in them crying out. People are so afraid of "what society will say," but everyone is a child of God whether lost or found. Absolutely nothing a person can do in this world can keep them away from God and salvation if they come to themselves and really seek help. Acceptance of the person comes first and should be continuing. You have to deal with right and wrong *within* acceptance when an opportunity presents itself. The Bishop says, "Let them come to the altar; the Lord will turn them around." My church body has given guidelines for many kinds of decisions. I do my *own* thinking based on discussion in the church body and on the Bishop's teaching. I wouldn't go out and look for other resources. My son will soon be out of prison. Some of my neighbors, parishioners, and family might not accept him, but I will anyway. . . . He needs my support, as a minister, not just as a mother. I believe in service to Christ as being beyond the walls of the church—in the community . . . hospitals . . . jails . . . the sick and dying. . . . I minister to friends . . . cousins . . . of the people in my congregation, too. They call me in . . . they expect me to be there to help. A born-again Christian is committed to action . . . has a strong urge to come up to expectations of Christ and follow the footsteps of Jesus . . . gives service tirelessly . . .

She speaks of being called upon for both problem-solving wisdom and emotional support in traumatic experiences of personal loss and conflict. She sees this type of individual spiritual nurture as a central moral responsibility for herself as minister and for all "born-again" believers. The developmental thrust such personal ministry has for her shows in the following comments:

• I'm so interested in young people. I want to give them substantial spiritual training . . . good recreation. . . . If I could just help them understand what's right and wrong. . . . The right way is to follow Jesus. . . . I deplore the passiveness and permissiveness I see so much. But you really have to work one on one . . . or do rap sessions . . . or group therapy . . . maybe after other meetings. My own son is in prison, but maybe I can help others. He was always so critical when I helped down-and-outers and even had them in our home. Maybe he was jealous of the attention I gave people he thought were "fooling me." The ministry can be depressing; sometimes you think you've helped and things fall apart; you preach and they compliment . . . but where does it go in growth and change?
• The Bible is one of my moral decision resources—a primary one. I look at Jesus' modeling of caring . . . challenging injustices. I also gain knowledge from other resources. Most of my reading is stimulated by actual cases in church and my need to understand more. I consult theological journals, church statements, newspapers, news magazines, and newsletters of special interest groups. I often consult my daughter and her college resources . . . and other people . . . especially those with first-hand information or with counter-views. I read their recommended sources. . . . Meditating is a moral resource, too. I think about what I can live with. Does it have integrity with my sense of self and my direction as I understand it at the moment? It must be revisable. In counseling I don't say what my stance is unless a person *needs* to hear it. If they ask explicitly or seem to need the jog of an alternative to get off "stuck," I'll tell them where I stand. I'm not afraid of confrontation if I think they're deceiving themselves or involved in grossly

destructive behavior. Generally they already know where I stand on issues; they've heard it in sermons. My scholarly theology is imbedded in my understanding; then I make bridges into today's life. Someone who comes in with a guilt trip . . . I'm very directive in making room for them to be free to think and choose. It is important for them to know and clarify their *own* concerns in the situation. The biggest help I can give is to reflect their own thinking so they can see it. They must live with themselves.

• My ethical thinking is clarified best in bouncing ideas off open, sharing people. I move more toward consulting someone who's actively involved in an issue. If they put up a wall, I back off because it won't be helpful. I use reading resources in the absence of appropriate persons for dialogue. Reading is usually triggered for me by some speaker. I often go to hear some speaker feeling something of the "urging to consider" that was present in my call. I sort through issues by becoming involved. Sometimes I get in over my head and have to disengage and start again. I get upset and overwhelmed but not defeated in my search for justice; but I believe I must be engaged in trying. Sometimes I just scream to God and people and myself, "Where is justice?" In personal problems I wait for a person to seek me rather than intervening myself. I'm more comfortable offering help if there is an approach from others. I recognize that I'm not responsible for the sinner, but to the sinner. I'm giving help in a community substance abuse program and I'm concerned about ministering to people in a nearby gay community. I'm cautious with radicalism due to the need to keep contact with people. Neighbor kids in a bad family situation ask to stay overnight with me sometimes. I've gotten involved with the family through responding to the needs of the kids. I didn't want to intrude but I recognized the children's need for a friend and respected the parents' need to see me as a helper, not an adversary or competitor. My emphasis in ministry is empowerment rather than command . . . a journey together rather than "Thus says the Lord" . . . openness vs. closedness. I want to be the lover rather than the restricting parent.

• I get moral judgments partly from the way I was reared and from a conviction that there is a moral sense to the whole of life. Part of my calling is to say no to injustice. Every time injustice is not stopped a crucifixion results. I ask people to take their own responsibility rather than look to others. I tend to explore answers with people. I sense that mine is a more vulnerable ministry than most. I want to open up the possibility that authority figures are not just male, per se, and that God can be both [male and female] and beyond. It's more likely that vulnerable, unsure people would seek me out, but vulnerable people who have a need for a mask or wall shutting out threat, I will never see. They die of hurt behind a display of confidence worn as armor.

Incidentally, this last sentence pretty well epitomizes what the women think about the kind of minister who attempts to model human perfection rather than the struggle to be fully human.

• The democratic ideal operates not only for the church as a body but also the individual as a Christian. The moral axiom is a two-edged sword—a responsible person must be free and a free person must be responsible. Democratic decision-making should be based on truth and the larger good. The rule of the majority does not abrogate the rights of the minority. "The minority has the right to its views; and though these views may be at variance with those of the majority, they are of inestimable value in furnishing the necessary checks and balances apart from which a democracy cannot be effective."

The above is from a written statement presented by an informant to her church body as an ordination requirement.

• The church has had rules. The moral theologians have written. The moral theologians are more weighty with me than the church rules. I take those seriously, but in some things we can't make principled decisions because empirical evidence for application of the principles is unclear. I try to make decisions in the context of discussion and prayer. Nonviolence is a major absorbing concern and value for me. So is equality for women. A faithful believer is a caring, sensitive person. If I'm called to visit an elderly parishioner who's being cared for over a long period of time by a middle-aged daughter, I'd need to ask "Where does the daughter get relief? Who ministers to her needs?" I think I'm freer with feelings in expressing myself than most male ministers. It may make speaking with me easier. This isn't uniformly true, but it's a helpful, needed alternative for some.

An informant lists the moral imperatives she senses for believers:

• Submission to God's will; trusting in God even in death; thanking and praising God in the midst of trouble; having love and compassion and serving others; sharing, caring, and doing what they can do to help; feeling with others . . . as part of each other; able to "take a lot" and be patient; refusing to do what is against God's will.

Then the same woman says of her highest hopes for her life,

• I would like people to be able to say, "She was a true servant of God. Her ministry was about building up faith so that people can go out and serve God and make decisions well."
• I might, for myself, read or consult friends but for counseling I would go only to God. I can't make the decision for other people . . . interfere with others' lives. . . . I cannot solve the neighbor's problem. I can pray for guidance.
• When I make moral choices I look for guidance to trusted friends, mentors, people I look up to. The decision-making process boils down to my own understanding of a combination of that which I was taught growing up and which I learned myself through experience or my interpretation of the Bible or a book on ethics or secular sources on the nature of problems. On a question like abortion I'd consider my religious ideals about the sacredness of life, and I'd also weigh the part of our society and world that are still unredeemed and that affect situations . . . and then I'd decide to the best of my ability where I come down. I'd draw on my understanding of the forgiveness and loving kindness of God. And I'd look at secular sources to learn what impact abortion has had on people . . . medical facts . . . psychological factors . . . guilt. . . . Tension always exists between abstract principles or ideals and particulars of a situation. As a counselor I would hear the person's concerns, anxieties, fears. . . . I don't see my job as telling the person what to do but to reassure of God's care, mercy, forgiveness. I can share my understanding of Scripture, but every person knows their own experience and has to live with the consequences of their decisions. In the end, consequences for persons are most important for me in decisions . . . consequences for the decider, for people in the world. The issue that I'm trying to search out for myself and in my preaching is what's behind all the

things like anti-Semitism, war, racism, sexism. . . . Is there a basic attitude . . . a greed
. . . toward the givenness of creation that underlies all those other particulars.
• Moral resources? Other people . . . I must talk with them; my gut . . . I go with my gut
a lot; I'll read; I'll listen; and I'll pray. In counseling all I can do is say, "I've been
given a set of tools; if you want them you can have them." *Easy* answers are *no* answers!
People who come to get fixed I can't help. My tools are questioning, listening, self-
understanding, patience, referral, empathy, sharing common experiences. I can hold up
a mirror and help them look at themselves. I can talk about God, religion, and spirituality
as a "shrink" can't.
• My denomination teaches that moral decisions should be based on traditions, Scripture,
reason, and experience. I find I use all—and did even before I knew this was the official
teaching. I bring these resources to give to people who ask assistance. I have strong
moral opinions on many things from parental messages in early childhood. I see my job
in counseling as affirming individual responsibility to confront conflict in complex issues
like abortion. I know I am recognized as a "liberal" and as a crusader for the underdog.
I think a faithful Christian allows God's word to impel to *action*.

Another clergywoman images herself, her congregation, and Christ in *servant*
terms throughout her interview. She goes on to explain:

• It's not just "us here folks," but we're here to reach out with some good news in this
world . . . as servants, helpers, bringers of comfort and good feelings. Much of my own
personal growth and deepening commitment in faith are results of the associations surrounding death and burial. The two most important themes or components in Christian
ethics for me are love and reconciliation. Reconciliation and peacemaking at all levels
is a call for Christians. Not all aspects are under our control, but we can inspire, instruct,
and lead others in the direction of this call. I give moral decisions a lot of thought . . . a
lot of talk with my husband who works with the congregation's youth. The youth say,
"It all depends on the situation." I believe the situation is not the *primary* factor guiding
moral decisions, but a *relativizing* factor. I think we should use the best resources at our
disposal, pray, and act . . . humbly . . . knowing forgiveness is available. I pray *a lot!* I
read theological works and also secular information . . . social science, medical, economic.
In counseling I never make decisions for others. I offer resources . . . books, another
person's expert opinion, counseling services, attempts to negotiate with other interested
parties. Fact-finding is important; learn all you can. Then after gathering the facts, meditate
. . . pray . . . decide . . . act!
• My moral decision resources are Scriptures, prayer, experience, and the church . . .
other believers . . . face to face and in writings. I look for convergences in these areas.
Often you have to act without certainty; you mustn't pretend certainty you don't feel.
Men have been so into the doctrinal side of faith; I think women are more willing to
admit limits and weaknesses and to be vulnerable. Dialogue is crucial in working through
conflicts and making decisions. You give people the principles with which they can set
up dialogues with their concrete experience. I like the acceptability, as a minister, of
talking about God . . . and seeing people respond.

Theology student Rachel Richardson Smith has written a "My Turn" piece
for *Newsweek* magazine called "Abortion, Right or Wrong." It represents an

orientation toward moral choice, a type of moral dialectic characteristic of most (I would say all, but for the conceptual frame) of the women in this study.

I cannot bring myself to say I am in favor of abortion. I don't want anyone to have one. I want people to use contraceptives and for those contraceptives to be foolproof. I want people to be responsible for their actions; mature in their decisions. I want children to be loved, wanted, well cared for.

I cannot bring myself to say I am against choice. I want women who are young, poor, single or all three to be able to direct the course of their lives. I want women who have had all the children they want or can afford or their bodies can withstand to be able to decide their future. I want women who are in bad marriages or destructive relationships to avoid being trapped by pregnancy.

[. . .]

What many people seem to misunderstand is that no woman wants to have an abortion. Circumstances demand it; women do it. No woman reacts to abortion with joy. Relief, yes. But also ambivalence, grief, despair, guilt.

No woman can forget a pregnancy no matter how it ends.

Why can we not view abortion as one of those anguished decisions in which human beings struggle to do the best they can in trying circumstances? Why is abortion viewed so coldly and factually on the one hand and so judgmentally on the other?

[. . .]

How can we begin to think about it redemptively? What is it in the trauma of loss of life—be it loved or unloved, born or unborn—from which we can learn? There is much I have yet to resolve. Even as I refuse to pass judgment on other women's lives, I weep for the children who might have been. I suspect I am not alone.[2]

Among the informant quotations one sees a great deal of difference in some respects; how much of life experience and knowledge is envisioned as "going to God for help" is one of these. In other ways there is a great deal of commonality in the talk about moral perspectives and moral decision resources. The common themes that emerge from these data most vividly are (1) morality seen as *responsibility to care* for the world in personal terms—to be stewards of the healthiest developmental potential for ourselves, others, society, the universe; (2) morality seen as personal authenticity and full individual accountability for freedom in action choices; (3) morality seen as positive love and reconciliation in relationships rather than as avoidance of evil; (4) morality seen as noninterference with the growth and responsibility of others.

Moral leadership, then, is idealized not as perfect exemplary conformity to perfect rules of human goodness; not just as knowing a great deal about the official positions and defenses regarding right choices; not as prescribing appropriate religious compensations when the rules are disobeyed. It is rather idealized as authentic, exemplary struggle toward perfect caring community; loving life and people as best one can. All the women respect social (including religious) rules of conduct as important moral resources. But the impact of action on persons remains the essential evaluating criterion for them overall.

Responsibility and accountability are two sides of the same moral coin; several of the women reserve their harshest judgments for persons whose ''beliefs'' and actions don't ring the same tone—who allow themselves ''time out'' from accountability as though it were a ''work and leisure'' issue.

• If you're a mature minister you accept accountability for actions . . . you're not always expecting people to cover for you . . . take care of you . . . you don't lash out or cut out when the going gets tough . . . don't let impulses reign. . . . You take adult responsibility.
• I get frustrated with nonaccountable people . . . indifference . . . apathy . . . alienation.
• I am frustrated by people who come to church as habit or obligation rather than heart-faith or deep conviction . . . by ''lukewarm and hard-hearted'' people . . . by nonaccountable people . . .

Many of the women make clear that they see ministerial role enactment as a whole *saying* in faith. They intend to model a moral life stance that validates personal vulnerability, honesty, searching, authentic sharing of concerns and conflicts and confusions, empathy, flexibility, and sensitivity as ways of connecting with God, and with others' supportive strength. They think that this cannot be said or taught in mere words as powerfully as in lives lived openly as a quest for personal wholeness and creative community.

• I want to provide a concrete vision of what's possible as a professional . . . as a public authority figure . . . as a mother . . . as a wife. I'd like it if my epitaph read, ''Here sleeps someone who loved God and others . . . who was totally present to God and others . . . someone through whom others see God . . . a channel of God's grace.
• Since I've been here the senior pastor has leaned more toward my way of evangelical love—reaching out, for example, to those in prison, homosexuals . . .
• I want to be able to live with integrity . . . to have convictions . . . to act upon them . . . to be thought true to my concerns. As a parent I want to have given a hopeful child to the world . . . one who is hope . . . who gives hope . . . who has hope.
• It feels good when I hear members say, ''She lives her faith very carefully.'' They see a good relationship with my husband and they talk about it. They *love* him very much.

Those with feminist concerns see their clearest statement of both the need and the possibility for reform as residing in their role enactments as women and as professional ministers. The legitimized institutional role gives them a public way to show, day by day, how they can be assertive and competent without being controlling or adversarial; strong and steady without being rigid, unfeeling, or aloof; flexible without yielding to unjust exploitation. It is their intention to show whole humanness, or, more accurately, the struggle toward whole humanness.

When the emphasis is thus put on the most dependable process of moral deciding rather than on the best moral conclusions, the focus is on such matters as intentions, attitudes, the spirit of relationships, the liberation of human potential, or just ''helpfulness.'' The preferred teaching vehicles tend to be stories, poems, dramatization, and ordinary life, more than formal principles. Concrete decisions in concrete cases with their concrete consequences are seen as the existential testing ground for discernment of moral issues.

While the Christian ministers all refer to Jesus as their prime role model, they certainly are in agreement with the rabbi's statement that morality is better lived and described than systematized and applied.

• To me Judaism . . . Jewish law . . . is "the way in which to go" . . . a way of living. . . . The faithful Jew is a mensch . . . kindly . . . upright . . . with personal warmth . . . takes risks for people . . . praises . . . more interested in others than himself. I had role models . . . now I am a role model. I'm learning to deal with life on life's terms . . . living each day as best I can. I've got a way to help people in that. If they want it I'll show them how. The power of the clergy today is really the power of attraction because nobody has to come to temple . . . to church . . . and the problems we have are in balancing that with ourselves. I can't leave my rabbinate here in the office and go out and act like an idiot. Judaism is a religion of action. There are people with magnificent theologies that can't get off their butts to do anything. Knowledge is a gift to use, not a hammer to beat people. You have to treat people with kindness and honesty . . . but the kindness has to come first . . . and with dignity . . . and as full human beings.

No informant shows a tendency to think a moral leadership as essentially the passing on of an ethical code or the presiding over its enforcement in people's lives. All describe moral leadership and learning as occurring mainly in what sound to me like "apprenticeships" in moral choosing. That is, one lives alongside those one recognizes as *good people*—identifying with them, imitating, questioning, listening, accepting, rejecting, evaluating—refining judgments and responses in the direction of wise, beneficial actions. Perceptions are compared in mundane exchanges, formal study, conflict negotiations, or in just watching what people do and how things turn out. All of life, in a sense, becomes a workshop in the recognition of goodness—or God's movement.

• I'm only now realizing what strong role models my parents were for me. They did lots of praising; they were very positive. There were not many rules—simply the expectation of responsibility. . . . Mother kept right on growing with the times. She always understood the changes in the church. She's been so proud of my ministries . . . very supportive . . . very safe for conversation. My nickname is "Ma"; that comes from the caring I learned from my mother.

The women take themselves very seriously as role models in faith. They do not believe that their ministries are genuine unless the professional aspects are authentic expressions of their personhood.

• Scholarly theology is largely a personal resource for me. My desire is to model theology in experience. I want a ministry that fits full self-actualization.
• I don't like easy, glib answers to hard questions or cutesy, gimmicky religious packaging. . . . I have had a growing desire to be part of the struggle for a more humane world.

Frequent mention is made by the women of the importance of vulnerability and openness to their ministerial integrity. Many of them say they need to let their life struggle show because it is real for them, but also because it constitutes a reassuringly possible moral model in faith and draws them into the mutual ministering they desire for themselves and their congregations. Lest the talk about responsibility, struggle, and all that, begin to sound very serious and heavy, an important piece of the picture needs to be dropped into place. These are not glum women dutifully giving up enjoyment in favor of grim goodness. Whatever else may be said about them, the overwhelming majority appear genuinely to enjoy life. Their presentation carries a remarkable sense of vitality and enthusiasm for their work, as well as ready humor and a casual, straightforward confidence that tends to put others at ease.

As was my wont, I asked an informant at the close of an interview if there was anything she'd like to add or change. She said she thought not and then, after a pause,

• If there's anything I'd like to emphasize it's how joyful I feel in this work. I'm really happy . . . but with depth. [Laughing] I hope that doesn't sound too frivolous! I feel very blessed right now.

In Chapter 3 (especially in the sections on ''Nurturance''and ''Integrative Thinking'') we saw how ideas of ministerial and family caring tend to include each other, among the married informants. The informants do not seem to feel obliged to hide role conflicts as unprofessional from their congregations when wife, mother, and clergy roles vie for limited time. Nor do they seem to honor some hierarchy of roles wherein the demands of one role are given precedence systematically over the others.

Several women mentioned that parishioners are increasingly sensitive to such binds and cooperative in negotiating, on occasion, suitable alternative arrangements. But, more importantly, the clergywomen believe that sharing such mundane frustrations with members encourages the laity to tend their own valued relationships more publicly and responsibly.

In a time of much anxiety about appropriate family roles, the clergywomen want to evoke new possibilities for hopefulness in this central social institution. Yet they are reaching out for new learnings and help from others, too, as part of what they are willing to show in public.

• I'll lay my son's problem [his arrest] before the pastor-parish relations committee right away. They are my listening and consultation group.
• They see me as a concerned and caring mother [to her one-year-old]. I often ask advice from parishioners about parenting. Sometimes I'm ambivalent about it [parenting]. I find it demanding, rewarding, scary, and exciting. My husband and I trust each other most as parents. I think he's best with the little one.

Among the married women whose husbands are not clergymen, the mates are described as very active in church functions, and hence the relationship is very visible. The same is true for non-adult children, in general. Two of the clergy husbands also are well-known occasional participants in their wives' congregations. The informants report high satisfaction and joy from this interplay of family and ministry interests, and say that their families and congregations appreciate it also.[3] Family arrangements, with one exception, are highly innovative. They see exposing themselves to comment in the worship communities about such experimentation as conducive to responsible developmental choices for themselves and for others.

• My congregation values the family and they like my husband [a medical professional]. He teaches, takes nursery duty, etc. He's very loyal to the church. They feel we have neat kids, too. The children like the idea of my being a minister and participating in church activities . . . but they do regret that I'm not baking cookies more! People often say, "I don't know how you do it!" I'm aware of providing them with a concrete vision of what's possible . . . as a mother and as a public authority figure.

The ones who talk about this do not see modeling faith as "posing" or as inventing scenarios, but as living faith openly, hopefully, convinced that their most powerful influence is the way they live. Many of the "opportunities God provides" them for service arise because they "carry their ministries with them" into places where their self-expectations for responsible caring are continuous, though they may be among strangers and in an unfamiliar setting.

With regard to moral leadership I feel confident in saying that the women studied here represent their thinking about moral choice primarily in a normatively female way. That is, their core stance is holistic; they see all of faith and life as the moral arena for responsible caring, which is their central focus. However, their thinking shows that they have achieved epi-normative integration of concerns for both justice and caring. They see moral teaching as being done primarily (but not solely) through authentic and fully accountable modeling of a way to live in faith. In a sense, ministry is an ultimate show-and-tell time for them as persons.

As Gilligan points out, when male ethical standards are applied, women often seem defective and untrustworthy because they appear easily swayed by unique cases and discomfited by justice dispassionately meted out merely according to rules. Ironically, women are also often regarded as more pleasant and comfortable to be with, precisely because of their disposition toward personal caring and flexibility in relationships. Yet, conversely, women have been judged more virtuous and less comfortable to be with, insofar as commitment to radical responsibility causes them to suppress impulsive behavior inconsistent with their idea of healthy human development, and to be less venturesome where injury to some person is a possible consequence. (Mothers, wives, and female teachers have a folk reputation as "wet blankets" on "fun" and adventure.)

Encountering a paragraph like the above or just living in the society to which it refers are the sorts of experiences that have led many social thinkers nowadays to ponder the immensely fruitful moral synergy held at bay insofar as men and women fail to draw each other appreciatively into a dialectical movement toward fully human social morality. I shall return to this theme in Chapter 9, after first discussing the clergywomen's approaches to reality imaging.

The characteristic morality perspective among these women tends to find expression in their theologizing as well as in their administrative leadership. For many of them, integration of the God/truth vision, the ideal way to be in the world as a moral chooser, and the way to manage institutional organization is a very intentional unity.

The reader is already in touch with fragments of the evidence, from complex passages with multiple implications. Some of my best evidence in each area of the study also contains "best evidence" for related but different assertions. Again, the overlap in themes is everpresent. The crucial research function is served by specific pieces of data insofar as they do indeed speak to the concept in question. That they may *also* speak to other issues is gratuitous, though the fact may demand from the reader a discipline of precise selective attention in some cases.

NOTES

1. Critics have pointed out, and I think rightly, that these stages are better understood as stages in the *capacity for doing abstract thinking about moral questions*.

2. Rachel Richardson Smith, in *Newsweek*, March 25, 1985, p. 16.

3. See the data display in Chapter 3, under "Integrative Thinking and Intuition."

Chapter 8

Doing Theology

The view of God held by most of the clergywomen in this study is more that of a persuasively authentic Truth than of an invincibly dominant Control. Contemporary "process theologians" John Cobb and David Griffin (1976:43) capture this type of approach when they say,

> God is that factor in the universe which establishes what-is-not as relevant to what-is, and lures the world toward new forms of realization.
> [. . .]
> As a convincing notion of deity emerges that illumines human experience and coheres with our understanding of the world, the demand for an isolated and abstract proof diminishes. A theistic vision of all reality can gain adherence best by displaying its superior adequacy to other visions.

EXISTENTIAL THEOLOGIZING

Stimulated by the social forces of world modernization in this century, including such dynamics as accelerated broad-scale change, secular-scientific rationality, and human rights ferment, international scholarly theology has moved steadily toward what Peter Berger calls "the inductive possibility . . . taking human experience as the starting point of religious reflections, and using the methods of the historian to uncover those human experiences that have become embodied in the various religious traditions" (1980:115).

Individuals more than ever require credible symbols of shared reality for stabilizing adult identity. Social milieus present such variegation and flux that identity integration projects become problematic in the extreme. The rise of neofundamentalist religion and the attraction of rigidly authoritarian, life-ordering sects testify to the deep-felt need for stable, secure social arrangements. Yet explanations of life and personal meaning that ignore direct experience or obligate that experience to an arbitrarily imposed orthodoxy are unacceptable to most modern people.

Within relatively insulated organizations official dogma may be taken as truth and may offer personal security. But such protected environments are increasingly difficult to find or maintain, given the ubiquity of mass media and the general social and geographic mobility of populations. Accordingly, the most dependable modern person-stabilizing agencies (whether they be families, synagogues, schools, or whatever) are those that can model and symbolize the dynamic terms for healthy human growth and coping confidence, given the endlessly shifting environmental particulars. Few such agencies are widely available to persons now in ways that are apparent to them.

The hallmark of contemporary theologies is their tendency to consider both traditional knowledge and existential knowledge seriously in a fruitful dialectic of meaning-comparison. They are permeated with an idea of God as ultimate coherence, revealed potentially in *any* subcoherence (e.g., science, literature, history, marriage, farming, religion, sailing, music) and revealed best as believers in total coherence search out the reconciliation of its parts. Theology, then, is seen not as the "queen of the sciences" in a hierarchy of knowledge, but more as a bubbling stew of life-illuminating insights drawn from the various arenas of experience and subjected to each other's significance as a whole.

Labels like "process theology," "theology of hope," "story theology," "liberation theology," "dialogical," "dialectical," "existential," "creationist," "developmental"—all indicate lively movement in thought, a lack of absoluteness and finality in the culture forms of religious faith. The emphasis is on a trustworthy orientation toward reality—a way to truth, or a way in truth that may be followed with good experiential consequences for humans. Karl Barth is said to have commented that the interaction of the living God with the living and changing human scene makes doing theology a little like trying to paint a bird in flight.

From Martin Buber (1970:159–60):

> That before which we live, that in which we live, that out of which and into which we live, the mystery—has remained what it was. It has become present for us, and through its presence it has made itself known to us as salvation; we have "known" it, but we have no knowledge of it that might diminish or extenuate the mysteriousness. We have come close to God, but no closer to an unriddling, unveiling of being. [. . .] We cannot go to others with what we have received, saying: This is what needs to be done. We can only go and put to the proof in action.

[. . .]

The word of revelation is: I am there as whoever I am there. That which reveals is that which reveals. That which has being is there, nothing more. The eternal source of strength flows, the eternal touch is waiting, the eternal voice sounds, nothing more.

Cobb and Griffin (1976:29) speak of God-relatedness as "constitutive of every act of experience."

It is God who, by confronting the world with unrealized opportunities, opens up a space for freedom and self-creativity.

And, far from sanctioning the status quo, recognition of essential relatedness to *this* God implies a continual creative transformation of that which is received from the past, in the light of the divinely received call forward, to actualize novel possibilities. Although this divine power is persuasive rather than controlling, it is nevertheless finally the most effective power in reality. In Whitehead's words: "The pure conservative is fighting against the essence of the universe."

My informant group is in some ways like the man who responded to a description of prose by congratulating himself that he was already speaking and writing it with ease. For many of them, contemporary scholarly theology, though perhaps articulated with more sophistication than their own, is an approach to knowledge and truth long familiar to them as women. The dual socialization that is the ordinary lot for any non-elite social group sets up an existential condition tending to stimulate dialectical thought.[1] Trying to make sense of discrepancies between first-hand knowledge and cultural ideologies works against people's unquestioning acceptance of conventional truths. Often the women were involved early in prodigious efforts to reconcile conflicting cultural messages. The relativity of conceptual formulations of truth and goodness to actual experiences of truth and goodness is thus apt to be noted.

Entering professional religious leadership status has, additionally, precipitated dialectical consideration of the contradictions: (1) female, and interpreting traditions that normatively have ruled out females interpreting traditions; (2) leaders, and leading in institutional structures normatively incompatible with their styles of leadership; (3) moral choosers with an ethic of responsibility, in religious traditions normatively steeped in ethics of rules and roles.

Existentialist and/or dialectical approaches to knowledge have, of course, been around for a long time—long before any thoroughgoing intellectual articulation of their distinctive contributions to the perception of reality. Existential thinking is necessarily dialectical because of the nature of human thought. Perception and meaning occur in direct experience as the latter is referred to one's history of perception and meaning, one's habits of knowing. One has only the choices of imposing familiar images on a shifting (and, therefore, increasingly "obstinate") environment of phenomena or of engaging in dialectical resolution of contradictions as a decision for freedom in authentic experiencing.

American religion has been very "doctrinal" in its development and has tended, except for brief existentialist phases under the influence of charismatic leaders, to gravitate toward denominationally formalized belief systems super-imposed on activist social service (intragroup or otherwise). Religious Americans often seem to have more of a sense of "holding" correct beliefs than of partic-ipating in a search for truth. The latter position apparently has felt very risky to many believers and best left to the experts, especially during the "nation-build-ing" phase of U.S. history, though expert opinion was not necessarily adopted wholly or gullibly. Erich Fromm (1976:30–31) writes:

Faith, in the *having* mode, is the possession of an answer for which one has no rational proof. It consists of formulations created by others, which one accepts because one submits to those others—usually a bureaucracy. It carries the feeling of certainty because of the real (or only imagined) power of the bureaucracy. It is the entry ticket to join a large group of people. It relieves one of the hard task of thinking for oneself and making decisions.

[. . .]

God, originally a symbol for the highest value we can experience within us, becomes, in the having mode, an idol.

[. . .]

Faith, in the *being* mode, is not, in the first place, a belief in certain ideas (although it may be that, too) but an inner orientation, an *attitude*. It would be better to say that one *is in* faith than that one *has* faith. [. . .] One can be in faith toward oneself and toward others, and the religious person can be in faith toward God.

In what Fromm calls the *being* mode of faith, then, the God-content—the ultimate reality—is understood as always limited and skewed by the particularity of a person's orientation, and always in need of expansion and correction from others' views in an ongoing spiritual formation. Faith is a way to be most fully alive in life, not merely the most fully correct ideas to have about life, according to Fromm's perspective.

This existential grounding of faith, together with faith's relativity to both past and present cultural contexts, is assumed by the informants, whether implicitly or explicitly. They feel they are directly in touch with God. God, as known doctrinally, is contradicted by many aspects of life, including the self of the knower. They assume that greater knowledge of God emerges from confronting and attempting to resolve the contradictions toward a complex, unified con-sciousness.

Scholars (including theologians) have moved increasingly toward modes of knowing and testifying to experience interpreted as process. It is unclear to me as I listen to discussions of the works of Teilhard de Chardin, Küng, Buber, Nouwen, Cobb, Tillich, and so on, whether theologians by and large are noticing the special resonance of ministerial women to processual concepts; though it was men who early alerted me to the excitement in seminary theology that has come to their schools as a by-product of admitting women to professional studies.

A Roman Catholic seminary teacher recently told me about his experience with women students:

• Older women coming to seminary really take off on scholarly theology; then the men get interested in it as something *real*, which they didn't much sense before.

Some Protestant seminary personnel echo the above observation:

• There's just a higher interest in scholarly theology among the women who have come to us. They're good integrators; they have stimulated academic-intellectual life here.
• I think there's a deeper commitment to theological tasks and the dialectical development of theology . . . not so much among the real young ones.
• Parallel with ascendency of women's thinking in our seminary, interest in narrative theology is up . . . and there's a trend toward creationist rather than redemptionist theology. This affects both men and women and it's very hard to know the cause and effect sequence. The interaction among students is more equalitarian now, after some pretty tense times, and there's much more humor . . . appropriate humor, not hostile and sarcastic.
• I've gone from dealing with a coed college situation to an all-male seminary, and now coed seminary for a number of years. When it was just men in the seminary "getting it straight" was *so* important! The emotional level seemed underdeveloped and it was a humorless atmosphere.
• At first women seemed more difficult to get along with, but now it's more comfortable all around with both men and women. I see the benefits [from women in the seminary community] as more honesty in personal relationships, more openmindedness, and a more holistic view of life. In classes there's better discussion, more curiosity, less defensiveness. Teaching has changed for sure! Male teachers don't presume to speak for females as they once did.

I did not do any orderly canvassing of seminary faculty and administration personnel regarding opinions about women seminary students. I just talked with them whenever and wherever it was convenient, in connection with other scheduled activities.

Overall, the opinions I heard either reiterated the above quotations, emphasizing greater interest among women in dialectical theologizing and faith/life integration, or else they reflected an opinion that there are few important differences that stem from the presence of women students. In this latter group of faculty were some who felt any apparent differences were matters of changing times or individual variations.

The informants' theological perspectives show up clearly in their talk about the Bible, which is central in the religious traditions for all of them. Since this interview material about the Bible is so rich with information about their dialectical faith development, I shall quote from most of the interviews, and at considerable length:

• I don't go to the Bible with an expectation for immediate help; sometimes it's immediate but that's special. I go with a listening stance. Yesterday I opened to the story of Jairus' daughter's being raised to life. It spoke very powerfully to my recent experience of my mother's death. The Bible heightens awareness of God. . . . It's a *living* "Word of God." Scripture lives and changes because *I* live and change; it's a special source of God's

coming to me. I have strong feelings against a fundamentalist approach to Scriptural interpretation; literalism is dangerous; it fails to see the whole truth. It goes with self-righteous imposing of views on other people and it blatantly ignores scholarship. I don't look to the Bible for *proofs* of beliefs. It's not *prescriptions*, but *descriptions* of how to be—of what attitudes are helpful.
• God, I *love* the Bible! The Scriptures are a kick in the butt! What it is is a lot of really tough questions . . . wonderful stories . . . what matters . . . a dynamite document! My favorite theme is the humanity of the characters. I have to wrestle with a text like Jacob wrestled with the angel . . . have to fight it and fight it because it's so hard to understand. The thing makes no sense read as ordinary literature. Study. Show up and do the footwork. Don't expect guidance to come from simple reading; and scholarship may be irrelevant. Understanding comes in the dialectic between experience and Scripture. Did the Red Sea part? Who cares? The people thought it did and wrote it down for others to think about.

Another woman made the following reference to the Red Sea story:

• People have "Red Seas" in their lives . . . when their backs are up against a wall. A story like that can bring answers . . . different answers in different problems.
• People call me a "solidly biblical preacher." That feels comfortable to me. My illustrations come naturally out of my life, but comments indicate they touch a different set of responses than the illustrations the men use. They quote more from famous people.
• What did it mean then? What does it mean now? What are the connections? It's helpful in the interpretation of the Bible to know the interpretations made now by people in other cultural situations . . . poverty . . . Latin America. . . . It gives a counterpoint to our own experience of life. As a preacher, people say I give them fresh connections to ponder.
• I don't ask God to specially "light up" the Bible for me; that would feel like "using" God. Mainly I take the scholarly route. . . . I look at different translations. . . . I might go to poetic works for insight. The Bible begins and ends with God—God in relationship to creation in all its aspects. . . . It's the human experience of that relationship. I can't adhere to the total infallibility of biblical texts, but I see God as faithful to promises made. In an adult Bible study we got to discussing ERA [Equal Rights Amendment] and the "inclusive lectionary." We moved on to translation issues and God images. I shared from my understanding. I think it's very important not to destroy people's inner life "tapes." It turned into a very good exchange . . . helpful in expanding ideas.
• I went to a traditional Sunday school. The "Bible" we learned about was a limited Bible. At college, biblical studies were an eye-opener! I had a hard time learning how to relate to *that* God . . . or to put together the Old and New Testaments. My theology has changed with my life experiences. In some ways I guess I'm an existentialist believer; my theology is formed out of what I've experienced and know and can understand and can envision. The culture context of Scripture has been increasingly clear to me. It played a large part in the way the story was told. I see God now as living, fluid, acting—not just contained in a book. The Bible is a story of human growth and human interpretation . . . with multiple layers of information . . . and of understanding God. I used to see church people as perfect . . . or hypocrites. Now I see them as sinners, strugglers, questioners—as people always working through their own theology.
• The Bible is light in darkness; it shows me myself . . . and others . . . and direction on my path. It's God talking face-to-face—not every time, but often. It's not a rule book or a list of "do's" and "dont's." It's a living, active, embracing revelation. It accom-

plishes things; it "pierces your heart." God is there as sacramental presence . . . mystery . . . as water of baptism . . . more than what it appears on the surfaces . . . more than well-written words. The Holy Spirit who inspired the writing must also inspire the reading and understanding. The inspiration of Scriptures is like making love: persons were so penetrated by the love of God that a Word[2] was brought forth—an incarnation (just as Jesus was God and human). It's reliable . . . trustworthy because it's God in human form (subject to human limitations as Jesus was). Disputes about inerrancy are simply ridiculous!

• I believe very solidly in the inerrancy of the Word of God. However, I'm also very aware of the fact that its human writers were subject to all the laws of observation and interpretation of their relationships with God within the context of life as they lived it then. I interpret using a comparative approach . . . comparing with other parts of Scripture and then looking at the society in which I find myself . . . attempting to derive a principle or guide for life out of what is being said. I look at the literary and historical context and struggle with that. I'm not a literalist. I look at the total picture and recognize that there are questions and doubts left in my mind. I'm not always sure what it does say. I use much more of an inductive approach than deductive.

• The Bible is inspired to the extent that experiences with God caused people to want to write down their experiences.

• Scripture stays fresh in a powerful way—even across the class lines in my congregation. I don't take it to be literally true; it's inspired, not dictated magically by God. I see it as a record of faith. The Old Testament and New Testament are witnesses to what people see of God. It's written by real men, but yet they speak to us.

• The Bible is allegories . . . parables . . . comparisons . . . history. In my ministry I want to help people understand. The principles are good. Adam and Eve and the tree are about being "double-sighted" in life; God is absolute good but we can use that power in us to destroy or build.

• The Bible is a communicating tool for speaking about God and struggling to understand in a disciplined way. I encourage serious parish dialogues around the issues and crises of faith and life. It's neat that many people entering such dialogues come from social action groups that have tended to be anti-religious. In the Bible God speaks profoundly in changing ways to people who see new revelations out of their different situations. It's a living reservoir of stories that carry messages into each person's historic time. I'm intensely invested in rational analytical interpretations of Scripture; I also do just simple reading and seeing what it says in terms of the present situation . . . what it reveals now. It's not a dead rule book. God is always current in culture. Someday I want to write biblical criticism. The world can be healthier. People get alienated; I think that's not the inevitable way to be human. I want to help unlock biblical insights for a healthier humanity—more respect among people.

• I feel God doesn't judge whether we've got the exact right idea of Scripture.

• There is a record of interactions between God and the people of God in the Bible—a record of God seeking us out, though one sees people seeking, too.

• As a child I needed to know about Jesus. Why was he the way he was? Why does he want me the way he wants me? I always see me in the Word. The Bible is better than a psychiatrist's couch. I respect contexts of then and now. Basic principles remain the same and can be extracted from those situations. The closer one walks with Christ the more he reveals to you—the more insight you have in what you hear and read.

• It's a book we consider holy because it teaches us what God is like. It presents God in many images and in the variety comes fullness. Layers of richness can be extracted through careful study. I think it's irresponsible to go to the Bible to get minute instructions for specific daily tasks or decisions, but within the layers of meaning there's much help for daily life. I love Scripture study. I respect the culture context; then I bridge to the present time. I have a quarrel with people who interpret "inspired" as "inerrant" or "infallible." The Bible was recorded by people . . . inspired by God.

• It was written by people who were faith-filled. They spoke to their experience of God's presence; they were so touched by God that they were compelled to witness. There's human error . . . inconsistencies . . . paradox . . . humor. Much of the truth is in the inconsistencies and paradoxes. I always expect to learn what God is and was and will be like from the Bible. It shows God's love and patience. I learn a lot about people, too; and the culture perspective is informative. "Truth for all time" statements in history come out of extraordinary experiences and insights; but they emerge out of the lives of people in very ordinary circumstances. Interpretation uses their reason and ours.

• Official doctrine in my denomination is that the Scriptures contain all we need for faith, development, and salvation. I don't think they have answers for *everything* in daily life. I don't expect *direct* spiritual or intellectual assistance from devotional use alone. I hold texts in unconsciousness as I proceed with life and then I integrate it all with my daily observations. My congregation gives me high marks for my sermons because of this.

• The Church came first; the Bible is second . . . brought together out of the primary life of faith . . . among apostles, disciples, councils. It must be interpreted through the fellowship of the Holy Spirit. The canon[3] is not closed; it's the Church's book—that's what the canon is all about. The Bible is the true word of God . . . not infallible . . . not a book of science or economics. We mustn't pick out our favorite pieces to use as proofs for our beliefs. It's the story of salvation and a means to understand salvation. The Bible is one way God has spoken. It has to be interpreted in the light of experience.

If we divide theological perspectives roughly into authoritarian, or "correctness," theologies that emphasize having correct ideas approved by the correct experts, and existential, or "witness," theologies that emphasize a continuum of testimony about persons' immediate experiences in life, all 17 women would appear to come down squarely in the "witness" camp.

A few of them have had little or no exposure to formal existential and dialectical religious scholarship. Some use the idiom of orthodoxy, at least in part. Yet all assume that the primary religious reality is experiential. None expects truth to emerge except in the struggle to reconcile meanings: of the God/the person; the historic/the current; the concrete/the spiritual; even then, never with absolute finality.

The metaphors and conceptual categories of academic processual theology are familiar territory to most of the women. The other women develop and maintain an unself-conscious dialectical faith stance from simultaneous attention to immediate experience of God, needs of persons, cultural constraints, and human solidarity. Not one woman shows the slightest tendency that I can see to defend her own faith statements by citing only official orthodoxy. Each woman shows great confidence and freedom in giving testimony about her personal faith, and most of them voluntarily point to deviations from orthodoxy. No matter how small or large, such departures are presented matter-of-factly, without apology or defiance. Moreover, some deviation from orthodoxy is considered by them to be an essential factor in authentic faith and its communication.

• I don't have a big reform *agenda*; I see reform as intrinsic to my faith journey.

The tremendous need they speak of to share the "news" of what God does, is, or desires in the world, and to hear the "news" from others as well, blows them off the track of rigid orthodoxy. They may not articulate the dialectical approach, as such, in analytical terms. But they know that they are weighing multiple dynamics as a central exercise in faith. They regularly submit religious rules to judgment by personal needs and experiences, more importantly than the reverse, in their value hierarchies (see Chapter 7). If theological study has not given them the formal tools for intellectualizing the process itself, they are apt to use the more familiar language of exceptional cases, love imperatives, inner urgings attributed to God, social opportunities attributed to God, and sudden turns of events or awareness attributed to God.

The reader may remember an earlier quotation from a woman who describes her seminary education as contributing concepts more adequate for her long-term inner dialogue as a "biblical conservative and social liberal." Among these women the question does not seem to be whether dialectical thought or strict orthodoxy is operational in their faith. For all it is the former. The dividing question rather appears more to be whether the women conceptually will project the dialectical process onto the God-activity, in the main, or embrace it intellectually, within themselves and among others, as a necessary function of God-awareness.

With regard to the dialectic of theology, two other areas of ministerial concern seem worthy of attention. One is feminist issues (including language issues), where active reconciliation of tradition with experience is especially apparent in the lives of many of these women; the other is ethical leadership, which has been treated as a ministry-defining task in a chapter of its own.

FEMINIST THEOLOGIZING AND LANGUAGE CONCERNS

In the worldwide press for human rights, many categories of non-elite people have developed an increased awareness of sociopolitical factors contributing to their subordination. There has been rising motivation in such groups to share more equitably in the distribution of social benefits. Sexual liberation constitutes a peculiar case in this press, because traditionally women and men have been integrated emotionally, economically, and ideologically due to conventional aspects of the primary institution that normatively subordinates women: the family. The necessity of making an opponent of one's intimate companion and economic support source, as a condition of posing a challenge to oppressive social conditions, is a formidable restraint to such activity.

In *Dilemmas of Masculinity*, Mirra Komarovsky (1976) concludes that even the most intellectually liberated men in her study expected, in their own mating arrangements, to choose women who would defer to their husbands' choices and allow the husbands to pursue their chosen careers without substantial requirements of mutual negotiation.

With few exceptions, my informants evidence some degree of conflict and ambivalence about how to deal with traditional sexism as it exists in religious communities and in the society. One the one hand there is the thoroughgoing commitment to human justice; on another, the commitment to healthy personal development for all people; on still another, the willingness to be accepting and supportive to people as they are; and further, the prophetic vocation to declare to the world its need for revolutionary change on behalf of persons both as individuals and as members of society. Is it any wonder that this is the area in which I saw the greatest tendency, during interviews, to be cautious and to qualify remarks?

Other experiences (seminars involving, over a few years' time, several hundred mid-life clergy couples—mostly clergy*men* and wives) have alerted me to the high anxiety triggered in both women and men by merely identifying categorical differences according to gender, especially differences in social power. There are important ego-support, guilt, and intimacy issues for both sexes. Both sexes are caught up in either the need or the fear of finding "natural law" justification for sexism in the normative differences. Both seem afraid that the empirically based information will be used against them to demean, criticize, alienate; that the other sex will feel heightened threat and anger, and therefore escalate attempts to control; that, as individuals, they will either go on being dissolved in a sea of generalized abstractions about *real* women/men or be considered abnormal. But many women voice at last one other kind of anxiety: often they are invested heavily in ego-support for valued male partners (marital, professional, parental) whom they consider exceptional, and whom they wish to encourage or exempt or reward with regard to gender issues. For many there is deeply felt tension between their hope to bring fresh ideas, justice, and reconciliation into social processes at all levels and their hope to maintain solidarity among people. Several of the women in this study mention freely choosing to restrain their own expression from time to time so that others may not be overwhelmed or pushed to grow in ways or at paces for which they are not ready. They elect such concessions for the sake of building trust and negotiating community in diversity; but they know such restraint also risks losing the opportunities they hope thereby to gain.

All of the currently married informants place their mates in one of two categories: either very supportive or actively "feminist" by the men's own commitments. All but one of the currently single women say they would either prefer to remain single or would consider as a mate only a person capable of equalitarian partnership—a real friend-marriage. The remaining one says simply that she would like to be married to a good person who fits with her ministerial choice.

In the cases where informants work as assistants or associates with male colleagues, there is uniform appreciation for the men's unusual sensitivity and consideration, coupled with dismay that the custom of domination is so entrenched and unconscious. One voice already has been heard at length on this subject in the section on struggle. The others are similar.

• He treats me *very* well. There are excellent staff services and equipment made available to me and he's supportive of experimentation in ministry; but he's very much the boss in charge.

• He did a big education and interpretation job with the parish when I came. The interview was very thorough in acquainting me with the parish. Then the job broadened as my desires and abilities flowered. He likes working liturgically, as a couple, for the symbolism of it. I was convinced that a true partnership had evolved. But in a few years, after I took on a regional assignment that made him responsible to me for certain things, the "partnership" collapsed. He just said flatly, "I guess if somebody's going to be 'in charge' it's going to be me."

A retired bishop, whose tenure spanned two decades, recently talked informally with some church leadership people. His words are much sharper, though he is a gentle, soft-spoken man.

• I early advocated the ordination of women. When I saw them coming into the ministry I thought that they would first be wanted in multiple staff situations. Contrariwise, they were more acceptable (as were two-clergy couples) to rural parishes. Senior partners in suburbia see themselves as senior executive officers. They are comfortable surrounded with a covey of women serving them and carrying out their programs, but when you put a woman on the *ordained* staff, John Wayne falls off his horse!

It is the tenacity of the traditional double standard of gender power—held in place (though perhaps eroding) by the "inner tapes" of men and women, as well as by the society's institutional structures—that forces women clergy into the grinding gears where traditional assumptions mesh with immediate experience. Though with only an exception or two the informants do not identify themselves as feminists, they know they stand as highly visible signs of a new age in gender relationships. They see this as an opportunity to build credibility and to influence how that new age takes shape. But they see the opportunity as joined to a special set of pains and problems, too.

There are women among the informants who know well how to go against the grain of social convention and maneuver around obstacles, sometimes turning them to positive strategic advantage. Adversarial attacks may, for example, heighten visibility for modeling authentic nonadversarial responses. But, the turning of opposition, hurt, disappointment, and exclusion into *growth* and *ser-*

vice does not happen among these women without consciousness of objectives and cost, nor without intense theological questioning and interpreting. Such personal learning and social contribution come dear and are regarded often by the informants as God-directed.

They appear reluctant to address gender issues as an isolated area of alienation when a whole world of oppressive social customs requires new directions.

I despair of conveying to the reader adequately what was so strongly conveyed to me in the interviews: that gender reconciliation is crucial in the theologizing of most of the informants, but primarily as a showcase and workshop for *human* reconciliation *on all fronts*. They want it neither trivialized nor trumpeted adversarially or patronizingly. They desire solidarity with both male and female working partners in struggling through society's (and their own) complicated ambivalence about the distribution and use of social power.

Many readers will remember how the women's liberation cause was split off from the Civil Rights movement when committed women noted how male "human rights" idealism failed to penetrate the activist men's contempt for female "partners." Similarly, religious women are often jarred into consciousness that the "brotherhood of mankind under the Fatherhood of God"—in which they know themselves to be present—is, in fact, operating in society on a hierarchical basis, giving them secondary status.

• Emotionally seminary was very trying. I felt threatened and attacked as a woman by teachers and other students. I don't want the differences between men and women denied; I don't want them used for alienation. The degree of scrutiny was immoral! There is such a need in society to de-objectify *Woman* and to start real communication with real women among men . . .

The quotations above and below come from very young women who are polar opposites in assertiveness and in consciousness of the feminist agenda.

• I'm very grateful for the generally adequate support of family, friends, my church. The seminary professors were affirming, in the main. There was general acceptance . . . but still somehow special status that I could feel. I'm low-key and adaptable; I don't raise hackles much. I'm not a "women's libber," though I'm getting more assertive. . . . I just get to know the men on a personal basis; exposure itself may be more influential in social change than Scripture interpretation. Only occasionally are there negative responses to my presence or work. Among leaders I'm often the only woman present. I have to be so "on guard" all the time—so "up" to prove myself. At one church conference the discussion about women in ministry brought out very negative statements from clergy. I remember being very emotional; I went home and just fell apart.

While she describes "falling apart," she does not voice frustration about gender status. She is a confident, hopeful woman and she feels influential in her secondary status, which she knows she has learned socially but, at this point, prefers. She is aware of the dialectic set up in her between her spiritual integrity and her denominational experience. She suspects she will change much in the years to come. I suspect she is right.

Yet a much older woman, also, seems calmly accepting of what appears as a blatant injustice attached to gender. She has been in charge of a large parish for many years and is considered eminently effective.

• I think if I left now they'd want a man. In my church women tend to do the organizing of groups and when they become successful men take over.

I ask, "How does that feel?" She bypasses the question with a shrug and quietly comments,

• Well, that's they way the world *is*, though I have questions. . . . People support male clergy more . . . with gifts and help and money. . . . Maybe they look *up* to men from their understanding of Scripture. . . . Things may be changing some.

Qualified acceptance is an issue with numerous rankling variations.

• I was ordained in my local parish. It was a big celebration with much pride in me and support and love. On my visits home I preach or conduct liturgy . . . but they still treat me as an okay exception. . . . Probably they wouldn't hire a woman if they had a vacancy.
• When I hear, "No man would come for this salary," it really angers me; I feel devalued. I fight with an image that says men are worth more.
• I found that there were two levels of decision-making on the team. At one level I was officially included. At another level, the men did the *real* decisions and I was excluded.
• In the past a woman couldn't get a charge of her own unless she organized it and brought the congregation into the denomination. [This quotation is not from the same person as the similar one above.]
• Many women in my seminary shared their pain and frustration and the urgency of their calls to ministry. I felt I was one of few women in my denomination allowed to do much; I've had excellent working situations, comparatively speaking. Yet there are restrictions.
• This is a tough job. There's tons of administrative work heaped on. I didn't want it and felt ill-equipped for it, but a lot of pressure was put on by regional staff. They wanted me here as a showpiece for their liberality of leadership. I really wanted out the first year. . . .

Several women were "excused" from certain seminary requirements because of leadership's unwillingness to "push" a woman onto congregations for such practical experiences as preaching and internship. One informant mentions not being invited to participate in the local community's joint Good Friday service.

Some informants experience tokenism as a qualified acceptance, in that they become somehow depersonalized into a female "ingredient" in committees and boards and are understood to be delivering "the woman's point of view." Others speak of subtle but powerful pressures not to disturb the male club ambience of ministerial associations.

• I'm the only woman. I sometimes find myself responding and relating in "old boy" ways in my desire to be included. I have surprised myself laughing helpfully at dirty jokes which I've always hated and found uncomfortable.

There are few reports of overt intentional sexual harassment in the ministry. Only one woman mentions that for a brief time upon her entry into ministerial circles she was repeatedly propositioned by male colleagues for sexual acts. She thinks they were exploiting their assumptions about her as a divorced woman. Two others tell of distress over occasions in which they felt pressure to provide a good-buddy-type cover-up for the "moral nonaccountability" of male colleagues.

While the propositions were offensive and affect the reporting woman's attitudes toward the particular people involved, she does not describe them as compromising her integrity. By contrast, the informants who were pushed to withhold knowledge of professionally sanctionable behavior were not only offended, but also felt violated in their own integrity and highly conflicted over how to handle such situations most responsibly.

In one of the cover-up cases a male colleague, also privy to the matter, was sensitive to the informant's dilemma and went to bat for her in a pastoral, helpful way. He remains one of her valued ministerial models.

Such experiences tend to stimulate in the women a great deal of reflection about theological, ethical, and administrative aspects of ministry and what, of their learning as women, they can contribute to the spiritual life of their religious communities.

Overall, I was impressed during the interviews with the extraordinarily positive, appreciative attitudes toward men evidenced by at least ten of the 17 informants. None of the others was especially negative, but their references to men were put in more conventional terms that I found less revealing. Some of the women were quite explicit about their gratitude and delight that there are men with compatible spiritual vision.

• The struggle for wholeness is not an easy journey, but it is intrinsically worthwhile. I admire people whose faith and life are congruent. My husband is one of those people. He's so encouraging and gives me strength. He pushes me to move and develop in ways I might not without him. He gives very helpful criticism. He tempers my ideas about men because he's *such* an exception!
• Among my heroes are the men who have compassion on women. They are a great support. My co-pastor is one—and his sons and wife are helpful, too—and my own husband.
• I want to write liturgy and innovate. I think I see nuances men don't see. . . . But there are feminist men, also, who are sensitive to the implications of language and image.

An informant who willingly identifies herself as feminist (in the humanist sense) and whose husband is as committed to that kind of feminism as she is, credits him with freeing her to be more vocal than she likely would be without his support. She says they understand Jesus as a model for their position.

• I see Jesus as a truly liberated person . . . and a liberator. He is a model for faith and life . . . a friend . . . a brother. The stories he told sparked new thinking about God. He called into question traditions and models and images of his day. He brought sight to the blind, deliverance to captives. He is a spiritual discipline model. I titled a sermon I preached, "Jesus Was a Feminist."

Several women talk about incidents in their lives when sympathetic and helpful men countered the action of men who had been openly discriminatory. The informants express deep gratitude for such advocacy, along with keen awareness of what it says about women's continuing dependency on the good will of male allies in situations where the gender power differential remains entrenched.

• The senior minister was ailing and died the year I left the parish. He was a fine adult mentor . . . he helped heal the anger I had against the male clergy who had "junked" me. It was an empowering relationship.

The clergywomen informants place high value on credible congruence among intentions, ideas, and acts. This leads to discomfort for them as communication specialists when traditional theological or liturgical language carries meanings that distort or contradict the authentic faith they intend to convey. They treasure continuity with the past, but only for the sake of truth, not for the sake of the past itself, or for orthodoxy. Using male-skewed formulas now, without modification, in settings and on occasions celebrating "the worth of each person in the unity of all" seems truth-blurring and anachronistic to most of them.

Four of the informants use traditional religious language comfortably. They experience no stress from conventional assumptions that context determines when masculine language connotes males and when it connotes all people; and beyond that, they see little at stake.

The other 13 find that the realm of religious language is an area in which gender alienation is especially problematic, and in which their imaginations are most excited by the possibilities of redemptive innovation and fruitful dialogue. They try very hard to be clear with meanings and inventive with expressiveness as well as inoffensive and respectful of traditional idiom. They want to introduce language flexibility and expansion while minimizing discomfort in the transition to a wider range of terminology that better fits a single standard of human worth and caring. One woman speaks of the stumbling, the embarrassment, and the humor that can accompany serious attempts to transmit new awareness in faith and fresh theological insights.

• I take tradition seriously but not rigidly. Communicating things seems to go easily for me. Inclusive language is important even if it's awkward. Ten or fifteen years ago when I was investigating imagery, and religious language around God, I lapsed during a service and started a free prayer "Our Father . . . " and then [after a confused pause] added "and Mother." The congregation just cracked up; they knew I had messed up. I didn't have a lot of good alternatives for a long while, but I knew I was responding negatively to "great white grandfathers in the sky." I'm not into the goddess worship thrust. I search for innovative imagery for who God is and how God acts. I often use imagery from the Psalms. . . . water . . . the rise and fall of the sea . . . a river flowing.

It is clear to me from the informants' discussions of language issues that those who move away from traditional terms have little difficulty finding appropriate alternatives for preaching and teaching situations. Nor do they find forms of address in private devotions any problem at all. It is when they address God ceremonially on behalf of the congregation that they and others are apt to feel most groping and linguistically bereft. The tortuous struggle for meaningful words to express the present full experience of God shows how nontrivial the issue is. If the whole of our language lacks fitting words for a major area of consciousness, something new, indeed, is happening and the words *will* come; but it may be a long time before today's tinkering settles into an unself-conscious vernacular for this problematic area of expression.

Still, there remains a yearning for just the right terms to address and describe God in ways that are authentic for both women and men of faith.

• My God imagery is parental but indirect. . . . I make references to us as children of God. I'm comfortable with father imagery. It's the way I think. But I want to free up the imagery. I draw more on the spirit side of God; it feels more feminine to me. I equate it with love . . . loving action.

• God the Father is big in my thinking, but I'm uneasy with the king image; it infects people's ideas of God with assumptions of arbitrariness and force. I went through an angry stage about father imagery . . . but it became very comfortable again. I use action images a lot . . . "causing to flower" . . . "looking for the lost one" . . . "shaping irresistibly, slowly, without wrecking"; they move toward mother-figure qualities . . . and sometimes I use organic nature imagery. The mother image functions more as my personal, private thought. I now tend to integrate the Trinity ideas and experience them together. Spirit images for God are strong . . . wind . . . flame. I never see fire or hear wind without thinking of it as the Holy Spirit. To refer to the Holy Spirit as "He" seems jarring. The Holy Spirit feels female to me. I can picture the Holy Spirit breathing and groaning and giving birth to me.

• I avoid the personal pronouns when I can. I want to open up the language for people's own images without the offense of occasional female pronouns which can make barriers in communication. It's a strategic question. I respect people's images—even if they're exclusively male; people have a right to their own images. I try to sense what they are.

• I dwell on adjectives . . . God as loving, merciful, etc. It's a gentler way to wean folks away from concrete male images.

• I choke on the prayer book. I think God needs to be *person*-ized. Male/female is a pragmatic blend I settle for.

• I struggle. I haven't come up with a pronoun that's comfortable. I say things like "Dear God, Creator and Sustainer of the universe and of our lives . . . "

• I have absolutely no problem seeing God as a woman—on hands and knees searching for us as for a lost coin.
• I'm getting more conscious of the mother part of God now. I find I'm starting to avoid the Father name sometimes, but I still *think* that way.
• My public and private imagery for God is different. In private there's mother . . . spreading wings . . . nourishment . . . softness, compassion. Publicly I back off from free use of female imagery because I don't always want to deal with the problems and criticism. I use more male imagery there out of respect for the roots and traditions of people. When I use "Father," it is with high consciousness and I often avoid the masculine pronouns when I mean "human." But I make *some* changes, and there is increasing openness of people to more feminine and inclusive imagery. I also use the biblical metaphor . . . light, water, wind, fire. God is there in nature for knowing and encountering. I'm "androgynous" with God but not with Jesus, because with Jesus there was an actual human form.

Others, also, mention that the concrete maleness of Jesus is, for them, a non-issue.

• Function terms like "harmonizer," "comforter," "redeemer" seem less culture-bound and sexually biased. Sexually inclusive language is very important to me. As a form of prayer address I often use "Oh Gracious and Holy One." I use "Father" and "Lord," too, and they are full of meaning for me, but I want to stretch rather than limit the understandings. Entry and acceptance of women pastors opens many new possibilities in faith, especially for women. The new balance in leadership is good. I see the need for reform as constant. Feminist reform is my most conscious aim. I think it is *true* to my tradition . . . inherent in it . . . but ignored. I've tried to introduce it in the parish in a nonthreatening way. They've been very accepting.
• The female imagery appeals to me personally, but I'm not fully comfortable with that in communicating. I'm frustrated with male imagery, but I use the language because one can't push in all directions at once with change. I have respect for traditions and the strength of traditional liturgies. I work to preserve them . . . and yet innovate . . . especially with the language. I'm beginning to see the thinking and needs of women converging. Self-consciously feminist women and self-consciously non-feminist women are moving together more. I get a lot of feedback on the imaging I do for people just by being a woman in ministry. I'm a model for female authority . . . female vocation . . . leading, serving, caring. People with daughters mention that I provide images for them. They like that.

Performance is an especially rich language, and the clergywomen are making important contributions to its range.

The clergywomen themselves had mentors and models for ministry who were mostly male, though the informants extrapolated behavioral ideals from "strong women," too—"women with backbone." Much of the informants' current theologizing grows out of their awareness that how they live their lives—how they comport themselves, how they choose, how they deal with people and situations—is now a model in faith, not just for women and girls, but also for men and boys.

The women are feeling notable freedom and success with innovation in special ceremonies. It seems to be the place where their inventiveness with language, broadly as well as narrowly understood, is most appreciatively received. It's in some ways their existential "playhouse" of faith communication.

The language of implication is often more powerful than the language of explication. The modeling aspect of new roles is especially influential. Ceremonial religious pageantry frequently combines words, acts, and life marker events. Skillful artistry with such ceremonies is a complex gathering of tradition and community to lift up and enhance a particular life moment.

• Women tend to have good sacramental sense. They're more in touch with their bodies . . . in touch with the power of the physical—loving touch, the visual—as a vehicle of grace. They like experimenting with liturgical art . . . dance, clowning, mime. . . .

(Additional quotations about ceremony appear in the section on nurture in Chapter 3.)

For the informants wrestling with the "language question," there are no exceptions to the rule that they are utterly serious about arriving at effective words for sharing their deepest and fullest experiences as women, in faith, with God. This is no frivolous pastime; nor is it, as language, their most important concern in ministry. It is painful for them to observe people judging the issue as a petty partisan pursuit or a merely administrative matter.

Since both the discomfort and vitality in this arena signal the cutting edge of their theological thought, it is impossible for the clergywomen to regard their striving as faddishness that will "quiet down" once their first big splash in the role has subsided. They are increasingly convinced that they are raising issues at the heart of society's most deadly dilemmas and also at the heart of their ministries. For example, some see the pathologies of sexism, criminal violence, militarism and ecological greed as intricately perpetuating each other in a cosmic pathology of adversarial self-interest and hierarchical power arrangements. Liturgical language is the "tip of the iceberg" for the women who concern themselves with this issue. They know the power of words to carry imbedded assumptions at the subconscious level, so it is not a matter they feel they can responsibly ignore. But they also know that new language must unfold with experience if it is to be useful and clarifying; so they are pledged to patience and sensitivity as they struggle to say what's true in their experience. It is this need to construct an effective and authentic testimony to their faith that impels the experimentation with language forms.

They feel affirmed by the many men who are also distressed about the hierarchical implications of traditional language usage. The clergywomen are keenly aware that the evolution of religious language, whether conscious or not, is a product of women and men together shaping culture.

At the World Council of Churches' Conference on "The Community of Women and Men in the Church" in 1981, General Secretary Philip Potter said:

[W]hat has emerged most powerfully for me is the need to rethink the whole question of authority and interpretation of Scripture. The more I meditate on it, the more I realize . . . the way in which the relations of men and women have been dealt with in the Scriptures themselves and the way in which we have interpreted what the Scriptures have said, have brought seriously into question how we understand the total revelation of God in Christ expressed in the whole canon of the Scriptures. We have systematically left aside as our criterion of judgment the central nature of God's revelation and have clung to all the things that strengthen and confirm our attitudes of domination and of hierarchical oppression. It seems to me that this discovery challenges the way in which we deal with the Scriptures, and we shall have to do some hard thinking about this.

Secondly, we have to come to terms with our ecclesiology, our understanding of the church. . . . If there is a fellowship, a real sharing of life with life in which we are all in council together, then it means both women and men are in council together, that decisions are made together, and that decisions are made by those who have the gifts required without regard to sex or culture.

[. . .]

And then there is our whole understanding of tradition and traditions. We have made a great sacred cow of our different traditions, but what I find, as a student of history, is an urgent need to rewrite church history as the history of women and men in mission and service. Our existing church history is largely a history of men. . . . [O]ur whole understanding of sexuality is challenged. We are called to take it more seriously, especially in our theology. (in Parvey 1983:25–27)

Relative to the assertion of one woman that "the canon is not closed," it is interesting that more than just a few of the informants expect Scriptures to expand over time to include the female experience of the Absolute. None of them sees "the female view" as a substitution for "the male view" or as a superior alternative. Rather, they see it as a redemptive completion of the human view of experience, a movement toward reconciliation of the alienated parts of creation. It is this vision that makes them wary of identifying with a narrowly construed "women's rights" position; and that makes them anxious when men respond as though they advocate a takeover of social control by women for women. It is this vision that also moves them into alignment (albeit unconsciously in some cases) with the intellectual abstractions that currently interest moral and theological scholars and social futurists (see Chapter 9).

In the recent past, Harvard Divinity School (whose student body now has roughly the same numbers of men and women) put out an anniversary edition of their *Bulletin* celebrating ten years of women's studies at HDS.[4] In that edition Constance Buchanan reminisces:

[F]rom the start at the Divinity School, the influx of women into this technological institution, into the church, and into its ministries was not understood as a question of access. It was understood . . . to be a question of transforming the study and practice of theology. . . . They called for rethinking traditional modes of theological inquiry, theological education, ministry, and institutional structures in faith communities themselves. And it was precisely in these terms that they first engaged the faculty, which was in the early 1970s almost exclusively male, in discussion about the significance of women in religion. . . . The second thing contributing in a major way to the ten years of institutional growth and change represented by the program was the seriousness of the response by faculty to the questions posed by the [women's] caucus.

In an issue of *The National Catholic Reporter*[5] devoted to "Women Doing Theology", theologian Rosemary Radford Ruether explains:

[F]eminism must reject all ideologies and social systems based on the assumption of male superiority and the superiority of those "qualities" called masculine, but it must also criticize social movements that romanticize the repressed—whether of women or other dominated people, or of repressed cultural attributes, or of bodiliness and earth—without overcoming the alienated dualism between the two.

One cannot assume that only the "masculine" qualities have been distorted and that the "feminine" qualities stand for spontaneous goodness. False dualism distorts both sides of any relationship. Hence, in seeking to liberate ourselves from patriarchal culture, we must overcome and transform both sides of distorted dualisms that have alienated us from our whole human potential as persons and people in community with each other, with nature and with God/ess.

Over 100 years ago, John Stuart Mill (1869) also talked about the developmental distortions resulting from oppressive social dynamics. The passage has the feel of a century past, but the insights are still *avant-garde*.

Standing on the ground of common sense and the constitution of the human mind, I deny that anyone knows, or can know, the nature of the two sexes, as long as they have only been seen in their present relation to one another. If man had ever been found in society without women, or women without men, or if there had been a society of men and women in which the women were not under the control of the men, something might have been positively known about the mental and moral differences which may be inherent in the nature of each. What is now called the nature of women is an eminently artificial thing—the result of forced repression in some directions, unnatural stimulation in others. It may be asserted without scruple, that no other class of dependents have had their character so entirely distorted from its natural proportions by their relation with their masters.
                                                [. . .]
Men do not want solely the obedience of women, they want their sentiments. All men, except the most brutish, desire to have, in the women most nearly connected with them, not a forced slave but a willing one, not a slave merely, but a favority. They have therefore put everything in practice to enslave their minds. The masters of all other slaves rely, for maintaining obedience, on fear—either fear of themselves or religious fears. The masters of women wanted more than simple obedience, and they turned the whole force of education to effect their purpose. All women are brought up from the very earliest years in the belief that their ideal of character is the very opposite to that of men; not self-will and government by self-control, but submission and yielding control to others. All moralities tell them that it is the duty of women, and all current sentimentalities that it is their nature, to live for others.[. . .] When we put together three things—first, the natural attraction between opposite sexes; secondly, the wife's entire dependence on the

husband, every privilege or pleasure she has being either his gift or depending entirely on his will; and lastly, that the principle object of human pursuit, consideration, and all objects of social ambition, can in general be sought or obtained for her only through him, it would be a miracle if the object of being attractive to men had not become the polar star of feminine education and formation of character . . . and resignation of all individual will into the hands of a man, . . . an essential part of sexual attractiveness.

Much social change has occurred since the above writing. Economic dependence and domestic careers for married women are no longer the rule in the same way. But the analysis of gender relations still rings true. The extensive entry of women into higher education and public careers provides an occasion for addressing such distortions, analytically and existentially, with an eye toward beneficial social transformations.

Men and women contributors to the gender analysis literature also continue to emphasize the crippling effects on males from conventional relations. At the 1981 conference on ''The Community of Women and Men in the Church,'' contemporary theologian Jürgen Moltmann had this to say:

It is the men who are mainly ''disconcerted'' by women who emancipate themselves from age-old subjection. Women should not cover up this fact out of love nor should men deny it out of pride. We are becoming insecure in the masculine roles which have been instilled in us. We have to relearn everything, and every existential experience of relearning is painful. But the problem lies still deeper. The man also feels that his manly pride is violated. His sense of self-respect is shaken. His patriarchal identity disintegrates. He no longer knows who he really is. One reaction to this is aggression. But the most common reaction is depression.

Women are experiencing their new identity, their dignity, and their liberation into complete humanity. The reason men find it difficult to follow them in this way is because, to discover the starting point for their liberation into complete humanity, they have first of all to return deep inside themselves. They have to break through the hard crusts of their alienation in order to reach the core of their human nature. Moreover, man must abandon self-righteousness if he is to learn to trust his humanity. To put it simply, the ruling ''lord'' in man must die so that the brother can be born, ready for honest friendship. (in Parvey 1983:38–39)

It is this ''reaching the core of human nature'' in order to struggle jointly as brothers and sisters for a new cultural norm in gender identity, that excites the feminist passions of the informants who address the issue. The others emphasize an individualized, caring approach to social issues, feeling more influential at that level of social concern.

Throughout the interviews there were repeated indications that they all walk a tightrope on this matter of sexual alienation. They are all concerned. They have all been hurt deeply, one way or another, by conventional sexual injustice. But they fear triggering the closure of dialogue in personal and public discussion if men (or women) (1) see their concerns only in adversarial or judgmental terms; (2) fail to catch the globally human significance of their concerns; or (3) are unwilling to join in a struggling partnership to develop more healthy sexual selves and relations. Almost all are skittish about identification with what goes popularly as "feminism," though they know that just *being* in the professional ministerial role as women is a strong feminist statement.

They say they *know* a God who *knows* them experientially as full persons; yet they minister officially in administrative structures and liturgical languages that do not always *know* them in this same full way, or even *allow* them fully. Most of the women (13 of the 17) aspire consciously to influence social change toward equitable gender arrangements throughout institutional structures.

A woman who has immense appeal as a model for ministry among clergymen[6] nonetheless makes this observation:

• My eclectic background is at odds with the maleness and the lack of spiritual articulation in the church. . . . Maleness at judicatory levels is *most* frustrating—*most* resistant to women. Such rational . . . heady . . . wordy formulas . . . *so* influenced by the business world . . . such lack of contemplation and spiritual discipline. It's all hierarchy . . . power . . . either/or . . . analytical/bureaucratic . . . with tasks more important than people. There's a refusal to just let women be who they *are*. . . . So much pressure to act like a man. Sometimes I think about alternate models. . . . Now, abstract principles are imposed on concrete situations that have to adjust. I see myself as a renewer of traditions . . . through working for a whole new saintly/secular spiritual consciousness in which renewal occurs as people try to adapt church structure to what's happening in society.

Another says:

• Both my dreams and my frustrations are all bound up in church and women issues.

I want to call attention to a set of differences following racial lines among the informants. All of the black women informants are quite comfortable with traditional religious language. None speaks of investment in combating sexism, except as individual cases. I get no glimpses of systematic feminist emphasis in either theology or language. They do not express their *theological* positions in reformist terms, though they have dynamic, developmental views of faith in all cases and evident social reform agendas. The white women are a contrasting group in this regard. Whether or not they identify with "feminism" or "women's liberation" as labels, they are committed to dealing with sexism as a *systemic* evil; and they show enthusiasm for deliberate theologizing as a central exercise in faith. All of the informants interweave the biblical traditions with contemporary life experience, but differ as to whether they are more inclined to dramatize or intellectualize the connections.

The crucial difference seems to be in levels or modes of articulation rather than in the basic orientation to life and ministry, though mutual formation of language and experience cannot be ignored; that is the whole point of the feminist language issue. I shall not attempt to explain these distinctions merely *as racial distinctions*, both because of the nature of this study and because other factors are correlated strongly.

The four black women range in age from the forties to the seventies, with a mean age between 55 and 60. Thus they are some of the older informants and they also represent the lengthiest tenures as professional ministers. They faced ordination requirements that exposed them to less or none of the rational-ana-lytical type theological study required of the white informants. It is this last factor, coupled with denominational traditions, that seems to me most likely to have importance in determining conceptual and linguistic styles. Here I take clues from the white women who "discovered" in dialectical theology a more fitting frame of reference for discourse about their spiritual development, pre-viously known and expressed unquestioningly in traditional metaphor (see Chapter 3, 61–62 and 64–65). I am also reflecting other contacts such as a sermon I heard preached recently, at the ordination of a Harvard graduate, by a young black woman whose mode of thinking and speaking was not so much like that of the black women in this study as it was like that of the white women.

During the second interview with the youngest of the black informants, I mentioned the racial difference I had noted with regard to comfort in the use of traditional religious metaphor. She responded with an insightful comment:

• I see many cultural differences between the racial lines in religious expression. I think this divides the groups religiously more than prejudice does now.[7] The traditional language has carried meaning for black people through the years far beyond any literal meaning. It has always been a code language for us to share the deep experience of desperation and hope.

Insofar as this is true, it may signal an exceedingly deep bond with traditional language, even though there is little disposition toward rigid, literal interpreta-tion.

Anthropologist Marvin Harris talks about cultural forms (including religion) as adaptive expressions in an environment—maintained until less costly, better, alternative solutions to recurring interests and problems appear as available and credible to a people (1974). This tie to experience is also emphasized by Clifford Geertz in his observation that religion is not the divine but a conception of the divine; what happens to a people happens to its faith. Michael Harrington (1983:183) comments:

As a result of discrimination, black people (and Hispanics) have been disproportionately excluded from the most "modern"—scientific, technological—sectors of the society. Indeed, while a participant-observer in the civil-rights movement of the fifties and sixties, I argued that "soul" was less an innate quality of black people than a characteristic of all groups who had not been though the capitalist cultural revolution.

Vittorio Lanternari (1963) specifically addresses the analysis of religious expressions among oppressed peoples (though he is not talking about U.S. culture) and shows the importance of historical origins, developmental factors, and concrete secular circumstances. He notes the unique blends of world religions such as Christianity with folk symbols and goals of various regions and with a group's distinctive existential hopes. Religious vitality appears to demand a rationality of faith that fits the ordinary forms of rationality operating in the worshiping community.

All this serves to underline the logic of expecting that until no significant differences remain in the cultural experiences of blacks and whites (or of women and men) in the United States, there will continue to be some recognizable differences in the characteristic religious expressions.

The larger cultural traditions and pressing needs of religious communities make a difference in leadership styles, too. Black churches appear to encompass many more aspects of black community organization and experience than do white religious groups; political, economic, and educational mobilization occur more frequently under the religious umbrella of black congregations. The continuing needs among black people to tap energies for strategic work on high-priority social reforms may tend to keep religious language and thought, as such, more simple, more specially religious, and more symbolically available as a rallying dynamic. White U.S. religion has become more organizationally specialized in the past century; it encompasses much less of the entire white social experience. Yet in much mainstream white Christianity and Judaism there is a growing tendency to encompass the whole world of social experience in theological reflection. As it were, audiences are presented with more sophisticated intellectual tools for integrating and making life sense from the everchanging meanings of modern existence.

With regard to feminist impulses and overt alignment with feminist ideologies or political strategies, many social thinkers have pointed to the important differences between the life situations of black women and white. I will alert the reader to some of these contrasts without being able to say how they may affect the views of the four black women and 13 white women in this particular group of informants. One thing is certain: the differences matter, and are of a sort to ensure that black women and white women ordinarily can identify only partially with each other's positions vis-à-vis *womanness*.

Diane Lewis (1977:243–46) traces the conflicts black women are apt to experience with respect to white "women's liberation":

Black women, due to their membership in two subordinate groups that lack access to authority and resources in society, are in structural opposition with a dominant racial and dominant sexual group. In each subordinate group they share potential common interests with group co-members, black men on the one hand and white women on the other. Ironically, each of these is a member of the dominant group: black men as men, white women as whites. Thus, the interests which bind black women together with and pull them into opposition against co-members crosscut one another in a manner which often obscures one set of interests over another. Historically, their interests as blacks have taken precedence over their interests as women. A shift in the power relations between the races had to come before changes in the structural relationship between the sexes.

[. . .]

Black women, on account of male exclusion from the job market, have been forced to share with black men marginal participation in the public work world of the dominant society through menial and ill-paying jobs. Their economic contributions have often been essential to their families. Their important economic role has assured them power over the limited resources available to a racially excluded group. On the basis of power over crucial resources, black women have held a relatively high position within a dominated society.

[. . .]

During the long period of male exclusion from the public sphere, black women shared the experience of racial oppression with black men.

[. . .]

[A]ttributes of the white women's status currently criticized by many feminists as examples of sexism were seen (and are still seen) by many black women as representative of the unique privileges of women of the dominant group.

Lewis maintains that there is growing responsiveness to feminism among black women who see the implications of sexism more clearly now, as blacks enter some higher-status positions in the society at large, and integrationist permissions from white society are seen to benefit black males more than black females. But she observes that black women continue to need their own special expressions of feminist ideals because of the unique conflicts they almost inevitably face. Black women remain attuned to the fact that their men often have been defined as threats to white jobs, homes, and women. They desire solidarity with the men and genuinely want to be supportive in the struggle for social- and self-respect.

The main points I want to emphasize here are that (1) the situations of black women and white women in U.S. society are different in important ways and might be expected to affect the point of view about gender discrimination and other matters; (2) the particular black women interviewed for this study happen to differ from the white clergywomen in other than racial ways (age, professional tenure, denominational affiliation, and type of formal theological education). Consequently, though the informants are split along racial lines with respect to intentional existential theologizing and feminist social reform, they may or may not be indicative of differences between the racial groups in the broader society.

I have some strong impressions from the interview experiences, beyond what I can show. The black women have high awareness of sexist injustice, and of racist injustice. They have high motivation to help bring about more fair and helpful conditions for human development. They have high respect for Scripture, and quote passages quite literally while at the same time displaying great freedom to interpret the references according to multiple layers of symbolic meaning. They think more personally than politically. All four are strong, confident women who have had many occasions to see the results of their individual influence. Hence, in the relatively meager contact they have had with a type of scholarly work that articulates logical and empirical relationships among different types of systemic social injustice, their own way of unifying their concerns and social strategies is to emphasize God's radical concern for respect and justice for all human individuals. They experience this focus on individual well-being as more fruitful, less adversarial in tone, and more conducive to creating necessary coalitions.

• I find it more helpful to consider the uniqueness of persons and problems and to work for specific concrete solutions.

Though younger, more classically educated or politically minded blacks often criticize the individualistic approach as soporific and ineffectual in social reform, ideological individualism does not seem to have dampened the ardor for social change or prevented the public effectiveness of these women. (One holds local, state, and national tributes for community contributions.) They tend to see the approach as freeing them for flexible helpfulness in affecting social outcomes. They do not see "individual" as *opposed* to "societal" but more as a microcosmic and operationally critical *version* of "societal".

• I try to keep the church from being satisfied with separated groups and small interests.

I conclude that all of the informants are busily engaged in *doing* dialectical theology as a continuing reconciliation of historic traditions and immediate experience. Not one treats the content of faith as a finalized belief-package that can be passed on effectively apart from living and growing in its meaning.

• There's no good theology if it doesn't apply to mundane concerns.

This integrative theologizing gives a characteristic cast to their moral and administrative leadership, as we have seen in previous chapters. And, as we shall see in the remaining chapters, it puts them in a position to make ordinary sense, to a wide range of people, out of new forms of spirituality and worldview.

NOTES

1. I am using the terms "existential" and "dialectical" very simply and broadly. I mean "existential" to convey "experiential," that is, known in direct encounter. I intend "dialectical" to mean mutually constraining dynamics that are forming in terms of each other's contradictory reality.

2. For many Christians "the Word" and "the Christ" are equivalencies in the sense of "the embodied God-content of the Bible and Jesus." For other Christians "the Word" is more literally understood as *the words* of the Bible. No one in this study understands it flatly or merely as the latter.

3. The books of the Bible officially recognized by the Church.

4. *Harvard Divinity Bulletin* 14, no. 2 (December 1983–January 1984), pp. 6–8.

5. *The National Catholic Reporter* 20, no. 25, April 13, 1984, pp. 4–6.

6. I interviewed her after a coffee break at a meeting where she had just made a presentation preparatory to leaving that region. The content of clergyman testimonials to which I was privy as a waiting bystander, and the level of gratitude expressed for the quality of her collegiality, were impressive.

7. While there are racially integrated religious communities, most parishes tend to be dominated by one racial group or to be single-race congregations. (Only one informant serves as pastor to a congregation characterized by a racial mix—in this case, four racial strains in an urban neighborhood.)

Chapter 9

Worldview Paradigm Shift

The clergywomen's views of life, as presented in this study, coincide in important ways with a worldview paradigm gaining credibility among social prophets inside and outside of organized religion. In this chapter I shall attempt to outline the main features of the ascendent orientation described by many scholars, and show its likeness to the informants' stated ministerial intentions. The similarity suggests that an increasing proportion of clergy positions filled by women holds potential for subtly shifting the course of institutionalized religion toward a way of spiritual searching congruent with the new paradigm's emphases.

Throughout recorded history there are indications that people have noted the drama attendant upon the realization that "the times are changing." Always people seem called upon to choose and adjust toward some end not yet seen and only dimly, if at all, imagined. Always there is risk of precipitating harm instead of benefit to oneself or one's group. Usually the magnitude of change and risk seem greater within the arena of present happenings, compared to some other time. Usually one's own time seems fraught with peculiar critical significance in the course of events.

Yet a careful look at history reveals *objectively* critical times in which truly new ways of ordering and experiencing life are forming around discoveries and techniques that penetrate and alter irrevocably the structure and meaning of social interaction. The past two decades have occasioned an amazing outpouring of literature arguing that civilization is already committed to the social dynamics that force a "turning point" in history—toward species destruction or toward a radically changed species behavior. The old and new reality paradigms are variously explicated and analyzed, but one does sense that the reviewing critics have at least watched the same "movie."

This chapter will focus on an array of quotations from well-known popular and scholarly writers. The selections are made with an eye to what they are saying about human species evolution—the direction of change desirable or discernible in the view people have of human existence (an unalterably social existence). I see considerable convergence in some aspects of the analyses. My major areas of interest are (1) what sort of paradigm shift they say is in process for imaging reality at the global or cosmic level; (2) what is in store for individuals, or required of individuals, developmentally, according to that paradigm; (3) what is in store for social institutions, or required of social institutions, developmentally, according to that paradigm; and finally, (4) how such persons as the informants in this study may connect with the paradigm shift described by the various authors.

The best work I know on the subject of paradigm shift (social reality transformation) is still Thomas Kuhn's book, *The Structure of Scientific Revolutions* (1962). Written about science, its insights are so penetrating and transferable that almost every student has it assigned in some class or other during a college career. I suspect that the revolutionary worldview shifts Kuhn identifies in science research (e.g, from Newtonian to Einsteinian physics) are different only in particulars from such foundation-quaking experiences as religious people have when they move out of an authoritarian, absolutist ethic toward a radical commitment to species caring.

Kuhn rejects the idea that growth in knowledge is a simple additive accumulation of discoveries. He claims that such a view only applies within limited time and place frames. He suggests that a more appropriate overview notes periodic crises in reality perspectives. Such crises erupt when important evidence cannot be accounted for and important problems cannot be solved using existing assumptions about the universe.

As anomalies challenge the trustworthiness of the theoretical base, people speculate about more fruitful and satisfying ways to *know* things. Innovative "sense," in unfamiliar terms, is often rejected as "impossible," "crazy," "demonic," or "unnatural." If, however, over time, it appears to offer superior coherence for a wide range of data and projects, and especially if it provides simpler ways to envision complex principles, the proposed reality model is likely to capture attention and win converts. People come, one by one, not to be able to see things in the old way any longer. They are aware of the old way and they understand it, but it is no longer *real* to them. The new model for knowing comes to dominate work and critical comment. It gains support and moves toward status as an assumption in posing questions and struggling to find answers.

In recent years much of social science has been directed toward worldview paradigm transition among people in U.S. society, and toward the content of the paradigms under which people live their daily lives. The complex megaprocess of world modernization has been operating to stimulate substantial erosion of trust in traditional institutions and values. The institutions themselves are in turmoil and flux. So it is no surprise that personal identity stability, implying a counterpoint of stable institutions, is a major twentieth century problem. Who am I? Where am I going? What is real? These questions appear with special poignancy now, along with pandemic, inchoate fears about present or impending crises: war, ecological disaster, economic chaos, educational failure, health care disarray, rampant crime.

The idea of "crisis" is of a "crucial turning point" in some dynamic process; that is, a fork in the road where the choice made casts the future toward destruction or rejuvenation, danger or opportunity, despair or hope, pathology or health.

Physicist Fritjof Capra, in *The Turning Point*, talks of a shift in worldview paradigm and world social order as an evolutionary inevitability. Others speak more in terms of what must be chosen in life if species calamities are to be avoided; they are less sanguine about the turn that will be taken.

I have selected excerpts from Capra's first chapter. I believe that they represent the pith of his ideas and give an initial feel for some of the futurist social thought of recent years. His work provides a reference point both for other citations and for some of my concluding thoughts. (Readers who are well acquainted with the contemporary literature of macro-social analysis and prognosis may wish to skip the lengthy quotations in this chapter.)

At the beginning of the last two decades of our century, we find ourselves in a state of profound, world-wide crisis. It is a complex, multidimensional crisis whose facets touch every aspect of our lives.[. . .] It is a crisis of intellectual, moral, and spiritual dimensions; a crisis of a scale and urgency unprecedented in recorded human history. For the first time we have to face the very real threat of extinction of the human race and of all life on this planet.

[. . .]

It is a striking sign of our time that the people who are supposed to be experts in various fields can no longer deal with the urgent problems that have arisen in their areas of expertise.

[. . .]

These problems . . . are systemic problems, which means that they are closely inter-connected and interdependent. They cannot be understood within the fragmented methodology characteristic of our academic disciplines and government agencies. Such an approach will never resolve any of our difficulties but will merely shift them around in the complex web of social and ecological relations. A resolution can be found only if the structure of the web itself is changed, and this will involve profound transformations of our social institutions, values and ideas.

The rhythmic recurrences and patterns of rise and decline that seem to dominate human cultural evolution have somehow conspired to reach their points of reversal at the same time. The decline of patriarchy, the end of the fossil-fuel age, and the paradigm shift occurring in the twilight of the sensate culture are all contributing to the same global process.[. . .] As individuals, as a society, as a civilization, and as a planetary ecosystem, we are reaching the turning point.

Cultural transformations of this magnitude and depth cannot be prevented. They should not be opposed but, on the contrary, should be welcomed as the only escape from agony, collapse, or mummification.

[. . .]

The Chinese philosophers saw reality, whose ultimate essence they called Tao, as a process of continual flow and change. In their view all phenomena we observe participate in this cosmic process and are thus intrinsically dynamic.

[. . .]

The Chinese gave this idea of cyclical patterns a definite structure by introducing the polar opposites yin and yang, the two poles that set the limits for the cycles of change. . . .

In the Chinese view, all manifestations of the Tao are generated by the dynamic interplay of these two archetypal poles, which are associated with many images of opposites taken from nature and from social life. It is important, and very difficult for us Westerners, to understand that these opposites do not belong to different categories but are extreme poles of a single whole. Nothing is only yin or only yang. All natural phenomena are manifestations of a continuous oscillation between the two poles, all transitions taking place gradually and in an unbroken progression. The natural order is one of dynamic balance between yin and yang.

[. . .]

In Chinese culture yin and yang have never been associated with moral values. What is good is not yin or yang but the dynamic balance between the two; what is bad or harmful is imbalance.

[. . .]

In the Chinese view, then, there seem to be two kinds of activity—activity in harmony with nature and activity against the natural flow of things. The idea of passivity, the complete absence of any action, is not entertained.

[. . .]

For our purposes these associations of yin and yang will be most useful:

YIN	YANG
FEMININE	MASCULINE
CONTRACTIVE	EXPANSIVE
CONSERVATIVE	DEMANDING
RESPONSIVE	AGGRESSIVE
COOPERATIVE	COMPETITIVE
INTUITIVE	RATIONAL
SYNTHESIZING	ANALYTIC

Looking at this list of opposites, it is easy to see that our society has consistently favored the yang over the yin—rational knowledge over intuitive wisdom, science over religion, competition over cooperation, exploitation of natural resources over conservation, and so on. This emphasis, supported by the patriarchal system and further encouraged by the dominance of sensate culture during the past three centuries, has led to a profound cultural imbalance which lies at the very root of our current crisis—an imbalance in our thoughts and feelings, our values and attitudes, and our social and political structure.

[. . .]

According to Chinese wisdom, none of the values pursued by our culture is intrinsically bad, but by isolating them from their polar opposites, by focusing on the yang and investing it with moral virtue and political power, we have brought about the current sad state of affairs.

[. . .]

The view of man as dominating nature and woman, and the belief in the superior role of the rational mind, have been supported and encouraged by the Judeo-Christian tradition, which adheres to the images of a male god, personification of supreme reason and source of ultimate power, who rules the world from above by imposing his divine law on it. The laws of nature searched for by the scientists were seen as reflections of this divine law, originating in the mind of God.

It is now becoming apparent that overemphasis on the scientific method and on rational, analytic thinking has led to attitudes that are profoundly antiecological. In truth, the understanding of ecosystems is hindered by the very nature of the rational mind. Rational thinking is linear, whereas, ecological awareness arises from an intuition of nonlinear systems.

[. . .]

Living systems are organized in such a way that they form multileveled structures, each level consisting of subsystems which are wholes in regard to their parts, and parts with respect to the larger wholes. Thus molecules combine to form organelles, which in turn combine to form cells. The cells form tissues and organs, which themselves form larger systems, like the digestive system or the nervous system. These, finally, combine to form the living woman or man; and the "stratified order" does not end there. People form families, tribes, societies, nations. . . .

[. . .]

Arthur Koestler has coined the word "holons" for these subsystems which are both wholes and parts, and he has emphasized that each holon has two opposite tendencies: an integrative tendency to function as part of the larger whole, and a self-assertive tendency to preserve its individual autonomy. In a biological or social system each holon must assert its individuality in order to maintain the system's stratified order, but it must also submit to the demands of the whole in order to make the system viable. These two tendencies are opposite but complementary. In a healthy system—an individual, a society, or an ecosystem—there is a balance between integration and self-assertion. This balance is not static but consists of a dynamic interplay between the two complementary tendencies, which makes the whole system flexible and open to change.

The relation between modern systems theory and ancient Chinese thought now becomes apparent. The Chinese sages seem to have recognized the basic polarity that is characteristic of living systems. Self-assertion is achieved by displaying yang behavior; by being demanding, aggressive, competitive, expanding, and—as far as human behavior is concerned—by using linear, analytic thinking. Integration is furthered by yin behavior; by being responsive, cooperative, intuitive, and aware of one's environment. Both yin and yang, integrative and self-assertive tendencies, are necessary for harmonious social and ecological relationships.

[. . .]

Our 1960s and 1970s have generated a whole series of philosophical, spiritual, and political movements that seem to go in the same direction. They all counteract the overemphasis on yang attitudes and values, and try to reestablish a balance between the masculine and feminine sides of human nature.

[. . .]

Perhaps most important, the old value system is being challenged and profoundly changed by the rise of feminist awareness originating in the women's movement.

These various movements form what cultural historian Theodore Roszak has called the counter-culture. So far, many of them still operate separately and have not yet seen how much their purposes interrelate.[. . .] We can anticipate that, once they have recognized the commonality of their aims, all these movements will flow together and form a powerful force of social transformation. I shall call this force the rising culture. . . .

[. . .]

For two and a half centuries physicists have used a mechanistic view of the world to develop and refine the conceptual framework known as classical physics.[. . .] Like human-made machines, the cosmic machine was thought to consist of elementary parts. Consequently it was believed that complex phenomena could always be understood by reducing them to their basic building blocks and by looking for the mechanisms through which these interacted. This attitude, known as reductionism, has become so deeply ingrained in our culture that it has often been identified with the scientific method.

[. . .]

In the twentieth century, however, physics has gone through several conceptual revolutions that reveal the limitations of the mechanistic world view and lead to an organic, ecological view of the world which shows great similarities to the views of mystics of all ages and traditions. The universe is no longer seen as a machine, made up of a multitude of separate objects, but appears as a harmonious indivisible whole; a network of dynamic relationships that include the human observer and his or her consciousness in an essential way. The fact that modern physics, the manifestation of an extreme specialization of the rational mind, is now making contact with mysticism, the essence of religion and manifestation of an extreme specialization of the intuitive mind, shows very beautifully the unity and complementary nature of the rational and intuitive modes of consciousness; of the yang and the yin. Physicists, therefore, can provide the scientific background to the changes in attitudes and values that our society so urgently needs. (1982:21–48)

Another existing attempt to illuminate human crises and social change from the perspective of physical science is Erich Jantsch's theoretical contribution of a "self-organization paradigm" for universal evolution. In *The Self-Organizing Universe* (1980) he develops sophisticated arguments for an evolutionary model that includes all levels of phenomena.

I shall not try to capture the gist of the book. But certain portions will indicate the significance for culture formation and individual existence.

He shows how science is gradually moving away from unitary focus on structure, adaptation, and equilibrium of systems, toward an understanding of how systemic *de*stabilization and the development of new forms occurs. The notion of system is coming to emphasize becoming and process-orientation, according to Jantsch, rather than merely stabilization and maintenance factors.

. . . . [A] system now appears as a set of coherent, evolving, interactive processes which temporarily manifest in globally stable structures that have nothing to do with the equilibrium and the solidity of technological structure. Caterpillar and butterfly, for example, are two temporarily stabilized structures in the coherent evolution of one and the same system. (1980:6).

Drawing on the thought of other scientists, notably chemist Ilya Prigogine, the Jantsch paradigm incorporates ideas such as "order through fluctuation" and "autopoiesis."

Autopoiesis refers to the characteristic of living systems to continuously renew themselves and to regulate this process in such a way that the integrity of their structure is maintained.[. . .] In the domain of the living there is little that is solid and rigid. An autopoietic structure results from the interaction of many processes.

[. . .]

This new type of science which orients itself primarily at models of life, and not mechanical models, spurs change not only in science. It is thematically and epistemologically related to those events which I have identified as aspects of the metafluctuation which rocked the world. The basic themes are always the same. They may be summarized by notions such as self-determination, self-organization and self-renewal; by the recognition of a systemic interconnectedness over space and time of all natural dynamics; by the logical supremacy of processes over spatial structures; by the role of fluctuations which render the law of large numbers invalid and give a chance to the individual and its creative imagination, by the openness and creativity of an evolution which is neither in its emerging and decaying structures, nor in the end result, predetermined. Science is about to recognize these principles as general laws of the dynamics of nature. Applied to humans and their systems of life, they appear therefore as principles of a profoundly natural way of life. The dualistic split into nature and culture may now be overcome. In the reaching out, in the self-transcendence of natural processes, there is a joy which is the joy of life. In the connectedness with other processes within an overall evolution, there is a meaning which is the meaning of life. We are not the helpless subjects of evolution—we are evolution. (1980:6–8).

In an eloquently theological epilogue Jantsch writes:

We stand at the beginning of a great new synthesis. The correspondence of static structures is not its subject, but the connectedness of self-organization dynamics—of mind—at many levels. It becomes possible to view evolution as a complex, but holistic, dynamic phenomenon of a universal dynamic unfolding of order which becomes manifest in many ways, as matter and energy, information and complexity, consciousness and self-reflection.

[. . .]

Life, and especially human life, now appears as a process of self-realization. . . . In self-transcendence, the opening up of new levels of self-organization—of new levels of the mind—, the chord of consciousness becomes richer. In the infinite, it falls together with the divine.

[. . .]

The God idea does not stand above and outside of evolution as an ethical norm, but in true mysticism is placed into the unfolding and self-realization of evolution. Hans Jonas . . . has given this evolutionary God-idea perhaps the most profound expression with the thought that God abandons himself many times in a sequence of evolutions in which he transforms himself, accepting all the risk introduced by indeterminacy and free will in the play of evolutionary processes. God is thus not absolute, he evolves himself—he *is* evolution. Since we have called the self-organizing dynamics of a system its mind, we may not say that god is not the creator, but the mind of the universe.

[. . .]

[T]he "God-structure" is neither form nor quantity, but the non-unfolded, the totality of undifferentiated qualities. It is pure potential. Each of the great process philosophies has found a different name for it. (1980:307–8)

I am reminded of the rhapsodic evolutionary mysticism of the priest-paleontologist, Pierre Teilhard de Chardin, when I read Jantsch's epilogue. In both men, "the objective urge to understand leads to the most profound subjective experience" (Jantsch) and "a last dualism" (between subjectivity and objectivity) "becomes dissolved" into synergetic complementarity. Jantsch identifies the most important task today as searching "for new degrees of freedom" to facilitate the living out of evolutionary processes in ways that indicate our acceptance of moral responsibility as creative participants in world design.

Other social thinkers are not all so highly theoretical as they analyze social trends. They employ a wide variety of approaches—political, journalistic, survey research, and religious, among others.

In *New Age Politics* (1978), Mark Satin lays out in cookbook style an array of action strategies for revised social order. The Jantsch and Satin books are altogether different and yet, when Satin ends a chapter with the following exhortation, we see the family resemblance in the self-organization theme:

Beyond hope and despair, then, there is something absolutely essential to do, and that is to live. To live with simplicity and intensity, gentleness and generosity, so that the idea of a freely self-developing humanity does not die, no matter how comfortable or "happy" or obedient the mass of the people may become. (p. 322)

Satin talks about a "six-sided prison"—the central aspects of contemporary social consciousness that are projected into our institutions and that hold us captive.

Dozens of New Age writers and activists have been trying to define our most basic beliefs, and if you put their writings together, you'll come up with this. Our basic beliefs make up a cultural complex whose six main elements are: patriarchal attitudes, egocentricity, scientific single vision, the bureaucratic mentality, nationalism, and the big city outlook.

I like to think of these six elements as making up a "Six-Sided Prison," partly because at least fifteen authors . . . have used the Prison metaphor in their own work, and partly because it is so apt.

[. . .]

Basically the Prison is a way of *seeing* the world, a mental construct (as sociologists would put it) or an illusion (as Eastern philosophers would) that we create every day anew.

Political people have tended to disagree—often quite bitterly—over the question of whether it's "better" to work from within the system or outside it.

[. . .]

There is, however, an emerging consensus among New Age people that suggests that the question is being posed in the wrong way. The point, they say, is first to get in touch with your self, and then to begin to simplify your personal life and life-style in a way that can reflect and deepen your new understandings. From there, each of us "should go where our hearts tell us to go," as David Spangler puts it, "hopefully without prejudgment. . . ."

Some of us will break away from the mainstream of society; others of us will work from within. Still others of us will find some kind of middle ground. (p. 192)

Satin has a penchant for lists. Here are his "four New Age ethics": the self-development ethic; the ecology ethic; the self-reliance/cooperation ethic; and the nonviolence ethic.

The final paragraph of *Seven Tomorrows*, by Paul Hawken, James Ogilvy, and Peter Schwartz, states:

Because we have insisted on retaining a passionate commitment to individual freedom combined with unrestrained desires, we have created a paralyzed society adrift without vision in a turbulent and often dangerous world. If we continue on our present course, we will most likely encounter an increasingly authoritarian, war-ravaged future. If, instead, we recognize that freedom is more than the individual liberty to shrug off the needs of others, then we can learn to act cooperatively to take more control of our lives together. We can learn to give more and expect less. We can recognize that empathy, compassion, and security are inevitable handmaidens, and we can see through the fallacy of total victory in a diverse and pluralistic world. (1982:228).

The book jacket of John Naisbitt's bestseller, *Megatrends* (1982), says it is a "primer for the eighties that outlines where our sophisticated technology is taking us, how we will be governed, and how America's social structures will change." Inside the book Naisbitt describes ten restructuring trends moving U.S. society from the old era to the new. Some of the shifts he identifies, such as the population migration from the industrial Northeast to the South and West, are of little concern for our purposes. I shall not list them all, but rather quote selectively from his series of "bottom line" statements:

With the coming of the information society, we have for the first time an economy based on a key resource that is not only renewable but self-generating.

[. . .]

We are moving from the specialist who is soon obsolete to the generalist who can adapt.

[. . .]

We must learn to balance the material wonders of technology with the spiritual demands of our human nature.

[. . .]

The more high technology around us, the more the need for human touch.

[...]

The globalization of our economics will be accompanied by a renaissance in language and cultural assertiveness.

[...]

As our top-heavy, centralized institutions die, we are rebuilding from the bottom up.

[...]

People whose lives are affected by a decision must be part of the process of arriving at that decision.

[...]

Hierarchies remain; our belief in their efficiency does not.

[...]

In the network environment, rewards come by empowering others, not by climbing over them.

Naisbitt further comments:

Although the time between eras is uncertain, it is a great and yeasty time, filled with opportunity. If we can learn to make uncertainty our friend, we can achieve much more than in stable eras.

In stable eras, everything has a name and everything knows its place, and we can leverage very little.

But in the time of the parenthesis we have extraordinary leverage and influence— individually, professionally, and institutionally—if we can only get a clear sense, a clear conception, a clear vision, of the road ahead.

My God, what a fantastic time to be alive! (1982:252)

Veteran survey researcher Daniel Yankelovich talks about the "new story" Americans are beginning to compose as new ways of thinking about life arise spontaneously from the great mass of common people and enter into their decisions and aspirations. In *New Rules*, Yankelovich points to evidence that Americans have abandoned the traditional ethic of self-denial, but also the more recently popular ethic of self-centered self-fulfillment. He sees strong movement toward an "ethic of commitment" as a more mature understanding of self-fulfillment. He notes much experimental energy directed at finding the most satisfying ways to secure relational ties. He also anticipates deep and disturbing social fissures, through to the end of the century, as the "culture plates" shift.

[B]y the mid-seventies a majority of the American people had reached a conclusion comparable to that reached by intellectual critics of industrial civilization in earlier years, namely, that our civilization is unbalanced, with excessive emphasis on the instrumental, and insufficient concern with the values of community, expressiveness, caring and with the domain of the sacred. Characteristically, with an outpouring of energy and enthusiasm that matches the drive for material advancement, Americans are now striving to achieve a new balance.

[...]

The new shared meaning bears a resemblance to the old one. The old one said poverty is not destiny. The new one says, instrumentalism is not destiny. The old meaning insisted that political freedom can co-exist with material well-being and indeed enhance it. The new meaning insists that the personal freedom to shape one's life can coexist with the instrumentalism of modern technological society and can civilize it. It took several hundred years and boundless energy to bring the old meaning to fruition; the new meaning is just at the start of its long journey.

[. . .]

[F]or a successful social ethic to take hold, people must form commitments that advance the well-being of the society as well as themselves.

For this to occur people must receive clear and distinct signals from the larger society—from political leadership, the mass media, institutional leadership . . . and from informal interchange of views with friends and neighbors. These signals should convey the terms of the new giving/getting compact. . . .

[. . .]

The new values embrace greater autonomy for both men and women; more freedom to choose one's own life style; life as an adventure as well as an economic chore; leisure; self-expression and creativity; a greater concern for past and future; a more caring attitude; and a larger place for the awe, mystery and sacredness of life (1981:232–33, 259, 263).

Michael Harrington (1983) outlines hopeful alternatives to increasingly technocratic, elitist, and manipulative consciousness in the social order. He advocates struggling to bring about a worldwide political reformation conducive to human spiritual development. He lists the four main elements of a new integrating consciousness as the recognition that (1) no law is binding unless people have had effective participation in its formulation; (2) communitarianism must transcend functional specialization; (3) moral motivation in common and official action must be based on solidarity rather than greed and gain; and (4) the consensus must involve the whole world society already implicated in our economics, science, and technology. The envisioned reform is, thus, a reform of no less than individual and species identity.

What I propose is not a world view which will be imposed upon society by political means but one which will develop spontaneously out of a social process of self-definition.

Does that mean, then, that one sits contemplatively and hopes that the masses will find some new values? Not at all. If political religions are dangerous and contradictory, politics can take into account those economic and social measures which are more likely to create an environment in which individuals and communities can work out their own values.[. . .] And that permits us to recognize, and actively seek, a new design which will create, not a new spirituality, but the social and economic preconditions that make it possible.

[. . .]

My practical point is that men and women of faith and anti-faith should, in the secular realm at least, stop fighting one another and begin to work together to introduce moral dimensions into economic and social debate and decision. That means that the structures of corporate "rationality" will have to be challenged in the name of a human rationality.

[. . .]

[T]he political and social God of the Western tradition is dying. An atheism of fools could rejoice in the emptiness of the heavens he leaves behind; a theism of fools could keep on singing the old hymns. But the real issue is whether the horizon is being wiped away, not how it is defined. No politics can answer that question—and only a politics of all those concerned with the survival of the spirit, whether it is said to be holy or only human, can work to create the social structures in which people are more likely to answer it for themselves. (pp. 217–18)

Analytical conclusions and prognosis perspectives differ widely. Sociologists Charles Glock and Robert Bellah edited a group of writings under the title, *The New Religious Consciousness* (1976). It is an attempt to assess the effect on U.S. religion of the social unrest of the 1960s and early 1970s. The aftermath of materialistic quietism that had already emerged by the time of publication led them to bridle their hope that a great reform was in the offing. Yet they present material suggesting, at the least, the continuing erosion of the traditional religious value consensus, and the pervasive need for institutions and individuals to arrive at a new consensus of social meanings that offers nontotalitarian unity in the life experience. The final paragraph in the book is Glock's:

The position advocated here is that the end of the open rebellion did not mark the end of the process of which it is a part. All that has gone before in this volume is testimony that the search for alternative realities continues. (p. 366)

Bellah's contribution discusses both the loss of traditional legitimating assumptions and some possible scenarios for the future of U.S. social coherence.

The question of why the old order began to lose its legitimacy just when it did is not one we have felt equipped to answer.
[. . .]
The deepest cause, no matter what particular factors contributed to the actual timing, was, in my opinion, the inability of utilitarian individualism to provide a meaningful pattern of personal and social existence. . . . I would thus interpret the crisis of the sixties above all as a crisis of meaning, a religious crisis, with major political, social, and cultural consequences to be sure.
[. . .]
[O]ut of the shattered hopes of the sixties there has emerged a cynical privatism, a narrowing of sympathy and concern to the smallest possible circle, that is truly frightening.
Moralism and verbalism and the almost complete absence of ecstatic experience characterized the middle-class Protestant churches. The more intense religiosity of black and lower-class churches remained largely unavailable to the white middle-class members of the counterculture.
[. . .]
The future that most people seem to expect and that the futurologists describe with their projections is very much like the present society only more so. This is what I call the liberal scenario. American society would continue as in the past to devote itself to the accumulation of wealth and power. The mindless rationalization of means and the

lack of concern with ends would only increase as biblical religion and morality continue to erode. Utilitarian individualism, with less biblical restraint or facade than ever before, would continue as the dominant ideology. Its economic form, capitalism, its political form, bureaucracy, and its ideological form, scientism, would each increasingly dominate its respective sphere.

[. . .]

Another distinct possibility is worldwide economic collapse bringing social convulsions in train. No matter how the breakdown of the "modernization" syndrome might occur, Heilbroner envisages a relapse into traditional authoritarianism as the most likely result—providing, that is, that the worst outcome, total destruction of life on the planet, is avoided.[. . .] Technical reason, because it is concerned not with truth or reality but only with results, not with what is but only with what works, is ultimately completely sub-jective. That its domineering manipulative attitude to reality in the service of the subject leads ultimately to the destruction of any true subjectivity is only one of its many ironies.

[. . .]

There remains a third alternative, however improbable. It is this that I am calling revolutionary . . . because it would bring fundamental structural change, socially and cul-turally.[. . .] Such a new order would involve, as in the case of traditional authoritari-anism, an abrupt shift away from the exclusive dominance of technical reason; but it would not involve the adoption of a reified objective reason either. In accord with its concern for ends rather than means alone, such a revolutionary culture would have a firm commitment to the quest for ultimate reality. Priorities would shift away from endless accumulation of wealth and power to a greater concern for harmony with nature and between human beings.

[. . .]

Perhaps only a major shift in the established biblical religions, a shift away from their uneasy alliance with utilitarian individualism and toward a profound reappropriation of their own religious roots and an openness to the needs of the contemporary world, would provide the mass base for a successful effort to establish the revolutionary alternative. To be politically effective such a shift would have to lead to a revitalization of the revolutionary spirit of the young republic, so that America would once again attract the hope and love of its citizens. This outcome too at present seems quite utopian. It may be, however, that only the implementation of a utopian vision, a holistic reason that unites subjectivity and objectivity, will make human life in the twenty-first century worth living. (1976:339–51)

In an earlier set of essays, Bellah (1970) sounds the theme that Harrington reiterated over a decade later:

[I]n the present situation a politics of the imagination, a politics of religion, may be the only sane politics. There is no hope in any of the competing absolutisms. . . . [P]erhaps the only responsible politics is to unmask the pretensions of all the contending parties and give witness to the enormous possibilities in human experience, in a word, to waken the actors out of their trance. To this end a human science can perhaps join with a human religion to help create a human politics. (p. xviii)

Scientific corporate management and the analysis of bureaucratic entities is a major focus for research and analysis. Here, too, are many signs of recognition that unmitigated application of abstract systems designs to human endeavor comes to be counterproductive, personally and even economically. P. R. Lawrence and J. N. Lorsch (1967) conclude that future viable organizations must be characterized by, among other things, experimentation, ferment, and change; and that high adaptability to rapid change requires a high level of democratic worker participation for efficiency. Leadership personnel must demonstrate interpersonal skills generally rooted in early personality formation as well as methodological training.

Henry Jacoby (1973) claims that the emphases of power centralization and individual isolation are mutually reinforcing in worldwide bureaucratization, and they endanger both democratic principles and bureaucratic efficiency itself as they produce a characteristic state of mind: a sense of disassociation from other persons. He comments on the irony that as individual legal rights and protections have grown, sources of identity support have diminished. The bureaucratic spirit comes to dehumanize as it turns workers into representatives of ''it,'' manipulates them to ''its'' advantage, and makes them dependent on ''its'' well-being as a juristic abstraction. He sees some minimal hope for rehumanization of bureaucratic organizations through attention to information rights and expressive needs of individual workers.

Rensis and Jane Likert capped decades of studying the human dynamics of organizations with the publication of *New Ways of Managing Conflict* (1976). They talk about diversity of orientation and difference of opinion among workers/ members as positive sources of ''fruitful friction'' in organizational problem-solving. They conclude (as do several of my informants) that authoritarianism, rather than enhancing efficiency, obstructs optimal work performance. U.S. society is steadily legitimizing rights of self-determination which now require extensive interaction-influence networks for operationalizing. The networks need multiple overlaps for sturdy linkage. The Likerts claim that the nature of a society—its basic values and philosophy—is reflected in the strategies and principles it uses for dealing with conflict in its organizations, all the way from families to governments. They have devised an elaborate framework for measuring and describing organizational systems in terms of carefully defined variables. The following is a summary of principles used by the ''highest-producing managers'' studied:

The human organization of a [high-producing] firm is made up of interlocking work groups with a high degree of group loyalty among the members and favorable attitudes and trust among peers, superiors, and subordinates. Consideration for others and relatively high levels of skill in personal interaction, group problem solving, and other group functions also are present. These skills permit effective participation in decisions on common problems. Participation is used, for example, to establish organizational objectives which are a satisfactory integration of the needs and desires of all the members of the organization and of persons functionally related to it. Members of the organization are highly motivated to achieve the organization's goals. High levels of reciprocal influence occur, and high levels of total coordinated influence are achieved in the organization.

Communication is efficient and effective. There is a flow from one part of the organization to another of all the relevant information important for each decision and action. The leadership in the organization has developed a highly effective social system for inter-action, problem solving, mutual influence, and organizational achievement. This lead-ership is technically competent and holds high performance goals. (p. 16)

Looking to a future that in their estimation calls for worldwide, coordinated, win-win solutions to problems, the Likerts comment:

A problem can be suppressed for a period of time by the win-lose method, but this leads to a fear-charged stalemate accompanied by growing hatred. The win-lose method, consequently, aggravates and intensifies conflicts but does not resolve them. Enduring solutions to these serious, complex problems can be achieved only by problem-solving methods that yield solutions acceptable to all parties to the conflict. (p. 327)

In an unpublished 1981 paper reviewing the work of ten scholars studying large-scale organizations I observed:

Either past thinking has been too simplistic in assuming mutual repulsion of bureaucratic and democratic principles or . . . the nature and conditions (both internal and environ-mental) of bureaucratic success have undergone change. At any rate, there is accumulating credibility for the claim that rationalized authority need not be authoritarian for efficiency and, indeed, tends to obstruct efficient organization of work performance if it is.

[. . .]

The Likerts view democratic participatory conflict resolution as a superior order of corporate discipline, rather than as some permissive departure from disciplinary rigor.

[. . .]

The very real possibility that juristic and natural persons could be mutually enhancing in bureaucracies is certainly worth serious investigation.

[. . .]

I suspect that equalitarian conflict resolution skills are about to emerge as crucial requirements for efficiency in organizing the modern world's vast array of projects. . . . Such skills operate at a pivotal point for the personalization of the arena of the rational and the rationalization of the arena of the personal.

Sociologist J. Milton Yinger (1970) points out the need for any society to have high congruence, over time, among the forms of social structure, culture, and character it produces and maintains. Otherwise, social disruption and per-sonal distress become intolerable. He sees in world modernization a great turning point in history—humans have structured a technologically unified world and are tied together in economic, political, military, and communication systems, but have not developed appropriate culture systems for socializing persons who are truly at home in such a world. The whole world cries out, according to Yinger, for fresh, deeply satisfying rituals of community and dependable tech-niques for positive bonding and conflict resolution among persons. He speculates about the possibility of a continuously self-revising religious system that can offer coherence in an era of rapid and complex social change where discrepancies among structural, cultural, and personal elements of society have become *normal*. He notes the widespread ache for beliefs, rites, and practices that may reassure that (1) justice will flow *and* failures will be dealt with adequately; (2) suffering will be abated *and* sense can be made of what remains; (3) intellectual possibilities are developed *and* we can have peace and meaning in the absence of comprehension.

This desperate need for a credible, trustworthy, revisable, ultimate coherence, embodied in the acts of social institutions and persons, is now a familiar component of social analysis and prediction. It is an essentially religious need, of its very nature, and my informants seem attuned to it.

Brigitte and Peter Berger, along with Hansfried Keller, have written a wonderfully lucid book (1973) about the contemporary feeling of being lost. They locate the source of the dislocation in the forms and pace of rapid and extensive social change.

Technological production and bureaucratic organization are themes of modernization seen by Berger, Berger, and Keller (1973) as having diffused into the general symbolic realm, where they have become not just cultural techniques, but shapers of perceptual reality. Thus specialization and fragmentation of experience have come to typify our way of life and our problem-solving mode. Moral issues tend to be handled as administrative matters. Integrative specialties, such as the realms of personal intimacy and religion, become isolated, privatized, and significantly degraded as priority concerns, resulting in experiential meaning voids. With privatization, the areas of personal relationships and religious faith become intensely subjective and conversion-prone—a sort of Rorschach for secular salvation dreams they are ill-suited to fulfill.

Perpetual identity crises seem epidemic—though not inevitable, it must be said. Futurists note those persons who "ride the crest of change" with exhilaration and confidence. And Abraham Maslow (1962) many years ago proposed that, instead of counting how many people do this and that, social scientists should snoop out the obvious "good choosers" who live wisely and nobly— full of good will and good cheer—and document how they do it.

The late social systems theorist, Talcott Parsons, lists acute problem areas in the evolution of modern societies (1971) as (1) the need for rational integration of the varied consequences from the industrial, democratic, and educational revolutions; and (2) the need to mobilize widespread motivation for somehow achieving social solidarity in a pluralistic society.

In an earlier work (1966) he observes that increasingly high-energy conditions for human physical adaptation to the environment (such as we now have in technological societies) require matching high-information controls that can provide relatively stable cultural integration of meaning for the shifting concrete circumstances of life. It is this overarching value generalization stage of development that is traumatically overdue in modern societies. A number of the authors quoted in this chapter think they see it on the horizon now.

The concepts and practices of new, culturally coherent approaches to life do exist here and there at a relatively mature and sophisticated level. But, so far, they have not spread into common cultural understandings largely because existing authoritarian traditions (which are antithetical to the needed value system) impede the flow of such knowledge and tend to isolate it in elite expertise or in the life stories of exceptional individuals. People in everyday life need a general orientation that provides a sense of confidence in coping with the social conditions they regularly face. And they need ritual ways to reassure each other that the orientation is shared.

The picture of social realities, requirements, trends, and possibilities laid out in this chapter provides a clear convergence of opinion that social life in the modern world now functionally demands behaviors and ideals at all levels of expression that are maximally equalitarian, cooperative, holistic, and flexible. The traditional, more hierarchical, competitive, fragmented, and absolutist arrangements are judged by these scholars to be literally antisocial. That is, such arrangements are deemed to be opposed to the best interests and well-being of persons and of social collectives at this point in time. The viability of societies and their individual members represents a mutually derivative bill of health. So it is important to note that the character formation that fits the projected institutional needs is the very character formation most frequently associated with ego maturity and mutually satisfying relationships in the estimation of a large group of professional psychologists, personality therapists, and human development specialists.

A sociology implies a psychology. The external order of societies enters persons as they, from birth, unconsciously construct conscious perceptions in response to patterned social happenings. The internal order of persons enters and structures the environmental phenomena through patterned behaviors of various sorts. And, in addition, the recurring patterns (and systems of patterns) of meaningful interactions come to take on a life of their own—as culture—as an objectified pattern for being human.

For me, Peter Berger's insightful and thorough treatment of how the mutual formation of persons and societies occurs remains the most helpful (1966, 1967). But he is by no means the only social thinker emphasizing the presence and significance of such dialectical social reality construction. Karl Mannheim (1936) thought it impossible to live consistently, over time, by the light of brotherly love in a society not organized around that same principle. And Erich Fromm at the close of his landmark psychology of totalitarianism, *Escape from Freedom* (1941), includes the following statement:

The social character results from the dynamic adaptation of human nature to the structure of society. Changing social conditions result in changes of the social character, that is, in new needs and anxieties. These new needs give rise to new ideas and, as it were, make men susceptible to them; these new ideas in their turn tend to stabilize and intensify the new social character and to determine man's actions. In other words, social conditions influence ideological phenomena through the medium of character; character, on the other hand, is not the result of passive adaptation to social conditions but of a dynamic adaptation on the basis of elements that either are biologically inherent in human nature or have become inherent as the result of historic evolution. (pp. 326–27)

Throughout his analysis Fromm maintains that ego security built from dependency on either domination of others or subordination to others is the same failure of courage to be *free* as humans—freely responsible for acts, freely accountable for acts, freely connected to the well-being of others.

This declaration that only in free, equalitarian relating can true confidence, intimacy, trust, or justice merge is a common theme in modern psychologies and therapies. Equalitarian respect (single standard human ideals) is repeatedly designated as the foundation for enduring social justice or cooperation, whether intimate or international. Much support could be gathered for a statement such as this one from Jeanne Block (1984:16), echoing the essential thrust of Fromm:

The present cultural emphasis in the United States on masculine machismo and feminine docility appears to impede the development of mature ego functioning. Because children are socialized early into culturally defined sex-appropriate roles, introspection and self-evaluation, which appear to be essential catalysts for psychological growth, are discouraged. Further, there appear to be significant personal costs paid by both sexes when the socialization of sex-appropriate behaviors, defined in such narrow terms, is "successful."

During recent decades many of our most respected psychologists have suggested that relationships based on maintaining domination of one party by another (whether racial, economic, national, or sexual (1) are socially maladaptive for both, in that valuable personal resources and flexibility are lost; (2) are psychologically destructive for both, in that possibilities for building personal confidence, trust, and autonomy are denied; (3) are politically dangerous for both; and (4) are spiritually stifling for both. Personal therapies have emphasized the ego-development benefits from authenticity of self-expression, awareness of feeling responses, spelling out intentions clearly in negotiations, goal clarification, creative use of responsive feedback, willingness to be vulnerable for the sake of intimacy, willingness to risk some pain for the sake of self-knowledge and growth, empathic openness to the reality of others, active listening and non-judgmental acceptance of others. Over and over we have been exhorted to tune in and relate to our own personal truth, the other's personal truth, the truth of our relationships, the truth of our environment; to connect with the whole of the world and life as a dimension of our own well-being; to regard ourselves as neither more important nor less important than others; to know and relate to self and others as beings rather than instruments or functions; to be responsible for our own choices but refuse responsibility for others' choices.

Points similar to these appear not only in scholarly literature, but in a motley array of self-help books, articles, and columns that are directed at persons trying to negotiate ego and relationship development without traditional supports and guides. Variety and mobility in social experience increase options and encounters at such a rate that negotiability becomes a central characteristic of personal autonomy.

Childhood socialization, except for a relatively small percentage of the population, still does not prepare people well for constant, confident, intentional negotiation of their freedom. Yet the kind of world we have brought about requires us to participate this way in its formation and ours. The word is out that certitude must now emerge from trustworthy ways of being together as humans on a journey whose significance, course, and destination are always unfolding. It seems to be how we learn to know and treat each other as "traveling companions" that counts most in clarifying and unifying the meaning of the trip.

So negotiation, conflict resolution, and "struggle" become the heart of successful modern identity formation and institutional strength, rather than merely "troubles" held at bay to preserve stability. But our cultural images have not yet provided most of us with reassurance that we and our world will not fall apart under such "uncertain" conditions for living. Though dynamic models for integrating experience are embraced as "certain" and helpful by an increasing number of people, such models still seem literally unimaginable (or unthinkably exhausting!) to many.

Psychiatrist Scott Peck, whose writings have recently been immensely popular, recognizes the immobilizing fears that can overwhelm persons facing the demands of a positive morality, worked out and thought through constantly (ugh!) as a free, truthful, and responsible partnership in life. He subtitles his book, *The Road Less Traveled*, "A New Psychology of Love, Traditional Values, and Spiritual Growth" (1978). After having discussed the intricate relationship of truth-telling to responsible care-taking, he adds his opinion that the rewards are well worth the costs:

All this might seem like an extraordinary task, impossible to ever perfectly complete, a chronic and never-ending burden, a real drag. And it is indeed a never-ending burden of self-discipline, which is why most people opt for a life of very limited honesty and openness and relative closedness, hiding themselves and their maps from the world. It is easier that way. Yet the rewards of the difficult life of honesty and dedication to the truth are more than commensurate with the demands. By virtue of the fact that their maps are continually being challenged, open people are continually growing people. Through their openness they can establish and maintain intimate relationships far more effectively than more closed people. Because they never speak falsely they can be secure and proud in the knowledge that they have done nothing to contribute to the confusion of the world, but have served as sources of illumination and clarification. Finally, they are totally free to be. They are not burdened by any need to hide. They do not have to slink around in the shadows. They do not have to construct new lies to hide old ones. They need waste no effort covering tracks or maintaining disguises. And ultimately they find that the energy required for the self-discipline of honesty is far less than the energy required for secretiveness. The more honest one is, the easier it is to continue being honest, just as the more lies one has told, the more necessary it is to lie again. By their openness, people dedicated to the truth live in the open, and through the exercise of their courage to live in the open, they become free from fear. (p. 63)

Changeover from traditional values and ideals, which imply a more or less static hierarchical order, to dynamic, rolling ideas of truth and goodness, which imply an ongoing species opus, represents a cultural conversion project that may require decades, even centuries. Yet it seems to be what the technological world unmistakably requires for gathering its diverse and changing events into mean-ingful cultural symbols of shared truth and intentionality. There are those who through biographical quirks have grown into the newer forms of stability and can show the way; but many more feel rudderless and mapless and anxious. Mirra Komarovsky's study of Ivy League male students (1976) is especially revealing:

The overwhelming majority of the seniors attributed the strains in relationships with women to personal inadequacies. In this the men were similar to women in the 1950s, when only a minority of women recognized the social roots of their frustrations. This recognition, on the part of men, will be slower in coming than in the case of women. The very reforms which might alleviate the strains experienced by the seniors inevitably entail yielding some power and privileges and few possessors of power can be expected to yield it lightly. [. . .] But vested interest in masculine superiority was not the only source of resistance to change. The interviews revealed that the seniors were trapped (as are the rest of us) in certain dual classifications and were caught on the horns of a false dilemma because they could not conceive of a third option. The only alternative that came to the young men's minds when the traditional sex roles were challenged was simply reversal.
[. . .]
"If the husband is not going to be the mainstay, the leader, the dominant partner—will the wife then be the boss? If women are not to be reared to be loving, warm, supportive, will they be hard, competitive, and aggressive?"
[. . .]
Models of egalitarian sexual relationships, especially in marriage, were simply not available in reality or in literature on a scale to shape their imagination and free them of the false dilemma of power.
[. . .]
We need to present to both men and women more vivid models of egalitarian rela-tionships between the sexes in order to replace the traditional ones so deeply etched in social consciousness. But the agenda for needed reforms is far broader and more radical than this consciousness raising. In order to translate pious egalitarian pronouncements about wider and more equal options for men and women, we shall have to reorganize several institutions in a far more profound way. . . .
A major ideological roadblock still remains before serious efforts at institutional re-organization are undertaken. This obstacle may be first illustrated by the attitudes of the seniors in our study. [. . .] The vast majority no longer questioned women's rights to equal access to promotions and rewards in the most highly valued occupations and political positions. But this enforcement of equal opportunities coexisted with one traditional

principle: "The major responsibility for child-rearing is the mother's." For all the co-operation they were prepared to offer, their wives were expected to be the child-rearers and the homemakers. (pp. 248–50)

And from Lillian Rubin's study of female/male friendship patterns (1983) comes this analysis:

Intimacy, companionship, sharing, communication, equality. These qualities we now look for in our relations with each other still elude us too much of the time—not because our intentions are ignoble but because the traditional structure of parenting comes together with the developmental tasks of childhood and the cultural mandates about masculinity and femininity to create differences in the psychological structures of women and men. Inevitably, then, the core of identity is different for each of us and, therefore, our ways of being in relationships—whether with lovers, children, or friends—are dissimilar enough so that we're often at odds, often have trouble understanding each other.

What are we to make of our relationships, then? Dare we hope that the changes we seek can be ours? The answer is not an easy one.

[. . .]

[T]he wellspring of those things we would change about ourselves and our relationships lies buried deep in our social and psychological structures.

If this book has taught one lesson only, I hope it is this: Society and personality live in a continuing reciprocal relationship with each other. The search for personal change without efforts to change the institutions within which we live and grow will, therefore, be met with only limited reward. And the changes we seek will not be fully ours unless and until we understand where the roots of our problems lie. (pp. 205–6)

Sociologist Max Heirich at a professional conference recently summarized the emphases of the many "new age movements" by saying that they seem to be serious attempts to counter one-dimensional technologism; they promote ideas of holism, liberationism, ecological interdependence, power as magnetism rather than coercion, and the greatest pragmatism as equated with the greatest spiritualism.

This understanding of reality (that Capra calls the "rising cultural paradigm") is remarkably congruent with the perspectives of the clergywomen in the study. Where they do not hold the entire view explicitly they, at the very least, represent the orientation and implied character formation said to be needed for balancing the pathological skew toward bureaucratic technologism. The whole of the interview data displayed in the study supports this point.

Now it must have been noted by the reader (possibly with some surprise, satisfaction, or amusement) that the worldview put forth in this chapter rests on the scholarly work of men. Initially, I neither sought nor avoided this circumstance. The bulk of scholarship still represents male thinking; male thinking is still less easily dismissed by readers as biased or insubstantial; and my own intellectual formation has been heavily in response to male thinking, which, I learned early, stimulated my own in a particularly balancing and fruitful way.

I have not sought to correct my project toward inclusion of more of the exciting work now coming from female scholars. As it stands, the skew serves to make a point: The new paradigm perspective is neither a narrowly female perspective nor a rationalization of partisan women's rights agendas. But, without a doubt, women are in a strategic social location to embody and articulate both the missing dimension of public life and also to help bring it about as a bottom-up, consensual (rather than totalitarian) unity, a social freedom rather than a social imposition. One church report reminds that "leadership from below cannot change the power structure if it tries to imitate the image under which suffering was experienced."

Many years ago I happened upon a small book by Florida Scott-Maxwell. In *Women, and Sometimes Men* (1957) I recognized a kindred spirit and supportive presence. Searching out that writing after all these years, I recognize also an early voice speaking clearly in the new paradigm.

There must always have been women of marked individuality who lived their wholeness naturally, but now a new thing is among us. It is happening all about us, and it amounts to nothing less than women taking on their own individuality. Not living only as a function to others, but standing between their good and their own bad with a centre, a painful and brave centre of awareness, where they know they are themselves. They are attempting, and of course failing and also happily succeeding, in the integration of their masculine thought and will, adding these to devoted acceptance. It is perhaps part of the new integration that is taking place in both men and women, a new responsibility for the conflict in the soul of the individual.

[. . .]

It may be that woman's long-tested ability to contain opposing things, and her new ability to do it consciously and creatively is the very essence of the cultural task required of her. Out of necessity, and out of tenderness woman has learned to hold good and evil together, since the pain of doing this needs love. It could be nothing less than this that society now asks of her.

The very need of the times and the best quality in woman seem to synchronize so the task she must apparently undertake gives her her creative possibility.

[. . .]

It is truly as though a concept of wholeness were appearing among us, to counterbalance division and destruction.

[. . .]

In the human heart the new morality seems to be compassion, we could almost call it the morality of inclusion. It has much of the feminine in its care of the weak, in its dislike of definition, and in its large indulgence; also in its valour of the heart, and it may be the feminine offering to our troubled time. (pp. 201–7)

Women are now in greater numbers developing and expressing more of their human potential than formerly. While this often throws projects of male/female intimacy into high self-consciousness and anxiety, in general it feels good, expansive, exhilarating, and freeing to the women.

On the other hand, the complementary process of fuller development for males may not *feel* expansive and freeing and *more* powerful to many men. Dualistic assumptions and norms of domineering power conspire to color the "fully developed male" weak and restricted by conventional standards.

A good example of this is in how men and women tend to hear the meaning of "negotiation" and "communication." Anne Wilson Schaef talks about this in *Women's Reality* (1981), but I have noted the same tendencies in countless informal and formal conversations.

At one seminar I remember, a heated exchange that was dividing quite acrimoniously along gender lines only became productive of understanding when someone noted that we seemed to be hearing the word "negotiation" in very different ways. Men tended to hear it as a goal-directed adversarial power contest in which parties with conflicting agendas strategized to concede as little as possible of their own autonomous control over the outcome before striking an agreement with the opponents that would allow them to proceed. Women tended to hear it as an information-sharing process out of which might come understanding of the situation leading to action maximizing mutual well-being, including developmental freedom. From the male view here "equalitarian" discussion is seen as a stalemate. From the female view, competitive leveraging dams up crucial information.

Given such differences, until there is more evident change, it is understandable that men would not want to trade familiar controlling entitlements for endless "negotiation" of life circumstances. What looks to many women like freedom to be included as participants in life construction (freedom to draw close and build trust—freedom to make a creative contribution—even fun!) may very well look to conventional males like loss of control over life rather than the gain of growth possibilities.

Several factors converge to dispose women toward experiencing expanded gender understandings positively as release, opportunity, wholeness.

First of all, objectively, they stand to gain more concrete social benefits in the transition—economically, politically, and educationally. Second, the double-socialization of non-elite groups works to heighten their awareness of and identification with socially valued aspects of male norms, along with their own more distinctively female experience. Third, characteristic holism disposes them toward incorporation of the other's reality rather than competition for prime reality status.[1] Fourth, conventional valuing of intimacy with males and caring for males tend to result in generalized respect and encouragement for men's ways of being in the world.

Thus, while women may not be the most prominent theorists about where world society and culture are headed, or about which paradigms are most congruent with the projected technological future, ordinary women may very well be in a position to contribute the balancing perspectives and qualities required, simply by being who they are much more freely, visibly, and influentially in the public sector.

The key word here is *balance*. The force of authentic maleness is not being condemned by the "new age" theorists. What is challenged is a pathologically uncorrected version of maleness careening destructively through history less and less in touch with its own potential fullness and health. Authentic femaleness is not being condemned, either. The challenge is to a pathologically uncorrected version of femaleness simpering and suffering destructively through history, alienated from its own potential fullness and health. The message is that each of us as sexual beings develops best when we confidently embrace the freedom to incorporate and nurture the finest qualities of humanness (male and female) *within* our whole development. Then women and men become joint models for what is best in humans.

Ordinarily, and perhaps inevitably, this developmental journey starts for men and women from different primary orientations and completes itself in the other. So gender uniqueness is likely to continue and thrive, even if conventional prescriptions and proscriptions recede or disappear.

Dusk and dawn are very different concepts and have their own words. It means something quite different to be moving out of day toward night or out of night toward day. To be moving in maleness toward completion in femaleness is not the same in its subjective and objective social significance as moving in femaleness to know completion in maleness. Each is its own kind of dynamic, non-absolute wholeness. Androgyny understood this way is no human neutering, no rigid template, no doubling of developmental chores. It is freedom to be. It is a celebration of full-gendered uniqueness for persons.

As I understand the way most scholars are coming to use the term *androgyny*, it means the free personal choosing of appropriate human responses and developmental characteristics without rigid restriction of options according to sex. I am aware that there is widespread fear in some quarters that what is intended is a reduction of gender distinctions to a bland human uniformity, destroying the beauty and interest of contrapuntal sexual relations. It seems to me that such a fear fails to understand androgyny as it is now mostly put forth in gender analysis literature; but, more importantly, it fails to comprehend the depth of the gender uniqueness.

As I write this I am reminded of an experience that occurred just yesterday. A social commitment took me to a degree-awarding ceremony preceded by two candidates' (strangers to me) describing their practical dissertation projects in their respective congregations. These middle-aged male ministers reviewed for the assembly their experimentation in their religious communities with, in the one case, male-to-male expressions of caring and, in the other case, models from the ''new physics'' for articulating religious views. Later, at a reception, as I exchanged some brief comments with both men, we were aware of how extensively our points of view about many things coincided. Yet, as they had made their presentations, which I admired, I kept thinking, ''*I* could not bring together the material *this* way.'' And I thought it had to do, in part, with gender. Likewise, a male colleague recently said about some of my writing in this study, ''Only a woman would say it like this.'' His tone was not negative.

An African woman, Rose Zoé-Obianga, declared, in a presentation at an international religious conference:

If then it is up to women themselves to define their own identity—as men have done—and still do . . . and their own participation in the community life, this is by no means to say that women will transform themselves into men, still less make the world solely and completely feminine. But rather, they will incite and lead men and women to play the card of *complementarity* to the very end. (in Parvey 1983:69–70)

Maslow (1971) talks about transcendence of dichotomies in self-actualization, the binding of separates into a unity.

Any dichotomy may be used as an example; for instance, selfish versus unselfish, or masculine versus feminine, or parent versus child, teacher versus student, etc. All these can be transcended so that the mutual exclusiveness and oppositeness and Zero-Sum game quality is transcended, in the sense of rising above to a higher viewpoint where one can see that these mutually exclusive differences in opposites can be coordinated into a unity which would be more realistic, more true, more in accord with actual reality. (p. 274)

And Ruth Nanda Anshen in her introduction to Erich Fromm's *To Have or To Be* (1976) observes:

[W]e seem to inhabit a world of dynamic process and structure. Therefore we need a calculus of potentiality rather than one of probability, a dialectic of polarity, one in which unity and diversity are redefined as simultaneous and necessary poles of the same essence. (p. viii)

Returning now to the intentions for this chapter, outlined at its beginning, I shall order my conclusions accordingly.

1. The thinkers whose works I quoted say that something different is happening in the world; history is taking a crucial turn. Revolutions in world-level social order, cultural integration, and personal consciousness are, and must be, in process in order to carry the human species viably into the next evolutionary era, given the changes from worldwide modernization. The major premise is that the healthy development and creative functioning of any unit of life must be understood in terms of the other parts and the whole. A balance must be maintained between the integrity of component parts and the integrity of the organism, for the full functioning of each. Through external and internal processes parts and wholes are seen as intrinsic to each other. Societies and individuals and universes are each other's life-forming processes.

2. For satisfactory ego-maturation and social participation, a new order of consciousness is said to be required of individuals. Their knowledge and intentions in experience—even their feelings and values—need dynamic conceptualizations that are at home with trust, hope, and faith rooted in a truth about reality that is always, to some degree, uncertain in that it is always unfolding in its revelation, just as we are always

unfolding in our comprehension. Certainty becomes an ongoing community quest. The new order of consciousness must be coupled with a new order of relationship techniques. Equalitarian conflict resolution skills must move beyond the realm of therapy and come to be an intuited dimension of the socialization process. Cooperative solidarity can then emerge as a negotiated order of species life, from familial to cosmic. "Synergy" needs to transcend fad-word status and become the generalized assumption about partnerships, so that adversarial idealisms and projects are recognized as pathological rather than normative. A dependable, positive, non-absolutist morality of responsible caring needs to be modeled and internalized. It must emerge from the recurring responses of holistically oriented persons to human need at all levels.

3. What is required of new-paradigm institutions is simply a different level of the requirements for individuals. Mid-level social orders must be articulated with caring attention to the participatory welfare of internal human "parts" and to the surrounding environment as well.

4. The interview data exhibited earlier allow me to make some simple claims relative to the informants: Their worldviews clearly lean to the holistic. They show strong awareness of the complex dynamism of modern social change and the need to take it seriously in their ministries, though levels of explicitness vary. With just a few uneasy exceptions in certain areas of concern, they are non-absolutist and process-oriented in their conceptual approaches to truth and morality. The full participation of persons in their social arrangements is a high-priority consideration for the women. All of them place responsible caring at the heart of their moral commitments. As they talk about intentions for shaping institutional structure, all profess attention to how it serves individual members' needs; most profess attention also to how it serves the world level of human need.

Since these informants, for the most part, were chosen with consideration for their non-marginal status (their relative "success" in the ministerial role) and since their colleagues are still mostly male, it is reasonable to assume that any bias in gender orientation would lean in the direction of male norms or androgynous development. Rosemary Ruether and others have voiced the concern that women may be entering the professional ministerial role as "one of the boys" and suppressing a distinctively female point of view in the desire for acceptance and colleague cooperation. My data suggest otherwise. The women are, without exception, highly androgynous, though they lean toward a conventionally female orientation toward life.

They appear well suited to articulate the yin qualities said to be underdeveloped, undervalued, and undernoticed in public life, and also to articulate the crucial valuing of wholeness and balance itself in social arrangements.

The pulpit and the ministry may turn out to be a particularly opportune location for imaging, disseminating, and modeling unified (not uniform!) visions of reality. If this can be done by men and women in an idiom that is accessible and credible to ordinary people beyond just a narrowly religious frame, it may help crystallize the much-needed cultural integration of social forces.

NOTE

1. It is unwise to ignore the potential for female holism to activate in males primal dependency desires as well as fears of being ''swallowed up'' by females; this intrapsychic imaging parallels the potential for male instrumentalism to activate female fears of being co-opted and used impersonally for male projects.

Chapter 10

Concluding Thoughts

The time has come now to review the completed research findings in a sociological frame and say what may have been accomplished.

A truism of sociology is the interconnectedness of social phenomena—the mutual influencing of internal orders of personal identity and external orders of group behavior; characterological ideals and bureaucratic structure; economic institutions and political institutions; family relationships and religious beliefs; sexual choices and economic choices; education and leisure activities.

[M]utual influence between social structure and attitudes and values . . . makes the prediction of future developments . . . difficult. Changes in one may bring unforeseen changes in the other. Structural factors may lead to value changes. . . . [. . .] At the same time, value changes may lead us to reconsider our assumptions about what is natural and inevitable. Changing values can be an impetus to changes in social structure. (Davidson and Gordon 1979:277).

Possibly no one has contributed more to the understanding of this interconnectedness than Peter Berger (1966, 1967). In his work we come to see the various interdependent "moments" of human experience. He shows how personal integration, built with social integration, projected on the universe as ultimate integration, plays back on consciousness as religious truth, which legitimates value systems, validates human identity and thought systems, and focuses attention on an ideal reference point that appears objectively stable and appropriately absolute. Individuals and societies thus "inhale" and "exhale" each other via the conceptual patterns of culture, including their images of ultimate (i.e., religious) reality. Human experience is intrinsically social, meaningful, purposeful; and ways in which one part of the complex dynamism influences another are infinite. Some shared sense of what the whole of reality means is necessary for the healthy developmental stability of both persons and groups.

Beyond the known factors of ordinary social encounter, people recognize the existence of relatively inaccessible dimensions of experience with which they are somehow connected. How such unfathomable dimensions are imaged interacts, over time, with the nature of personal and species events and development. So the envisioning of the beyondness is not inconsequential or irrelevant in daily living.

Symbolic acts, ceremony, and ritual are a currency of shared meanings attached to the imagined nature of the infinite. Such rites emerge where people have a sense of belonging together and knowing something of what to expect from each other at critical points in life.

Clifford Geertz (1968) says of sacred symbols that their function is to provide orientation for the human organism, which cannot live in a world it is unable to understand. Karl Mannheim calls every concept a "crystallization of group experience" (1936).

Emile Durkheim concludes that knowledge coherence implies societal coherence—the unity of the collectivity—and incoherence in one is reflected in the other, over time (with Mauss 1963).

Whatever we think of given religions or beliefs, the need for a vision of what is ultimately true and worth our loyalty remains an essential (and essentially religious) requirement of human existence, according to many scholars, though it may or may not be expressed in traditional, institutionalized ways.

Berger and others, including theologian Hans Küng, point out that claims that God or eternal life are reducible to *merely* psychological or sociological phenomena are logically indefensible; by the same logic, atheism is *merely* the projection of persons' emptiness onto the universe. Küng observes that if the gods are products of projection or wishful thinking, it does not follow that they are *only* that which persons put into knowing them.

Max Weber's (1930) critique of the mutually forming dynamics of European capitalistic enterprise and the Protestant Reformation alerts us to the complexities of social change relative to ideas of ultimacy. He saw what was happening in the realm of religious beliefs as more than some simple adjustment to the presence of capitalism; he rather judged it a critical shaping force in the new world economic view. The structures of social actions and of conceptualized ideals are inextricably interwoven, according to him.

Weber refers to the spirit of capitalism as "an historic individual"; that is, a complex of elements in historic reality gathered into a conceptual whole because of their joint cultural significance. The complex, as he saw it, included a set of sanctions which were rooted in religious beliefs and practices and gave rise to a certain direction in practical life conduct (1930).

Weber refuses to reduce either ideas or social structure to each other. He feels that motivations and attitudes governing action choices reflect not ideas, as such, but ideal *interests* along with material interests. In other words, the effective social imagery of ideal goals that capture people's desires for their lives seem to him to affect the course of history beyond just the struggle to secure material benefits that has been the absorbing focus of Marxist analysis. He is not disposed to treat certain social conditions as determining others, but as selectively supporting their survival, once choices are available. He also observes that for new religious conceptions to emerge, people must not have unlearned how to face life with their own real questions or how to experience astonishment (Bendix 1960).

Using Weber's terms for some of the supporting evidence in this study, we can say that another "historic individual" is gradually emerging in the modern world. It is a relatively new combination of ideal interests and energies focused on humanizing and unifying a world order severely fragmented and endangered by hierarchical, adversarial, specialized, and instrumentalized relations in a bureaucratically organized technological society. The new view is put forth as a positive, creative model for renewing world order.

In this study I have gathered an extensive review of contributions to the envisioned "rising paradigm" by excerpting and summarizing key ideas from the literature describing current social crises and projected developments. The various scholars and commentators cited speak of a cultural deficit in integrative images of reality and in ways of organizing public life to support personal identity.

At different levels of social experience the yearnings, intentions, and species imperatives these authors mention point toward a model for social reality idealizing part/whole balance and cooperative existence.

Absorbing questions in the rising paradigm are: (1) What worldview is most credible, given the empirical evidence? (2) What view of individual responsibility promises a fruitful balance between satisfaction to persons and species vigor? (3) What image of the future can draw persons most hopefully and helpfully toward creative growth and social contribution as they make choices? (4) What kind of truth and confidence can be stabilized in personal, non-absolute, non-hierarchical terms? (5) Can human societies learn to socialize individuals with the necessary skills for negotiating cooperative interpersonal arrangements at all levels (much as ancient China socialized individuals into the subtleties of the elegant gestural repertoire)?

Emerging "answers" to such questions assume both the necessity and possibility of equalitarian, holistic, and cooperative knowledge/action ideals. The universe is seen as a system of systems functioning as an ecology of dynamic units, each of which is a valuable contributor to the entirety. Whether human or otherwise, components are understood to have potential for mutual supportiveness and synergy. Knowledge and morality are looked upon as socially constructed commitments to chosen realities for which knowers and doers are personally accountable. Truth under this model is the highest possible coherence in the resolution of traditional and existential meanings. Authoritarian certainty is indefensible by the new paradigm's assumptions, which, instead, imply an ongoing communal project of clarifying what's truest to think and best to do.

World order is demonstrably in need of ways to regulate in global community the already advanced interpenetration of regional interests. The design, implementation, and stabilization of such an order requires (literally) interminable good faith negotiations among regional and corporate representatives intent on maximizing species well-being.

Institutions that learn to organize their prodigious social power as "juristic persons" along lines of democratic rather than authoritarian information distribution can thereby tap and direct the free flow of corporate intelligence in ways that minimize tragic waste of creative potential. Corporate power rationalized as human service (rather than domination) is already a well-researched possibility with numerous fruitful experimental instances.

There are substantial cross-cultural benefits implied in the new paradigm from normative embodiment of equalitarian discourse skills and conflict management at all levels of experience. The various social realms are humanized and harmonized significantly when commitment to responsible caring suffuses communication and penetrates the social fabric beyond mere sentiment or obligation. At the level of individual personal exchange, equalitarian negotiation of trust is the essence of healthy identity formation within primary relationships. Mutually satisfying intimate associations carry implicit demands for freely chosen mutual accountability and mutual openness to criticism. Especially when begun at an early age, respectful contemplation of others and their points of view not only supports personal security and trusting relationships, but also provides invaluable apprenticeship in the art of critical analysis. Sophisticated judgment, whether developed through scholarly or mundane pursuits, is a complex conceptual tool that helps prepare a person to deal rationally and courageously with conflict, trauma, social novelty, or complex role demands. Many psychologists and therapists conclude that personal confidence rooted in receptivity to critical challenge and cooperative negotiation can grow sturdy and flexible; but confidence propped with attempts to avoid, trick, or compel the opposition remains precarious.

Human social effectiveness and life satisfaction depend on a relatively high degree of congruence among expectations in personal, institutional, and cosmic realities. For various reasons many people are cynical about possibilities for achieving a humane world order; and they doubt the wisdom of proposing an ideal they consider impractical. Those (myself included) already unable to envision a viable human future except according to the "rising paradigm" see such an order as the one toward which society is being impelled by its technology, and the only one toward which it can move, if the species is to survive, let alone prosper. They point to the fact that when any way of existence is possible to *some* humans *some*place, it is potentially achievable among *enough* people in *enough* places to tip the reality-construction balance. Meanwhile, for those who discover the intrinsic values of unfettered thought and action on behalf of human health, the reward is an exhilarating sense of meaning and purpose, as well as likely delight in life.

What potential a reality paradigm has for dominating what people take for granted about the world over time depends on exceedingly complex and subtle social dynamics, most of which are easier to trace historically from some future vantage point than to predict. Robert Friedrichs observes (1970) that social revolutions in ways of seeing things occur only when an alternative paradigm and its advocates are primed and ready.

So far we can see that such is the case with the "rising" view. But that is not enough for a revolution to occur. Jantsch (1980:294) adds:

To bring the vision into a possible form is not the only task. This form has to be conceived at a level which is generally recognized, at least within the framework of a specific culture. It has to correspond to the innermost experience and memories of the performing artist as well as the audience. It has to express not only the life of the creative artist, but equally the life of those other people sharing in the act. In other words, the form has to be related to a common human basis.

Borrowing an analytical construct from Robert Wuthnow's discussion of religious change in social context (in Bellah and Glock 1976), we can say that for a view to capture ideological loyalties and become a "natural" orientation dominating a society it matters a great deal (1) how much knowledge people in general have of the view, (2) whether it has appeal for them, (3) whether they participate in situations where the view is operating as reality, (4) whether the proponents and converts tend to be "bellwether" or "backwater" in the society at large.

All of the above are variables affecting the influence of the women in this study. They do not think of themselves and their ministries as promoting "the new paradigm view," any more than they, by and large, identify with feminism as a cause. But we have seen that they do, in fact, embody many aspects of the new paradigm approach. And they occupy an institutionally accepted position for articulating normative ultimacy. Traditionally religious institutions are looked to and counted on for lending stability to life in troubled times. But they themselves are changing in fundamental ways. The admission of women to leadership is one of them. In admitting women to official religious influence, groups already indicate some redefinition of reality, in that it signals both a changed outlook among existing authorities and the incorporation of new authorities with a different perspective.

The vulnerability of organized religion to change from shifting resource availability in clergy personnel may, according to evidence presented in this study, portend the entry of U.S. religion into a fresh dialogue with persons and institutions focused on new paradigm imaging of human spiritual experience. Insofar as secular society tries to reclaim the spiritual dimension of existence and religion tries to take secular knowledge seriously into account, a new mutual relevancy can be explored and may prove exceedingly fruitful.

Though the major scholarly proponents of the new paradigm aren't women, and aren't necessarily connected with organized religion, the religious women in this study seem oriented in the same way as the worldview writers. To the extent that persons such as the informants have influence in religion, they help bring the classic institution for value formation into the current societal value reformulation as a dynamic participant.

Important catalysts in paradigm shifts are (1) charismatically credible authorities who are operating consistently and effectively within the rising orientation; and (2) an increase in both prestigious and mundane uses of the view.

For religious views to spread beyond narrowly religious associations, the views must interpenetrate the secular realm, drawing and offering coherence beyond what is accessible to people with conscious faith commitments. If both prestigious religionists and ordinary ministers come more and more to work within conceptual frames that assume developmental models and personal accountability for truth, morality, and world, then something new is taking shape in religion, expressing and influencing something new that is taking shape in society. Religious people are seeing a new, freeing way of being in faith. Nonreligious people are seeing a new way of being religious. Holistic, developmental models for truth and responsible living may again offer a sacred/secular synergy for a credibly transcendent unity based on the valued uniqueness of contributors and their information.

That is the hope. The actuality is not yet realized. This study tries to imagine, from the assembled data, the position clergywomen may occupy and the part they may play in a tipping of the balance toward widespread social reality definition by a new paradigm.

The women in this study integrate life and tradition in an area (religion) where integrative thinking is the traditional essence. They aspire to authentic self-presentation, responsible caring for life, and mutual trust-building in an arena where all of the above are considered the traditional marks of obedience to God. But they are introducing nonauthoritarian, developmental, world-tending articulations of the traditions that shift the ground considerably and open their religious communities to possibilities of participatory, personal truth-building. Those women mostly responded to traditional religious formulations and early in life committed themselves to "radical obedience" to God. The ensuing commitments to humble human service, courageous truth-telling, and personal integrity carried interpenetrating imperatives that led them toward faith positions of increasing force and flexibility (and decreasing dependency on authoritarian legitimation). Their faith positions are still expressed as radical obedience to God, not primarily (if at all) as social change strategy.

However, their perspectives coincide in crucial ways with the new-paradigm characteristics put forth by important secular futurists and religionists. Whether or not they are aware of it, the informants embody a worldview alternative that seems to be gaining acceptance in some "bellwether" social locations. It is a point of view, for them, rooted in and developed from the social experience of being female. Now, at this point in history, it appears to be an orientation needed for balancing world order and for articulating the balance as unity rather than power parity.

As men and women ministers perform their traditional function of defining reality, responsibility, and ideal community, they might agree substantially on their objectives and still represent distinctive operational approaches. Since men far outnumber women in church leadership positions, we need to know where their ideal and operational values lie, relative to the "rising paradigm," in order to see the overall response or contribution of the religious sector in any widespread social change.

One thing that is especially striking among the informants is their emphasis on what Karl Marx (in Tucker 1978) calls praxis in social change—that is, practical critical activity with reference to all that exists. Marx says that the truth of all thinking—its reality and power—must be proved in praxis (Marx and Engels 1938). Though the women may have little or no exposure to Marxist thought, they are strong in the belief that ideas must be tested in action, with full critical attention to real consequences. Likewise, they would agree with Michael Polanyi's statement that truth can only be thought by believing it and ideals can only be known in following them (1958).

It is this very seriousness and intensity of existential integration that may give the informants' ministries potential impact on colleagues, congregations, and the public far beyond any words they say. Insofar as there is actual congruence of thought, word, and deed in their ministerial performances, and insofar as their ministerial and personal identities are well integrated, they provide the requisite modeling and articulation packages for public imaging of new options. If, in addition, they represent, in an ordinary way, what people are hearing about occasionally from celebrities and scholars, perhaps on TV or in a magazine, the cumulative force may escalate. Martin Marty, a well-known commentator on U.S. religion, said in a recent lecture: "Interpreting isn't all talk; the vividness of action is inviting to others. Mainline religion could 'recover' if it had a collective story to tell—a clarity of confession. There must be conscious attentiveness to the experience of the presence of God."

The general secular need for some transcendent life-sense converges with the religious institutions' need for a faith base credible to modern, secularized constituencies. Thus the pervasive hunger for a new cultural integration of social experience—a believable meaning frame—could conceivably stimulate the emergence of a human "story" rooted in both traditional meanings and modern experience, as sacred and secular realms open to each other's discoveries. If they take each other's cultural contributions seriously in a nonhierarchical struggle to know more truly and live more fully, then the collective "story" of life that emerges and becomes generally acceptable to people will certainly have a new flavor and likely would look, in crucial ways, much like the view most of the informants share.

I shall attempt to summarize the main points of that view as revealed in the data from this research project. It centers in the commitment to responsible caring for people; and, for some, extends very consciously to responsible caring for the universe. This commitment appears to be rooted in the normative female orientation to life learned in childhood. The development toward public articulation of the view is connected, in their lives, with an ego-structure that, from early life, was epi-typical, in that it included strong agentic qualities; and such ego structure came to be combined with religious interpretations of human service to God.

Using as reference criteria the generally accepted findings of the gender analysis literature, I analyzed the interview contents for indications of primary orientation to life. I conclude that, while the orientation is epi-conventional in development, at core it is normatively female without a doubt. That is, the clergy informants (1) identify trust-building, intimate associations as the arena they depend on for identity support; (2) exhibit a personal focus for making sense of life in thought and action; (3) expect life satisfaction to be intrinsic to responsible living and valued relationships; (4) emphasize caring in concrete situations where choices are required; and (5) think integratively (holistically, which sometimes means intuitively) about events, processes, and relationships.

The informants are unusually confident, outgoing, appealing, lively, able women. Ideal authority for them, in most cases, is imaged as personal magnetism and convincing performance rather than as official clergy prerogative. Equalitarian enabling is the favored image of leadership among them; and authentic, straightforward self-revelation is seen by them as crucial in effective administration, since it is a necessary condition for building trust.

The themes of struggle and growth recurring in the interview content signal the interactional process approach the women generally have toward arriving at reasonable clarity regarding truth, responsible goodness, and community solidarity. Truth and morality are treated, among them, as ongoing dialectical resolutions of honored traditional life interpretations and existential encounter. The articulation varies, from woman to woman, in the extent to which each idiom (traditional or existential) is employed. However, all of the informants agree that they must do their pastoral communication primarily in the everyday language familiar to their congregations.

They are highly motivated to work for a world organized for individual benefit, and for a personal identity norm oriented realistically toward species benefit, at the very least. Most of them are explicit about a belief in a unified reality, continually under correction from its parts. Though they assume an absolute unity with which they are sustained and informed, they reject, by and large, absolutist interpretations. They firmly rest their confidence on ultimately limited and uncertain interpretations of a unity that they believe warrants their trust and is best revealed in open, community-based, nonadversarial sharing of views and concerns.

Of course, the women themselves do not use such abstractions to describe their positions; but I conclude that the summary I make is true to the data at hand.

All of them rely heavily on the embodiment of beliefs in ordinary acts and in personalized ritual occasions of group solidarity for conveying much of their ministerial message. Administrative action is considered by them a part of such embodiment. The preferred view of executive style, among the informants, is as central facilitator, helping to bring about an organizational structure that best fits the intended functions of human service, personal nurture, and communion in the group.

While some of the informants experience conflict between personal and ministerial tasks, no important discrepancies appear in the data between personal and ministerial outlook and identity. Self-image, professional image, and ultimate preoccupations in life seem well integrated, in the main, for these women. It is rare in the data to find any implied burdensomeness from being accountable in personal life for the ministerial role. Most of them express great satisfaction and joy in life and ministry.

This high level of identity integration doubtless has a positive effect on their appeal and influence as ministers. And it would tend to confirm their reliance on charismatic credibility as an authority base, insofar as interpersonal trust works for them in establishing and maintaining their ministerial effectiveness.

A few sociological observations here from several sources may illuminate and help weigh the factor of charismatic credibility as potentially influential in a shift of worldview paradigms. Bryan Wilson (1973) says that charisma is a sociological, not a psychological phenomenon; it says less about the person than the relationship; it contains the acceptability of a leader to a following. Karl Mannheim (1936) implies a similar understanding when he declares that what is new in the achievement of "charismatic" individuals can be utilized for change in the collectivity, only if it attaches to some important current issue with which members are attempting to deal.

Weber has already been cited as thinking that ideal interests, not ideas, per se, influence action choices. Max Scheler, going a step deeper, thinks (as does Michael Polanyi) that knowledge already involves a desire and choice by the knower to know that which is known. Scheler declares that "valu-ception" precedes perception; one *feels* something toward objects of attention and cognition. And Durkheim concludes that emotional values play a preponderant part in how ideas come to be joined and separated.

Sociologist Rodney Stark comments that religious effects in society are clearly a function of peer associations. Religion matters only as groups give it the power to matter. To rediscover the effects of religion we must rediscover the moral community.

These are tiny glimpses into extensive considerations of the social foundations of religious influence. They stimulate, for me, some speculative thinking: Could a set of potentials be gathering force as a new "historic individual"? Can a revolutionary worldview be taking shape "in the wings" and preparing to come "stage center"? Perhaps, *if* the following things continue and build momentum:

If people at many levels of U.S. society are groping for a satisfying new understanding of life—a credibly modern sense of reality that ignores neither secular knowledge nor religious knowledge;

And *if* an attractive alternative to the currently dominant reality paradigm is coalescing out of the thought of many scholars in many disciplines, but as yet is articulated in terms either too sophisticated and abstract for mass attention and appeal, or too idealistic and holistic for acceptance among people steeped in hierarchical dualisms (even if the attraction of a harmonic universe ideal is great);

And *if* religious institutions at the level of scholarly theology convert largely to the rising paradigm;

And *if* ministerial women, with the gender-normative groundedness of their spirituality in mundane relationships, give concrete embodiment to the central dynamics of the new paradigm and "pull it down to earth" for people to encounter experientially as a real option in sacred/secular knowing;

And *if* in a transitional time for persons, institutions, and societies women are somehow well adapted, overall, to provide ministries according to existing pastoral ideals and also well positioned in their development to open up consciousness, through their influence at the grass-roots level, to a spirituality both honoring religious traditions and grounded in the modern society experience;

And *if* the religious commitments and ideals of clergymen make clergywomen's ways very appealing and appropriatable as models.

Other types of study will be needed to describe the complex dynamics of culture shift as it may unfold. I claim nothing more here than that, based on my evidence, clergywomen arc uniquely situated to provide an important piece of the action, should the proposed new culture integration come to pervade modern consciousness in U.S. society.

Women such as these informants are in a spectacularly visible location for modeling ways to be in the world, in faith, in relationships, in marriages, in parenting, in authority, in vocation, in ministry, in community, in conflict, in learning, in growth—as people and as women. And the commonalities in the ways these 17 women look at life and image their ministries coincide remarkably with major aspects of the worldview favored by many social thinkers as appropriate to the reality of our age.

In painting pictures there are moments when the artist establishes general color and space relationships with broad strokes, very roughly; there are other times when highly concentrated attention to precise detail may be required. In this study I am attempting a very large-brush description of social phenomena that seem to me to have profound significance in our time. Insofar as such description is true to the empirical evidence, provides explanatory frames, suggests hypotheses, or stimulates sociological imagination, it is fruitful.

This investigation has had strictly limited intentions and conclusions. I set out to document the empirical reality of 17 clergywomen's subjective experiences of their ministerial roles. In addition, I gathered their autobiographical accounts of early childhood, youth, education, and entry into professional status. My objective was to provide a deep encounter with a small group of informants for the intrinsic value of such knowledge in illuminating human experience; also for its function in revealing the commonalities and exceptional cases that stimulate questions for further study.

Some commonalities that emerge in my findings are clear. In spite of the variety represented in the informant group, the shared characteristics are not generalizable over the population of all clergywomen. The data suggest the need for determining statistically verifiable levels of incidence among other women ministers. The patterns noted also raise issues for addressing in comparative investigation. Minimally, the interesting comparisons are with clergymen, with women in secular vocations, and with clergywomen at different points in time. Complex combinations are particularly intriguing: Are there significant differences between the moral stances of clergywomen and clergymen? What kind? How large? Are there significant differences between the moral stances of clergywomen and women in secular professions? Clergymen and men in secular professions? What kind? How large? Are there moral stance shifts over time in each of the groups? What is the direction of movement? Are the genders converging? Diverging? Are the vocational categories converging? Diverging? Do the convergences/divergences differ by gender? By vocational category?

The following are core hypotheses that emerge in the data at hand, providing a base for future research:

Clergywomen are most commonly the oldest children or oldest daughters in their consanguine families.

Clergywomen most commonly report memory of a parenting combination featuring a mother who showed unusual personal competency and a father who showed unusual personal warmth and openness.[1]

Clergywomen come from families in which religion was well integrated with the life experience during their childhood years.

Clergywomen tend to combine high personal confidence and life satisfaction with an epi-normative, androgynous version of female gender identity.

Clergywomen regard their real authority as rooted primarily in charismatic credibility.

Clergywomen rely on personal care, personal integrity, authentic self-disclosure, and equalitarian negotiation skills as the primary tools for exercising administrative leadership in religious communities.

Clergywomen approach moral decisions using a primary criterion of responsible caring.

Clergywomen arrive at their beliefs about what's ultimately true through an ongoing process of reconciliation between traditional meanings and direct experience.

Clergywomen hold a worldview that emphasizes holism, cooperative existence, and personal responsibility for freedom.

Beyond the research possibilities that may branch off from consideration of the above hypotheses, there are other areas of inquiry suggested by the data. In this study we have been looking at a given role occupancy. But we have looked at its complexities in a simple way, from the standpoint only of women occupants describing their experience. We should at least balance these findings with a parallel phenomenological study of clergymen. Additional insight into role expectations and role enactments could then flow from qualitative and quantitative analyses of other dimensions of role development.

How observers describe the ideals, intentions, and performances of clergymen and clergywomen is an important piece of the picture. It is especially likely that members of religious congregations, same-gender colleagues, other-gender colleagues, regional administrators, and seminary personnel can contribute clarifying perspectives on the evolution of the clergy role if they become informants beyond the casual way they appear in connection with this study.

It would be interesting to examine the content of subjective role expectations for women and for men (including the content they assume for society's ideal, and the modifications they have made, intend, or desire as occupants), along with the level of integration of the ministerial role into personal identity structure. This is especially intriguing, since the traditional male clergy ideal is somewhat androgynously defined (e.g., caringly patriarchal and mystically rational).

In a different vein, content analysis of sermons can yield a rich harvest of information regarding theology, morality, authority, and worldview—implied or stated. Such studies may be constructed as longitudinal and/or gender comparisons (or racial, denominational, educational, etc.).

Sociographic studies could map and compare articulations of congregational leadership and community maintenance functions in connection with male and/or female clergy. National and regional judicatory levels may be observed for evidence of structures congruent or discrepant with those in local congregations and for changes, over time, possibly connected with a shifting gender ratio in top-level judicatory roles.

I am assuming that, in the future, social science will implicitly acknowledge its current skew toward yang-type research designs by gradually including a wider range of investigative approaches until a more fruitful balance is struck (Stanley and Wise 1983.) We may be nearing a time, according to the literature cited in Chapter 9, when scientific attention to the dynamic social construction of human meaning will again seem critically important and professionally central, though doubtless with a new specification of empirical connections. Consequently, my proposals for further research suggest both quantitative and qualitative analysis possibilities. I would be especially interested in seeing the results from any research that investigates the ways male and female professionals in any institutional sector may come to structure the equalitarian development and use of each other's primary strengths and contributions.

The words with which one informant describes an ideal minister can serve, in the new-paradigm perspective, to determine an ideal social scientist as well:

• [S]omeone who always knows how to open the door . . . to new light . . . new thinking . . . fresh air.

NOTE

1. Incidentally, this hypothesis is predictable from Jeanne Block's (1984) findings that the most confident, full-functioning females tend to have relatively androgynous parents.

Bibliography

Bellah, Robert. 1970. *Beyond Belief*. New York: Harper & Row.

Bellah, Robert and Charles Glock, eds. 1976. *The New Religious Consciousness*. Berkeley, CA: University of California Press.

Bendix, Reinhard. 1960. *Max Weber*. Berkeley, CA: University of California Press.

Berger, Peter. 1967. *The Sacred Canopy*. Garden City, NY: Doubleday.

———. 1980. *The Heretical Imperative*. Garden City, NY: Anchor Books.

Berger, Peter, Brigitte Berger, and Hansfried Keller. 1973. *The Homeless Mind*. New York: Random House.

Berger, Peter, and Thomas Luckman. 1966. *The Social Construction of Reality*. Garden City, NY: Doubleday.

Block, Jeanne. 1984. *Sex Role Identity and Ego Development*. San Francisco, CA: Jossey-Bass.

Bronowski, Jacob. 1973. *The Ascent of Man*. Boston, MA: Little, Brown.

Buber, Martin. 1970. *I and Thou*. New York: Charles Scribner's Sons.

Capra, Fritjof. 1982. *The Turning Point*. New York: Simon and Schuster.

Carroll, Jackson, Barbara Hargrove, and Adair Lummis. 1983. *Women of the Cloth*. San Francisco, CA: Harper & Row.

Chafetz, Janet Saltzman. 1974. *Masculine/Feminine or Human*? Itaska, IL: F.E. Peacock.

Chodorow, Nancy. 1978. *The Reproduction of Mothering*. Berkeley, CA: University of California Press.

Cobb, John B., Jr., and David Ray Griffin. 1976. *Process Theology*. Philadelphia, PA: The Westminster Press.

Davidson, Laurie, and Laura Kramer Gordon. 1979. *The Sociology of Gender*. Chicago, IL: Rand McNally.

Dewart, Leslie. 1966. *The Future of Belief*. New York: Herder and Herder.

Dinnerstein, Dorothy. 1976. *The Mermaid and the Minotaur*. New York: Harper & Row.

Durkheim, Emile, and Marcel Mauss. 1963. *Primitive Classification*. Chicago, IL: The University of Chicago Press.

Erikson, Kai. 1976. *Everything In Its Path*. New York: Simon and Schuster.

Foucault, Michel. 1972. *The Archeology of Knowledge*. New York: Harper Colophon.

Friedrichs, Robert. 1970. *A Sociology of Sociologies*. New York: The Free Press.

Fromm, Erich. 1941. *Escape from Freedom*. New York: Avon.

———. 1976. *To Have or To Be*? New York: Bantam Books.

Geertz, Clifford. 1968. *Islam Observed*. New Haven, CT: Yale University Press.

Gilligan, Carol. 1982. *In a Different Voice*. Cambridge, MA: Harvard University Press.

Glaser, Barney, and Anselm Strauss. 1967. *The Discovery of Grounded Theory*. Chicago, IL: Aldine.

Glock, Charles, and Robert Bellah, eds. 1976. *The New Religious Consciousness*. Berkeley, CA: University of California Press.

Gouldner, Alvin. 1970. *The Coming Crisis of Western Sociology*. New York: Basic Books.

Harrington, Michael. 1983. *The Politics at God's Funeral*. New York: Holt, Rinehart and Winston.

Harris, Marvin. 1974. *Cows, Pigs, Wars, and Witches*. New York: Random House.

Hawken, Paul, James Ogilvy, and Peter Schwartz. 1982. *Seven Tomorrows*. Toronto: Bantam.

Jacoby, Henry. 1973. *The Bureaucratization of the World*. Berkeley, CA: The University of California Press.

Jantsch, Erich. 1980. *The Self-Organizing Universe*. Oxford: Pergamon Press.

Komarovsky, Mirra. 1976. *The Dilemmas of Masculinity*. New York: W.W. Norton.

Kuhn, Thomas. 1962. *The Structure of Scientific Revolutions*. Chicago, IL: The University of Chicago Press.

Küng, Hans. 1981. *Does God Exist*? New York: Vintage Books.

Lanternari, Vittorio. 1963. *The Religions of the Oppressed*. New York: Alfred A. Knopf.

Lehman, Edward, Jr. 1985. *Women Clergy*. New Brunswick, NJ: Transaction Books.

Lewis, Diane K. 1977. ''A Response to Inequality: Black Women, Racism, and Sexism.'' *Signs* 3 (Winter), pp. 339–62.

Likert, Rensis, and Jane Likert. 1976. *New Ways of Managing Conflict*. New York: McGraw-Hill.

Lofland, John. 1971. *Analyzing Social Settings*. Belmont, CA: Wadsworth.

Lorsch, J. N., and P. R. Lawrence. 1967. *Organizations and Environments*. Boston, MA: Division of Research, Graduate School of Business Administration, Harvard.

Maccoby, Eleanor Emmons, and Carol Nagy Jacklin. 1974. *The Psychology of Sex Differences*. Stanford, CA: Stanford University Press.

Mannheim, Karl. 1936. *Ideology and Utopia*. New York: Harcourt Brace Jovanovich.

Marx, Karl, and Frederick Engels. 1938. *The German Ideology*. London: Lawrence and Wishart.

Maslow, Abraham. 1962. *Toward a Psychology of Being*. Princeton, NJ: D. Van Nostrand.

———. 1971. *The Farther Reaches of Human Nature*. New York: Viking Press.

Mill, John Stuart. 1869. ''The Subjection of Women.'' In *Three Essays/John Stuart Mill*. London. Oxford University Press (1975 edition).

Miller, Jean Baker. 1976. *Toward a New Psychology of Women*. Boston: Beacon Press.

Mills, C. Wright. 1959. *The Sociological Imagination*. New York: Oxford University Press.

Naisbitt, John. 1982. *Megatrends*. New York: Warner Books.

Parsons, Talcott. 1951. *The Social System*. New York: The Free Press.

———. 1966. *Societies*. Englewood Cliffs, NJ: Prentice-Hall.

Parvey, Constance, ed. 1983. *The Community of Women and Men in the Church*. Philadelphia, PA: Fortress Press.

Peck, M. Scott. 1978. *The Road Less Traveled*. New York: Touchstone.

Polanyi, Michael. 1958. *Personal Knowledge: Toward a Post-Critical Philosophy*. Chicago, IL: The University of Chicago Press.

Reinharz, Shulamit. 1979. *On Becoming a Social Scientist*. San Francisco, CA: Jossey-Bass.

Rossi, Alice S. "The 1983 Presidential Address: Gender and Parenthood." *American Sociological Review* 49, no. 1, pp. 1–19.

Rubin, Lillian. 1976. *Worlds of Pain*. New York: Basic Books.

———. 1983. *Intimate Strangers*. New York: Harper & Row.

Satin, Mark. 1978. *New Age Politics*. New York: Delta.

Schaef, Anne Wilson. 1981. *Women's Reality*. Minneapolis, MN: Winston Press.

Scheler, Max. 1980. *Problems of a Sociology of Knowledge*. London: Routledge and Kegan Paul.

Schur, Edwin. 1980. *The Politics of Deviance*. Englewood Cliffs, NJ: Prentice-Hall.

Scott-Maxwell, Florida. 1957. *Women and Sometimes Men*. London: Routledge and Kegan Paul.

Stanley, Liz, and Sue Wise. 1983. *Breaking Out: Feminist Consciousness and Feminist Research*. London: Routledge and Kegan Paul.

Stockard, Jean, and Miriam Johnson. 1980. *Sex Roles*. Englewood Cliffs, NJ: Prentice-Hall.

Teilhard de Chardin, Pierre. 1959. *The Phenomenon of Man*. New York: Harper.

Tillich, Paul. 1964. *Theology of Culture*. New York: W.W. Norton.

Weber, Max. 1930. *The Protestant Ethic and the Spirit of Capitalism*. New York: Charles Scribner's Sons.

Whitson, Robley Edward. 1971. *The Coming Convergence of World Religions*. New York: Newman Press.

Wilson, Bryan. 1973. *Magic and the Millennium*. New York: Harper & Row.

Yankelovich, Daniel. 1981. *New Rules*. New York: Random House.

Yinger, J. Milton. 1970. *The Scientific Study of Religion*. New York: Macmillan.

Index

About the Author

Martha Long Ice resides in Moorhead, Minnesota, where she teaches sociology at Concordia College.

She received her B.A. at Capital University, Columbus, Ohio, in 1947. In 1974 she completed a social science divisional M.A. at the University of Chicago. Her Ph.D. program in sociology at the University of Michigan resulted in a 1985 degree. She specialized in the cultural belief systems of science and religion.